Dreamer-Prophets of the Columbia Plateau

The Civilization of the American Indian Series

By Robert H. Ruby and John A. Brown

Half-Sun on the Columbia: A Biography of Chief Moses (Norman, 1965, 1995)

The Spokane Indians: Children of the Sun (Norman, 1970, 1982)

The Cayuse Indians: Imperial Tribesmen of Old Oregon (Norman, 1972)

The Chinook Indians: Traders of the Lower Columbia River (Norman, 1976)

Indians of the Pacific Northwest: A History (Norman, 1981, 1988)

A Guide to the Indian Tribes of the Pacific Northwest (Norman, 1986, 1992)

Dreamer-Prophets of the Columbia Plateau: Smohalla and Skolaskin (Norman, 1989, 2002)

John Slocum and the Indian Shaker Church (Norman, 1996)

Esther Ross, Stillaguamish Champion (Norman, 2001)

Dreamer-Prophets of the Columbia Plateau

Smohalla and Skolaskin

by

Robert H. Ruby and **John A. Brown**

Foreword by

Herman J. Viola

University of Oklahoma Press : Norman

Dedicated to
The LeRoy Johnson Family
and to
Jake and Charlotte

Library of Congress Cataloging-in-Publication Data

Ruby, Robert H.
   Dreamer-prophets of the Columbia Plateau : Smohalla and
Skolaskin / by Robert H. Ruby and John A. Brown ; foreword
by Herman J. Viola.—1st ed.
   p. cm.—(The Civilization of the American Indian series ; v. 191)
   Bibliography: p.
   Includes index.
   ISBN 0-8061-2183-1 (cloth)
   ISBN 0-8061-3430-5 (paper)
   1. Smohalla, d. 1895. 2. Skolaskin, ca. 1839-1922. 3. Wana-
pum Indians—Biography. 4. Sanpoil Indians—Biography. 5. Wan-
apum Indians—Religion and mythology. 6. Sanpoil Indians—Re-
ligion and mythology. 7. Indians of North America—Northwest,
Pacific—Religion and mythology. 8. Indians of North America—
Northwest, Pacific—Biography. I. Brown, John Arthur. II. Title.
III. Series
E99.W3S567   1989
979.5′00497–dc19
[B]   89-5292
                                                                 CIP

The paper in this book meets the guidelines for permanence
and durability of the Committee on Production Guidelines for
Book Longevity of the Council on Library Resources, Inc.

2   3   4   5   6   7   8   9   10   11

Contents

Illustrations

Maps

Foreword

By Herman J. Viola
Director of Quincentenary Programs
Smithsonian Institution

A century has passed since the Seventh Cavalry and the Sioux fought for the last time at an obscure spot on the Pine Ridge Indian Reservation called Wounded Knee. The so-called Battle of Wounded Knee, usually described as the last chapter of the Indian wars, was more a pogrom than a battle. Its victims were a band of starving, dispirited Sioux believers in the Ghost Dance religion whose only crime had been to pray for a return to their traditional way of life.

Because of Wounded Knee two men achieved immortality. One was Big Foot, the Sioux leader. The photograph of him lying dead in the snow will forever scar the American conscience. The other person is Wovoka, a Paiute shaman, who preached a strange religion compounded of Christian doctrines and Indian mysticism. It was the distortion of Wovoka's peaceful message by his desperate Sioux followers that led to the tragedy that unfolded in the sand hills of South Dakota a century ago.

Unfortunately, scholars have paid so much attention to Wounded Knee and Wovoka that they have largely ignored the other Native American messiahs who gave hope and purpose to their dispirited followers. Indeed, Wovoka was but one of dozens like him, Prophets and Dreamers who sought by means of religion to save their homelands from the European invaders.

The Indian messiahs were typical of the religious innovators who have appeared frequently in the history of mankind. Historically, messiahs have emerged in times of severe social and cultural stress, when members of a community have needed psychological and moral reorientation in order to cope with new stresses and situations for which their traditional beliefs do not provide adequate answers. Christianity, Islam, and Buddhism each had its reformers; the American Indian messiahs, who sought to revitalize their people through religion, were no different.

This insightful analysis of the Native American Dreamer-Prophet phenomenon tells the story of two of these Indian messiahs, Smohalla and Skolaskin. Both lived in the Pacific Northwest; both were Dreamer-Prophets in the classic tradition; and both raised unrealistic hopes among their followers while inspiring unfounded fears among their white neighbors. Hitherto, neither of them has been as well known as Wovoka because their followers were able to avoid a catastrophic confrontation like the one that occurred at Wounded Knee. Robert H. Ruby and John A. Brown have filled this void in our knowledge by making Smohalla, Skolaskin, and the times in which they lived better known to the reading public.

Preface

Among the Pacific Northwest Indians, of whom we have written for the past quarter-century, none have interested us more than Dreamer-Prophets. Thus we were pleased to prepare this account of these visionaries who endeavored to save their race in this region from the onslaught of white American society. Recent writers chronicling the struggles of American Indians have often glorified the warriors at the expense of the prophets—although the seers sometimes inspired and even led the warriors into battle. Those of whom we write armed themselves and their people only with spiritual weapons of dreams and visions.

The primary subjects of our study are two nineteenth-century Native American prophets who personified the highest aspirations of their race. The influence of the first, Smohalla of the Wanapam tribe (of the Shahaptian linguistic family), spread widely from his mid–Columbia River homeland to other areas. Skolaskin, Smohalla's contemporary among the Sanpoils (of the Salishan linguistic family) on the upper Columbia, has received less attention than he deserved.

In writing about the lives of these two men, we were faced with the historian's dilemma of placing in proper perspective the influence of events on them and of their influence on events. We take issue with those who would portray them as mere pawns in a contest of which the outcome was predetermined. We also take issue with those who stress the role of culture while neglecting the importance of individuals, and we are disturbed at the modern trend toward quantifying cultures. Our approach is primarily biographical. Otherwise, we believe we could not adequately relate the story of these personages of vision, whose charisma and cunning enabled them to enunciate their goal of

Indian salvation. Although they believed in the divinity of their missions, we find that they suffered the foibles and frustrations common to ordinary man. They usher us into the world beyond the mundane where special leaders in every time and place have been in the forefront questing for a better day for their people.

We are grateful to those of the Indian community who provided us with information about these two Prophets and the religions that they espoused, as we also are to librarians and archivists in our own region and back East. The knowledge gained from these sources provided us not only the basic facts about the Dreamer religion and its Prophets but also a better perspective on them. We would not fail to thank those who over the years have given us their readership. Without such, our efforts would have been in vain.

ROBERT H. RUBY

Moses Lake, Washington

JOHN A. BROWN

Wenatchee, Washington

Dreamer-Prophets of the Columbia Plateau

1

Introduction: *The Dreamer-Prophet Milieu*

> All the dead men will come to life again;
> their spirits will come to their bodies again.
> — *Smohalla to Captain J.W. MacMurray*

> Each one must learn for himself the highest
> wisdom. It cannot be taught in words. . . .
> Men who work cannot dream, and wisdom
> comes to us in dreams.
> — *Smohalla to Captain E. L. Huggins*

In the eighteenth and, particularly, the nineteenth century the forceful dilution of Native American cultures by the influx of Euro-Americans in the Pacific Northwest encouraged native prophet-leaders who advocated maintaining, restoring, or changing the traditional lifeways. The natives of the Pacific Northwest were under pressure from alien socioreligious systems which were forcing their forms and rituals on the various tribes, as well as from disruptive changes within their own societies. In this situation the Indians sought the leadership of the prophets whose ministrations linked the traditionalist past with a messianic millenarian utopia. The cult leaders promised their followers happiness in a pristine state in which the ancient past would be combined with a hopeful future. Some of these prophet cults simply petered out. Others were engulfed by more powerful religions.

Discussing the process among primitive people, Philleo Nash stated that nativist cults arise among deprived groups following shifts in value patterns caused by domination by external powers; the leaders of such movements attempt to restore original patterns by constructing fantasy situations. The anthropologist Ralph Linton asserted that for a nativist movement to preserve and restore culture in a society, the society must make a "conscious, organized effort," and for that to occur, its people must be aware of the presence of another culture and its erosion of their own.

The effort merely to survive may inspire participation in some revitalization movements. For example, the tribes that participated in the western Ghost Dances of 1870 and 1890 had declining populations, which was an indication of the deprivation of their cultures. Scholars, such as David F. Aberle, recognizing the possibility that deprivation alone may precipitate the rise of such a cult, have suggested that all societies respond similarly to cultural deprivation, whether or not there is contact with external powers. Christopher L. Miller has emphasized the effect of climatic change and other natural forces that add stress to an already overstressed society, forging new metaphysical arrangements. Such phenomena, in his view, gave impetus to the Dreamer-Prophets of the Pacific Northwest's Columbia plateau, which lies largely in the United States between the eastern foothills of the Cascade Mountains and those of the Rockies, extending from the southern British Columbia interior to the Great Basin.[1]

The Dreamer-Prophets were important as their followers' advocates, as spokespersons for their tribes' revitalization. The Dreamers addressed the concerns introduced by the Indians' cultural adversaries, the Americans. A most important element in the Dreamer cult was the frenetic corps of faithful who heeded the promises of the self-proclaimed, heaven-mandated Prophet-leaders and followed them implicitly. In transition from despair to delight, these followers often failed to recognize motives of self-aggrandizement in their leaders, whom they accepted as celestially accredited intermediaries between themselves and higher powers.[2]

Earlier Native American Prophets

Before examining the nineteenth-century Prophet phenomenon in the Pacific Northwest, a little should be said about others of the same stamp in America at large. Large-scale white settlements had begun more than a century earlier in eastern North America, where various American Indian religious leaders under pressure from alien white cultures attempted to undo or incorporate the compromising effects of cultural change. During the period between 1760 and 1770, for example, at least four prophets arose in the Delaware tribe alone. One of the better known was Neolin, who from 1762 to 1765 gained converts not only within his own tribe but also among the Shawnees, the Ottawas, and other groups. Among those influenced by Neolin's teachings was the Ottawa chief Pontiac, who rationalized his assault on the British stronghold at Detroit by espousing Neolin's message. After Pontiac fell, the Delaware prophet Wangoment began preaching in 1776. Among the Shawnees, during the period from 1805 to 1814, the influence of Chief Tecumseh's brother, the one-eyed Tenskwatawa, spread among natives seeking to halt white expansion.[3] Between 1799 and 1815 the Seneca Handsome Lake, who was less nativistic than most other American Indian prophets, grafted Quaker teachings onto traditional beliefs. After a dissolute life, he "died and returned to earth from heaven," where he claimed to have received a series of visions in 1799 and 1800. Heavenly messengers conveying moral precepts helped him develop on a reservation a code that became a blueprint for Iroquois survival in an evolving technological and social world order. Scholars have seen Handsome Lake's code as an instrument in the development of religious and secular pan-Indianism.[4]

Like other prophets, Smohalla and Skolaskin on the Columbia plateau were influenced by the cultural legacies of their tribes as well as their own personal experiences. Their tribal pasts included two phases that we term the protohistoric, roughly from 1790 to 1800, and the mercantilist-Christian, from 1820 to 1840. These periods introduced the anti-American phase, from 1860 to 1890, in which our subjects played out their major roles as Dreamer-Prophets.

Little is known about native prophets during the protohistoric phase on Columbia plateau, since the records of persons and events left by their contemporaries are sketchy at best. What little information we have was gleaned by scholar observers during the nineteenth and twentieth centuries. From informants of those later times we have learned of such prophets as the Spokane Yurareechen ("the Circling Raven"). Like the neighboring Kalispel prophet Woesal, who "some five hundred years ago" saw in heaven the "good man of the East" (that is, God) and returned to tell about him,[5] Yurareechen heard his Creator in a burst of light tell him to prophesy to the people. Yurareechen kept his celestial vision to himself until about 1800, when the air clouded and the ground became covered with the "dry snow," the ash from erupting Mount Saint Helens far away on the southwest of present-day Washington state. Then Yurareechen revealed his prophecy, assuring the people that the Creator was not ending their earthly existence. They realized the truth of his words when the ash fall did not cause the end of the world. "Soon," Yurareechen said, "there will come from the rising sun a different kind of man from any you have yet seen, who will bring with him a book, and will teach you everything, and after that the world will fall to pieces." He identified the coming strangers as white men, whom the people would accept and would call the *sama*.[6]

Among Yurareechen's neighbors, the Flatheads, the prophet Shining Shirt told how white-skinned men with long black robes would one day teach them religion and change their names and lives both spiritually and materially. With their coming, Shining Shirt said, wars would cease, but there would follow an irresistible flood of white people.[7] Other prophets foretold of the evil ensuing with the whites' coming. One of them, Wat-tilki, a Wasco, told natives of the lower Columbia River that whites would change things and would overpower them with sheer numbers, choking the war trail with weeds and drifting sands, causing council fires to burn low and putting to flight the "wisdom of the Nation,"[8] In early times other prophets of the Yakima River, a Columbia tributary, had uttered predictions similar to those of Wat-tilki.[9]

The prophet Katxot itinerated on the lower Columbia predicting that the coming whites would cause natives to lose their homes. The "long time ago" of his appearance was possibly foreshortened in informants' accounts. Katxot may have been inspired to his prophecies by the appearance of the Meriwether Lewis and William Clark "Corps of Discovery" party, who in 1805 were possibly the first nonnatives in any numbers to traverse the lower interior as they pushed toward the Pacific Ocean.[10] Most likely Katxot was not the Upper Chinookan "Father Woods" of the lower Columbia whose Roman Catholic–like teachings stimulated the rise of other prophets. "Father Woods" may have acquired his teachings from personnel of the Hudson's Bay Company's Fort Vancouver, which was established in 1824.[11]

Smohalla and the other Dreamer-Prophets were greatly influenced by the earlier prophets who helped set the stage for them. One of these was Dla-upác. He lived near Wallula, below present-day Pasco, Washington, at or near the place where Smohalla was born. On the fifth morning of a five-day "death," according to Umatilla informants, Dla-upác was found singing, with his arms flexed at the elbows, and telling of having seen heaven. In a celestially inspired song, he predicted the end of the world by flood or fire and advised the natives to prepare to meet Xwampipama (God) and be counted among the worthy dead who would return to life shortly before the world was destroyed. He left a prophetic legacy not only to Smohalla's people, but also to others, especially the Teninos along the Columbia River below.[12]

Among the precontact Wanapams was the prophet Shuwapsa, who was born during a time of plenty when the people neglected to thank the Creator, Nami Piap, for the bounties of the earth. Troubled by such indifference, an elderly medicine man tutored Shuwapsa by relating the fall of the "animal people" because of quarreling, after which the family of "Nahtites" (Indians), the first human beings, had appeared on the sacred islands in the Priest Rapids on the Columbia, or Enchewana ("Big River"), on which Smohalla would live and from which he would extend his religion. The Wanapams' own name stemmed from their words, *wana* ("river") and *pam* ("river country" or "river people").

Over time, the Nahtites neglected to worship and the world turned dark. There was much fear, hunger, and despair. After a man told them to recall the words and phrases of the elderly, and after giving seven-fold thanks, the Creator returned with food and restored the light of the sun and moon. From then on the natives were to gather and prepare their own food as punishment for their thanklessness. Shuwapsa foretold the coming of the whites, who he said would be friendly at first but then would spread war and disease. The remedy against the evil ones, Shuwapsa warned, was to worship and dance in a prescribed manner on bended knees, chanting prayers and songs revealed to him from above. He also told the Wanapams to hold thanksgiving feasts for the coming of the new roots and first salmon and to avoid their past carelessness, which otherwise would force the Creator to punish them as he had their forefathers. Not the least of Shuwapsa's admonitions was that they should consider the sun, the moon, and the stars their sacred trinity.[13]

Because early prophets possibly had contacts with men of the Lewis and Clark party and the Hudson's Bay Company, critics contend that their predictions were based on empirical evidence rather than on supernatural powers. Natives of the interior were aware of white men pushing west on the American continent even before the coming of Lewis and Clark. After acquiring horses in the eighteenth century, the natives of the middle and upper Columbia River watershed had met whites while journeying as far east as the Middle West. For example, from their Bitterroot valley west of the Rocky Mountains in modern-day Montana, Flathead Indians annually visited the Mandan Indians of North Dakota, who in turn traded with the Frenchman Pierre-Antoine Tabeau.[14] In the later eighteenth century natives of the Pacific Northwest interior were aware of Euro-American traders on the Northwest Coast as they acquired goods through intertribal trade. The new goods passed into their region via the lower Columbia River and the northern Cascade Mountain passes such as Ross (Kaiwhat) and Cascade.

Obtaining these goods gave impetus to the emergence of various prophet cults which, in the words of anthropologist Deward Walker, were "clearly in anticipation of the arrival of whites," although of themselves, the material goods were insufficient grounds on which to formulate prophet teachings.[15] A new mix was needed, a material-spiritual mix that the Dreamer-Prophets created by fusing mercantilist-Christian cultural elements into their own native traditions. The result was the syncretic base for the mercantilist-Christian phase of Indian-white relations between 1820 and 1840.

The mercantilist era corresponds roughly with that of the Hudson's Bay Company in the region. Like the other fur companies that had preceded it in the Pacific Northwest, the Hudson's Bay Company found the natives more eager to purchase the whites' goods than they were to hunt furs to exchange for them. The disruptions precipitated by fur trading, although not as severe as other intrusions into their cultures, were sufficient to benefit the ministrations of native prophets.

There was no sharp break between the fur-trade and missionary eras in the Pacific Northwest. Hudson's Bay Company personnel were mandated by their London superiors to instill Christian principles among their native clientele, and chieftains' sons were taken by company officials to a mission school operated by Anglicans on the Red River adjacent to Fort Garry at modern-day Winnipeg. Their return to their peoples helped stimulate the Christian element in the Dreamer-Prophet religion, one sign of which was the quasi-Christian services that natives held near Hudson's Bay Company posts.[16]

Important in the mercantilist-Christian-nativist syncretism fostered by the fur trade were the Iroquois Indians, who helped introduce Christian devotional practices among Pacific Northwest natives. One party of twenty-four Iroquois, under Ignace La Mousse, left a mission near Montreal, wandered across the continent, and settled among the Flatheads in about 1820. The anthropologist Cora Du Bois confirmed Leslie Spier's contention that it was from the Flathead country that the Christian-influenced Prophet Dance spread onto the Columbia plateau, although she also pointed out that Christian influences could have reached that region from the opposite direction – from the Pacific Coast and up the Columbia River.[17] In any case, it appears that the fur companies hoped the Iroquois moving west would encourage western tribes to engage in the fur trade. How successful the Iroquois were in this endeavor is questionable, and the Christianity they extended was interlaced with native beliefs. Nevertheless, because they circulated widely among the natives, they perhaps exerted more religious influence on them than did the clerks and factors in fur company employ.

The most important evangelists of the Christian faith among the Pacific Northwest tribes were the Protestant and Roman Catholic missionaries who first appeared in the interior in the 1830's and expanded their efforts in the 1840's. The fur people, the resettled Iroquois, and the native tribesmen sent east to examine and inquire further into Christianity, all had played important roles in formulating the native prophetic message, but the missionaries coming during the second phase reinforced it. Subsequently, as Christopher Miller and Wayne Suttles have pointed out, there would be a "superficial similarity between the moral and structural elements of the Prophet cult and Christianity, reinforcing the legitimacy of the former, the acceptability of the latter, and the potential for the confusion of the two."[18]

The missionaries' efforts served less to separate natives from their former life-ways than they did to divide them into "praying" and "nonpraying" factions. Because of this disruption, the Dreamer-Prophets found more ground for their attempts to save native society from those who would harm it. Most threatening, of course, were the white settlers, many of whom had been motivated to come west by learning of the rich soils and other resources of the region from Protestant missionary reports. More than any other group, the settlers and their protective government posed threats to natives, precipitating the great rise of Dreamer-Prophets during the Anti-American phase from 1860 to 1890.

Stimuli and Response

Wars and other human and natural cataclysms, producing suffering and great social change, were the catalysts that produced the Dreamer religion under which Smohalla and Skolaskin taught resistance to Americanization. In that crisis time they could not afford to retire to mountaintops to ponder and prophesy, but instead mingled with and ministered to those seeking their help. More than ten thousand settlers traveled the Immigrant Road (the Oregon Trail) to the Pacific Northwest in the 1840's.[19] In the same period the Indians became disenchanted with the missionaries who had come before, and they were angry at the United States government, which in the 1850's imposed land cessions and defeated various tribes in war. Anti-Americanism reached its zenith in the postwar era when the federal government moved Indians onto reservations, opening their previously held lands to white settlers, whose ways the government wanted the Indians to emulate on those reserves. The ministrations of Smohalla and Skolaskin were most effective at this time when their fellow Indians realized that they had but two choices: to remain under American domination or to reject American policies and values by joining the Prophet-inspired struggle for a pan-Indian revitalization and restoration of Native American life.

The United States government and the American community that it sought to protect were opposed to, if not frightened by, the teachings of the two Dreamer-Prophets and their circle. In the Columbia River watershed alone, nearly two thousand Indians, disillusioned and threatened by approaching whites and government edicts, were drawn to Smohalla. Others farther away were attracted by his promise of the restoration of native society as it was before the coming of the whites. From his Columbia homeland, Smohalla's influence reached even the Northern Paiute Indians of Nevada, whose Ghost Dance spread throughout the West in the

1870's. Like a prairie fire, the Ghost Dance was to consume the
Sioux in their confrontation with the United States Army in the in-
famous Wounded Knee massacre of 1890. Less directly, Smohalla
influenced the Modoc warriors in their futile attempts to avoid capture by American troops in the Modoc War of 1871 and 1872.

Closer to home, the Palouse and Nez Percé Indians came under
Smohallan influence. Stung by differences between American governmental promises and performance, and by differences between
Christian preachments and practices, the younger Nez Percé Chief
Joseph and his band unsuccessfully resisted American forces in
1877, unlike most of their tribe, who simply endured the injustices.
To a lesser extent, Smohalla influenced the Bannocks, who in the
following year also fought the Americans unsuccessfully. But, true
to the isolationism of his religion, Skolaskin avoided giving direct
spiritual or material aid to the embattled tribesmen.

Smohalla's people called the whites the *suyapos*. The latter, in
turn, called his followers "renegades" for their refusal to submit to
confinement on the reservations established for them under the
terms of the 1855 treaties, which the United States did not confirm
until 1859, after three years of successful wars against the Indians.
These so-called renegades, although anticipating the bright future
promised them by their Dreamer-Prophets, sought to preserve traditional lifeways. In this sense they were the conservatives of their
time.

Among the more important factors stimulating the Dreamer-
Prophet religions were the diseases carried by Euro-Americans to
the North American continent. The origins of these epidemics,
which struck the Pacific Northwest in the mideighteenth century
and possibly earlier, are vague. Some perhaps came from Russian
settlements in the north.[20] The smallpox, spread from aboard
ships, was easily identified by the pock-marked faces of its victims.
Smallpox raced up the Columbia River in 1782 and 1783 to join
epidemics of the disease that were moving westward up the Mis-
souri River and across the Rocky Mountains, leaving a path of
human destruction. Many were left dead from shipborne diseases,
such as those venereal in nature, introduced to natives of the lower
Columbia River in the eighteenth century, and the "intermittent
fever" (identified as malaria or some form of influenza) in 1829,
especially on the lower river.

Smohalla recalled the rumor widely circulated among natives
that the Reverend Marcus Whitman had returned from the East to
his Waiilatpu Mission in the Walla Walla valley in 1843 with a
germ-filled bottle from which the Indians believed he spread
measles among them. The rumor possibly emanated from near the
mouth of the Columbia River, where Duncan McDougall of John

Jacob Astor's Pacific Fur Company (Fort Astoria, founded, 1811) allegedly opened a similar vial, threatening to destroy the natives. The measles was carried to the mission primarily by white immigrants in 1847, and the disease was a root cause of the Whitman massacre of that year.

In recalling the plagues, Smohalla stated that "strong and terrible diseases broke out among us,"[21] and grim, though tenuous, statistics bear out his words. Whereas Wanapams, or the "Sokulks," as Lewis and Clark called them, had been estimated at 1,900 souls in 1780, the tribe was reduced to a mere 300 in 1870.[22] The frustration, anger, and terror that the natives felt at such heavy losses of life were important in elevating Smohalla to spiritual leadership.

Another deadly catalyst in Smohalla's rise to leadership in the midnineteenth century was the disorientation among Indians caused by the introduction of liquor. Arriving with the fur traders, liquor had flowed freely during the early stages of the land-based trade between 1810 and 1821, as it did in the coastal trade. Despite attempts by the Hudson's Bay Company to regulate it, supplies were available from that company's competitors, mainly the Americans. With American immigration the liquor trade continued, causing violent confrontations between whites and Indians in which the latter lost things dear to them—their lands, their wealth, their health, and even their very lives.

Other trade items from white men, although less dramatic in their effects than liquor, were also upsetting to them. The incoming goods altered traditional patterns and routes of trade, and traditional roles were altered as established native merchants yielded to those more able to deal with whites. Shamans, who had enjoyed prominence and wealth among their peoples from fees obtained in healings, were replaced by those adept in dealing with white men. Some tribes even went so far as to allow fur companies to choose their chiefs and to offer their women as wives of company personnel.

Even before the area became American territory, the landtaking policies of the pro-American Oregon Provisional Government (established in 1843) threatened to destroy the natives' existence. Treaties effected by the United States with lower-interior tribes in 1855 alarmed them, as did talk of removing coastal Indians to the interior. Defeats in wars against the Americans left them in disarray, as did the centerpiece of American acculturation, namely, the reservations delineated in the treaties. Smohalla watched at close range as Indians exchanged their vast homelands for such reservations in the lower interior as the Yakima, the Nez Percé, the Umatilla and the Warm Springs. Nothing resulting from the American presence caused the tribes more anguish than did confinement on reservations for the "crime" of standing in the way of advancing Americans. The reservations became the focal point of the discontent of nonconforming Indians, as the so-called renegades struggled to salvage their former ways of life. Believing in a future deliverance from such confinement, tribesmen along the middle Columbia sought spiritual and physical salvation from Smohalla's teachings.

On the reservations the government sought to destroy Indianness by imposing its own socioeconomic system. An alien legal system was thrust on the natives in which they had no voice in courts of law. As early as the 1840's, an agent, Elijah White, had imposed American laws on the Cayuse, Wallawalla, and Nez Percé tribes, threatening to replace their traditional codes. With Americans firmly established in the region, the native custom of obtaining "blood-feud" compensation for killings inflicted on their people was replaced by incarceration and execution, often by hanging, the worst possible demise for an Indian. The government acknowledged the system of chieftain governance when it served its purposes, but otherwise the chiefs were not recognized. Influential chiefs had benefitted from the division of labor in plural marriage, but polygyny was banned, as were native religions and languages in government schools. Under governmental protection, whites appropriated and exploited Indian lands, some of which were sacred, and ancient subsistence patterns were destroyed in the process. Fenced-off tracts interfered with passage to traditional grazing, root, berry, and fishing grounds.

The Dreamer-Prophets Smohalla and Skolaskin

In response to stimuli imposed by white men, and inspired by former seers of their race, Smohalla and Skolaskin offered salvation to their peoples. To do so, they had to demonstrate divine approbation of their prophetic roles by exhibiting what they claimed were supernatural powers beyond those that native youths experienced during their dream-trances on spirit-power quests. The two Prophets found the key to unlock their own powers usually after periods of physical and mental exhaustion not unlike what the youths of their tribes experienced in those quests. The similarity between their spiritual experiences and those of traditional Indian power seekers ends there, however, for they claimed that they had experienced death and heavenly sojourns and that they were commanded directly by God to instruct their people. They claimed that only by obeying their divinely established positions and by adhering to strict rules could their followers enjoy the millenarian delights awaiting them.[23]

Smohalla and Skolaskin prophesied in the manner of shamans but differed in other functions. The curings so important in shamanism were virtually nonexistent in their ministrations, and although the two Prophets were sometimes called priests by their white contemporaries, they did not fulfill all the priestly functions found in the established religious organizations of other societies. As chieftains they were religiously inspired, and yet, although such motives were shared by other traditional native leaders, socioeconomic concerns often prevailed over the dynamic of all-engrossing religion that inspired these two Prophets to lead their peoples.

The careers of Smohalla and Skolaskin present a contrast, in that the former began as a shaman and became a Prophet because of his increasing popularity, while the latter began as a Prophet and became a shaman as his popularity decreased. Smohalla stressed a rebirth and resurgence of native culture that was to remove the offending whites from the earth. Less universal in his perspective, Skolaskin stressed that revitalization was possible only if his faithful escaped from the earth, which he, like some of his spiritual predecessors in the Northwest, believed would again be engulfed in flood. Skolaskin's religion also differed from Smohalla's because, although it was a part of the Prophet-Dance phenomenon, which Leslie Spier showed had wide influence in western Native American revitalization, it lacked typical native dance content.[24]

Because the two men gained their positions as Prophets by trance-induced otherworldly experiences, the whites gave them the name "Dreamers." Because they promised hope to their followers, they stood in the forefront of a nineteenth-century cult movement among the Indians of the Pacific Northwest, especially in the interior region of the Columbia River and plateau. Important in this corner of the earth as representatives of an age-old religious phenomenon, the two Prophets, like others of their stamp, combined native traditionalism with Christianity, as they sought to unshackle their peoples from white American dominance.

Smohalla and Skolaskin's message of utopian restoration for red people was, in essence, one of revitalization. Until recently such messages among Native Americans have received little attention from scholars, particularly those dealing with the American West. As Clifford E. Trafzer and Margery Ann Beach Sharkey have pointed out, Smohalla and Skolaskin, like other holy persons in tribal communities,

> were suspect, often characterized by the white contemporaries [secular and religious alike] and Indian historians as frauds, fakes, and charlatans. In other instances, native religious leaders were regarded as wizards, witches, sorcerers, and devils. Often, American Indian prophets

belied the intellectual framework employed by scholars who failed – or refused – to perceive correctly the pre-eminent role of these individuals.[25]

Smohalla and Skolaskin were born and died scarcely three hundred miles from each other. Smohalla lived below the vast semicircular Big Bend of the Columbia River where it hugs the western border of the southern Columbia plateau. Farther south the river flows southeast before turning sharply west to form the boundary between Washington and Oregon on the final leg of its journey to the Pacific Ocean. Skolaskin lived near the top of the Big Bend where the Columbia, flowing south from Canada, turns sharply to the west, slashing through the southern rim of the northern plateau and on south through central Washington.

The two men were important historically not only in Indian revitalization but also because of their unique personalities and the stratagems that they employed. Like the one-eyed Shawnee Prophet, they both suffered physical deformities: Smohalla was a hunchback, and Skolaskin had crippled limbs. Their debilities kept them from excelling in hunting and other activities requiring physical skills. They did not, of course, lack mental acuity and personal magnetism, and by capitalizing on threats from outside, such as the presence of the encroaching whites, they were able to attract, manipulate, and offer hope to their peoples through claims of certification from heaven. Smohalla exploited his followers' need for leadership to carry them along on waves of enthusiasm, but Skolaskin often forced his people to act against their wills.

Because of the vagueness of the hopeful future that they projected, Smohalla and Skolaskin were forced to exhibit proof of their divine acceptance in the here and now. They did so not only by reaffirming their supernatural experiences but also by prophesying natural phenomena. They never revealed the sources of the latter information, which, in the case of eclipses, they had learned from the observations of whites. Often, in any case, their successful prophecies appear to have been based on pure luck.

If nothing else, the stark drama attending Smohalla's and Skolaskin's telling of their experiences had an hypnotic effect on their peoples. To maintain control over them, lest their enthusiasm waver, and to reinforce acceptance of his divine mission, Smohalla repeated his trance experiences, and Skolaskin proclaimed a second revelation reiterating his initial heavenly sojourn and admonition from God. In their otherworldly experiences, however, they made no claim to being supernatural – only to be able to communicate with the supernatural.[26] Unlike the prophets of other religions, Smohalla and Skolaskin needed no credentials from church boards or other governing bodies to prove that their authority came directly from above. Both believed in a "covenant" not unlike that of Judeo-Christianity, to which they owed a debt. This covenant required that, since the Creator nourished his children, they in turn were obligated to use and gratefully protect the bounties so generously bestowed on them. Any threats to the relationship between them and the Creator, be they human or natural, required supplications and appeasements beyond those required of traditional worshipers. It seems ironic that, despite the similarity of the native prophets to those of Judeo-Christian tradition, they were never accepted nor acknowledged as having merit by adherents of those faiths.

Part One
Smohalla of the Wanapams

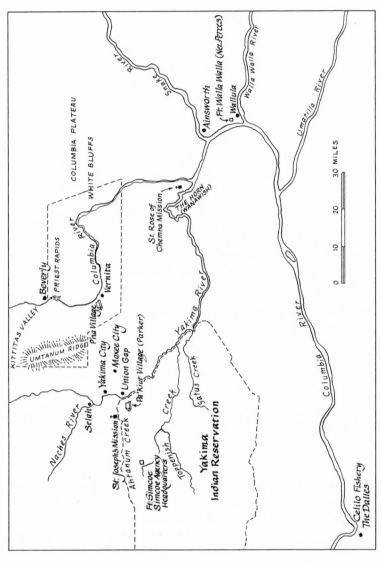

The Land of Smohalla and Its Environs

2

The Yantcha

God said he was the father, and the earth was the mother of mankind.

—Smohalla to Captain J. W. MacMurray

Little information comes to us concerning the birth and early life of Smohalla, whom his people called a *yantcha,* meaning a leader with strong spiritual qualifications. He was born sometime between 1815 and 1820[1] in the area of present-day Wallula, Washington. The Wallawalla word *wallula* meant "many small streams,"[2] and the future Dreamer-Prophet's birthplace was a mecca for numerous tribesmen who harvested salmon there before these fish escaped up the Columbia River and into its tributaries, such as the Snake, its largest, which entered it from the east. An early fur trader, with obvious exaggeration, described the Columbia shores in the Wallula area as so heavily populated in 1832 that scarcely was there "space enough between the lodges to allow a footman to pass."[3] In fairness to the trader, it should be said that the area was indeed heavily populated by permanent and temporary villagers who fished, traded, and socialized there.

Following the usual native practice, Smohalla would bear many names in his lifetime. At birth he bore the name Wak-wei, or Kukkia, meaning "arising from the dust of the Earth Mother." The names Smohalla, Smowhalla, Shmoqula, Smuxale, or "smo x El," as he once rendered it phonetically to a white man, were acquired after his majority when he rose to prominence as a *yantcha.* The names are from a word in his own Shahaptian tongue meaning "dreamer," although some sources render it "preacher." His people also called him Yuyunipitqana, "the Shouting Mountain," from their belief that, during his dreamings, revelations came to him from a mountain speaking inside his soul. White men would render the name as Big Talk on Four Mountains. Another name he bore was Waipshwa, or Rock Carrier.[4]

From birth Smohalla's head looked inappropriately big on his body. His frame, distorted by a hunched back and the attendant shortened neck and high shoulders, made his legs appear shorter than normal, and his body seemed like an assemblage of spare parts. Army Captain Eli L. Huggins, who visited him in the 1880's, noted that he was a "rather undersized Indian, about sixty years old, with a form inclining toward obesity, a reserved and cunning, but not ill-natured countenance, and a large and well shaped head" with manners "more suave and insinuating than is usual with Indians . . . [and] teeth . . . worn to the gums"[5] (very likely from eating salmon peppered with river sand). A similar assessment was given by Captain (later Major) Junius Wilson MacMurray, who visited Smohalla in the summer of 1884 and noted that he was "almost hunch-backed" with an "almost Websterian head, with deep brow, over bright intelligent eyes."[6]

MacMurray would have observed, as had other white men before him, that Smohalla's Wanapams were peace-loving, unlike some of their neighbors, such as the Cayuses on the southeast, a Waiilatpuan people who regarded those along the Columbia as their inferiors and sometimes raided them. Lewis and Clark had described the Indians of the Wallula area as "honest, worthy people."[7] Like other native societies, that into which Smohalla was born had a strong spiritual orientation. His people acknowledged the presence of a Great Spirit and lesser ones to whom they owed their subsistence and security, and whose powers and presence they acknowledged as encompassing all animate and inanimate things. This Dreamer came from a long line of *yantcha* prophets and shamans.[8]

Smohalla began his journey to spiritual maturity with the traditional spirit quest, the *wot*, like other native youth of the region. He was said to have received his spirit power atop the sacred mountain La Lac, which lies between present-day Prosser, Washington, and the Columbia River on the east. Informants claimed that he returned from his quest empowered to communicate with animals such as Crow (*Shah*) and Coyote (*Speelyi*), whose howlings warned of the death of a tribesman. By communicating with animals, Smohalla was said to have predicted good times and places for hunting and fishing. From his quest he also received special songs and symbols to implement his special powers.[9]

Important in Smohalla's rise to spiritual leadership, yet causing him great anguish, were the whites, whose arrival at the busy Columbia–Snake river confluence near Wallula was to alter the native society. Less touched at that time by white inroads were the Wanapam Indians living a short distance to the north near the Priest Rapids of the Columbia, to which Smohalla would remove to continue his ministrations. On their home grounds, the Wanapams had a record of friendliness toward whites going back to 1811, when they had met David Thompson of the North West Company and Astorians of John Jacob Astor's Pacific Fur Company. Both groups assessed the Wanapams as friendly in their relative isolation and their observance of traditional religious practices. The Astorians observed among them one whom they called Ha-quill-laugh, or "priest." It appears that he was so named because, in the Astorians' words, he performed for the "savages" "certain aspersions and other ceremonies, which had the air of being coarse imitations of Catholic worship."[10] Although it appears that this religious leader was more a shaman than a priest such as is found in more complex societies with organized churches, the Astorians named the rapids after him.

On the south, the North West Company (which replaced the Astor Company in 1813) established Fort Nez Percés in 1818 near the Columbia–Walla Walla river confluence in Smohalla's initial homeland. The fort brought natives of the Wallula area more directly into the fur nexus. Previously the Nor'westers traversing their lands had traded only casually with them. Hardly had any more changes occurred when missionaries arrived in the country than had occurred in native society with the fur trade. It was after the natives' brief enchantment with the missionaries' "magic medicine" that their disillusion turned to anger, precipitating a massacre at the nearby Whitman Mission in 1847, eleven years after its founding.[11]

In those changing times traditional shamans had little chance of retaining their former status, for on the heels of the missionaries came settlers and traditional shamans could no longer meet the threat that they posed. The times called for a new shamanism that would predict more than just the times of enemy attacks or the arrival of salmon—a shamanism that would inspire overwhelmed and shamed people who were unable to cope with the threats to their way of life. Special leaders were needed who promised more than the happy hunting grounds of heaven. The Dreamer-Prophets brought that heaven to earth by "dieing, going there and returning" with the spiritual power and the authority to offer the people revitalization. Smohalla was such a special leader. His ability to match the disturbing transition in native cultures with his own transition to higher, spectacular manifestations of spiritual power speaks much for his acuity and mental disposition, which sensed the fears and frustrations of his followers and promised them hope in their despair.

It is reasonable to assume that Smohalla's supernatural experiences were influenced by contact with those who espoused Christian doctrines or at least were aware of them. As the original

Christian resurrection was occasioned by a world in crisis, so was that faced by Smohalla. In his hands traditional shamanism was transformed to heal a threatened people. The Prophet's other-worldly experiences were not unlike those of two Christian saints, John the Revelator (Rev. 4.2) and Paul the Apostle (II Cor. 12.4), who wrote of having seen into heaven and returned to earth to tell about it. Sainted Christian dead were promised a return to life on a "millennial day."

Smohalla possibly learned of the Christian doctrine of death and resurrection from fur-company personnel such as the French-Canadian voyageurs, who espoused a primitive form of the Roman Catholic faith.[12] MacMurray was of the opinion that Smohalla had learned about that faith and had learned some French words as a lad when attending the Coeur d'Alene mission school in modern-day Idaho,[13] but that mission was not established until 1842 — too late for him to have attended it. James Mooney was more correct in stating that Smohalla would have learned about the Catholic creed and ritual at the Saint Joseph's Mission established by Oblate fathers in 1847 on Ahtanum Creek, a tributary of the Yakima River. To expose natives to their liturgy and langauges, priests from that mission traveled south to Zillah in the Yakima valley, as well as to the Selah and Kittitas valleys on the north and to the area of present-day Moxee City on the east.[14]

Although he did not attend the Coeur d'Alene mission school, Smohalla may have been aware of it, since fathers from Saint Joseph's Mission traveled there to purchase cattle and hogs for their own establishment.[15] The earliest contact Smohalla could have had with Catholic missionaries in his homeland was with the Reverends François Norbert Blanchet and Modeste Demers, who traversed the Priest Rapids in 1838 en route to the lower Columbia River. There is the likelihood that he also learned of the Catholic faith at the Saint Rose of Chemna Mission, established in 1847 in the lower Yakima valley, nearer his initial Wallula homeland.[16] Not unimportant in Smohalla's exposure to Catholicism would have been his awareness of Pierre Pambrun, the chief trader of Fort Walla Walla (formerly Fort Nez Percés), where Pambrun exerted among the natives not only a commercial but also a religious influence.[17]

Fur traders and priests were among the "all kinds of men" whom Smohalla told MacMurray that he knew. In recording his conversation with Smohalla, MacMurray interpreted this to mean that the earliest arrivals were French-Canadian voyageurs in the Hudson's Bay Company's employ. In Smohalla's ranking they were preceded only by the Indians in God's order of creation. Wanapams believed that the first members of their race had been born on their sacred island, Chalwash Chilini, in the Priest Rapids of the Columbia river. There the first men supposedly left their footprints on the rocks, and the Creator, Nami Piap, had called forth all the plants and animals, of which the first called were the salmon.[18] Third in Smohalla's ranking were Christian priests, who, according to Mac-Murray, had come to Priest Rapids with the Hudson's Bay Company. They were followed by the "Boston Men," the Americans, whom MacMurray stated had entered the Columbia River in 1796 (actually, it was 1792) on the ship *Columbia* (the *Columbia Rediviva*). They were followed by the "King George Men," whom MacMurray identified as "English" (British) soldiers; and lastly, by black men and Chinese.[19]

Smohalla's emerging leadership brought him into conflict with the influential Wallawalla chief Homily (Homli), who was jealous of his ascending rival. Unlike Smohalla, who saw their damaging effects on native culture, Homily tended to be receptive to whites, ambivalently holding onto their "medicine" with one hand and onto the native "medicine" with the other. He may have considered that his dual policy helped his people benefit from the two cultures, or he may have been motivated by self-interest. Native leaders often made no distinction between the two. It was shortly after 1850, following a three-day argument between the two leaders, that Smohalla and his followers moved north to Priest Rapids.[20] Besides his quarrel with Homily, we do not know if other motives prompted him and his people to move from the Wallula area. Possibly his antagonism toward Homily was matched by a desire to remove to a more isolated place to be free of the whites. Whatever his motives were for moving, natives freely passed along the Columbia in that area.

If credit be given to a story appearing in the *Overland Monthly* in May, 1889, Smohalla also incurred the wrath of the Wallawalla chief, Peopeomoxmox. According to the story, Smohalla had sought out that chief's youngest and most favorite wife. Discovering a tryst between the two, Peopeomoxmox flogged them to within an inch of their lives, sprinkled salt on their wounds, and left them tied for two days beneath a broiling sun. They were eventually ransomed by a clerk from Fort Walla Walla, after which Smohalla took his injured back and pride into the mountains. When Peopeomoxmox was slain by white volunteers in December, 1855, Smohalla was said to have attributed that chief's demise to his (Smohalla's) own "evil eye." Thereafter, the story concluded, mothers covered their babies' faces when passing the Prophet and adults feared to meet him alone.[21]

Smohalla's new home after his confrontation with Homily and his departure from the Wallula area was the P'na Village, which stood near a fish weir on the Columbia right bank at the foot of the seventh of the Priest Rapids, upriver from present-day Vernita, Washington. The village consisted of tule-mat houses set in wind-blown sand among fire-blackened rocks. Above it on the west towered the protecting Umtanum Ridge. There was little outward evidence of the changes that had occurred in the region since early in the century. The Columbia continued to test the Wanapams' navigational skills and to provide them with salmon, as did fisher-ies at the White Bluffs, which were below Priest Rapids, and at Wanawish (The Horn), about fifteen miles west of the bluffs on the Yakima River. The hills flanking the P'na Village furnished its people with roots and berries, which they mixed with salmon to make a nutritious food. They were not, however, bound to their homeland, for they gathered subsistence and traded with other natives in the surrounding valleys of the Kittitas and the Yakima on the west and the Columbia on the south, and on the plateau.[22] Before long the firearms brought into the region reduced the ani-mal population and forced the Wanapams and other natives to depend increasingly on fishing and gathering subsistence.

The Wanapams retained what Lewis and Clark had described as their "mild and peaceful disposition . . . in a state of comparative happiness."[23] They possessed that disposition even in relation to the rattlesnakes hissing along their riverbanks. Astorians saw them coddling these reptiles, whose fangs they extracted. When they were bitten, they applied herbs and ligatures and scarified the wounds.[24] They believed that, since animals had come before human beings on earth, the Great Spirit had delegated Speelyi, The Coyote, to prepare it in perfect form for human habitation; and prophets had foretold of the return of animals to live on earth with men in a future happy day. Coyote was believed to be a precursor of the Great Chief who would return to earth accompanied by the spirits of the dead, after which there would be no spirit land. Then all the people would live together, and the Earth Woman would revert to her natural shape and live among her happy children.[25]

In anticipation of that day, the Wanapams remained friendly toward those who did not violate their lands or persons. Their con-tinuing friendliness was evident, for example, on March 30, 1825, when their leader, "the Priest" (possibly the one for whom the rapids were named), and a hundred of his people smoked the pipe with Superintendent George Simpson of the Hudson's Bay Com-pany on the latter's return east from a journey to the lower Columbia.[26]

A quarter-century later, however, the increasing presence of whites and their threats to the natives' way of life forced Smohalla to continue formulating his religion. After telling Captain Huggins of the suffering that the whites brought to the Indians, Smohalla related to him the rumor that the Reverend Whitman had carried disease to them on his return from the East in 1843: "The Indians killed Doctor Whitman, but it was too late. He had uncorked his bottle, and all the air was poisoned. Before that there was little sickness among us, but since then many of us have died. I have had children and grandchildren, but they are all dead. My last grandchild, a young woman of sixteen, died last month. If only her infant could have lived. . . . I labored hard to save them, but my medicine would not work as it used to."[27]Neither had Smohalla's medicine worked well when his daughter had died earlier in adolescence. His failure to cure her and his deep anguish at the loss of other children must have given him more impetus to enunciate his message of hope and to shift to a Prophet role stressing revitalization as a panacea for death. The hope of resurrection of dead loved ones may have accounted for the absence of healings in Smohalla's ministrations. The Dreamer religion differed in this respect from the Indian Shakerism that sprang up in 1882 among the Squaxin Indians of southern Puget Sound under the sect's founder, John Slocum. Although Shakerism spread to the Columbia plateau, among other places, it is unclear to what extent it and Smohalla's Washani influenced each other.[28]

Smohalla was not averse to receiving medical aid from white doctors, even going so far as to let one of them patch him up when he broke three ribs in a fall from his horse.[29] As though wishing to cast aside his personal emotional and corporeal tragedies, which he may have regarded as expressions of the Creator's displeasure, he continually plunged into renewed spiritual activity. He was said to have received a revelation from the Great Spirit on the wings of a bird while influenced by thirst and hunger. From this experience he gained new power songs, reportedly as many as 120, and rituals to supplement those of his prophetic predecessor Shuwapsa. Both he and his followers claimed that he had died twice, each time being resurrected.[30]

To Smohalla, the most evident fulfillment of Shuwapsa's prophecy of the evil that the whites would bring was the Yakima War between 1855 and 1856, in which "hostiles" from the interior were defeated by the United States Army and Oregon and Washington territorial volunteers. This war was precipitated by the treaties which were to confine natives to reservations that were small when compared to the lands that they surrendered. Government officials expeditiously grouped bands together for treaty making, and in the process Smohalla's Wanapams were lumped with Yakimas and thus were denied an identity and a voice in the negotiations. There is some question whether one signer of the treaty under the Qamil-lema, or Kahmiltpah, standard was a Wanapam or was of a Salish people living around the Saddle Mountains, which, at least in later times, were a borderline between Shahaptian and Salish speakers.[31] Even if Smohalla had assumed leadership at that time, it is doubtful that he would have been party to such a transaction. Details of the treaties and the ensuing war may be found in other books.

The anthropologist James Mooney believed that Smohalla, whom he stated began preaching about 1850, materially facilitated the Indian war confederation. If he indeed stimulated warriors to action, they would have been members of more aggressive neighboring tribes such as the Cayuses, the Palouses, and the Columbia Sinkiuses—all tribes that the head war chief, Kamiakin, of the Yakimas, recruited to fight the Americans. According to Major Granville O. Haller, commander of the Fourth Infantry, U.S.A., which the Indian coalition defeated in the initial engagement of the war at Toppenish Creek in September, 1855. Indians from Priest Rapids were in the conflict, but it would have been most difficult for Haller to have identified most of his opponents. Several Priest Rapids Indians were huddled in the vicinity of Saint Joseph's Mission on the Ahtanum, trying to keep out of harm's way.[32] Also, the leader of the influential Wanapam So-Happy family (or Souiepappie, "stemming from the lineage of Shuwapsa") died at the hands of Yakimas for refusing to supply them with horses and enter the war.[33] Although Smohalla was said to have been a warrior in his early years, there is no evidence that he continued in that role in the Indian wars, much less helped organize the warring coalition.[34] The fur trader Andrew Pambrun claimed that the Indian "confederation" dissolved when its leader, Peopeomoxmox, was killed by white volunteers. In reality, it was the defeat of Kamiakin and his forces which destroyed any hope of continuing hostilities.[35]

The war and its ensuing treaties affected native society and Smohalla as much as they affected it. The government had laid down the gauntlet to them, claiming that they were illegal tenants on the land, and this proved a viable stimulus to the Wanapam Prophet to oppose the government. In the postwar era the power of traditional shamans, whose "medicine" had been unable to prevent Indian losses, tended to weaken, thus enhancing that of Smohalla and his new type of shamanism. He also encountered few challenges to his leadership among his own people. A possible contender, the influential So-Happy, was dead, and Mitchelle (Mischeil), the son of the elderly, infirm Mes-sow-wee, considered himself unfit for the chieftaincy.[36]

The greatest challenge to Smohalla came not from his own people but from the outside, in the person of Chief Moses of the

Columbia Sinkiuses on the north, whose wintering grounds at that
time abutted those of the Wanapams near the present hamlet of
Beverly. After the death of his father, the powerful Sulktalth-
scosum, at the hands of Plains warriors about 1850, and the death
of that chief's eldest son, Quiltenenock, at the hands of miners in
1858, Moses sought to be the leader of the middle-upper Columbia
River bands. With all the enmity of traditional chiefs towards the
Prophets, Moses believed Smohalla to be making especially strong
"medicine" against his life. His fears were understandable, since in
these Indians' cultures those who acquired prophetic and other
powers would safeguard them from rivals seeking to steal them,
even if it meant killing to do so. Moreover, the Columbia chief believed the Prophet to be proselyting members of his band.

According to a much publicized story, the two leaders engaged in
a fight that left Smohalla half dead; and left to die, he escaped to
journey as far as Mexico. From there he is said to have returned to
Utah, where he reportedly saw Mormon priests of the Church of
Jesus Christ of Latter-day Saints receiving commands directly from
heaven. Whether or not Smohalla did indeed visit the Mormons, he
would have had an affinity with them, not only because of their
practice of polygyny and their emphasis on the role of prophets but
also because of their antipathy toward American gentile society
and its government. He also would have had an opportunity to
learn about them without ever visiting their Deseret homeland.
Among the Mormon contacts with Pacific Northwest Indians was
Brigham Young's 1857 visit to the Mormon Lemhi Mission in east-
central Idaho where he sought to bring surrounding Lamanites (Indians) to his faith.[37] The Choosuklee (Jesus Christ), whom Klickitat
Indians in the 1850's said would come to drive out the whites, was
possibly a native prophet such as Smohalla, or possibly Young himself, who visited tribesmen of the eastern plateau.[38]

A correspondent of the *San Francisco Chronicle* may have been
among the first to publish the story of the Smohalla-Moses fight in
1878, at a time when the recent Nez Percé (1877) and Bannock-
Paiute (1878) wars had brought Moses and Smohalla to the attention of the white community, which was anxious to know if they
would send their braves against the Americans.[39]During the latter
war "hostiles" fleeing American troops sought sanctuary in Moses'
camps, and he was hard pressed to restrain his restless young men
from fighting.

In recounting his conversation with Smohalla, MacMurray freely
inserted his own story of the fight with Moses, as he also did Smohalla's improbable attendance at the Coeur d'Alene Mission school.
Those close to Moses, a man not above boasting, claim that he
never mentioned the fight, and Click Relander, a student, friend,

and chronicler of the Wanapams, stated that none of their elderly ever mentioned it.[40] In that day of poor communications, sensational stories in the press, such as that of the Moses-Smohalla confrontation, were often based on misinformation and rumor. For example, the March 9, 1866, issue of the *Weekly Mountaineer* of The Dalles, Oregon, reported that "Smoholor," or "Big-talk on four mountains," a "great rogue and murderer," had been killed near Priest Rapids by Yakima Indians around mid-February of that year. The story seems to have pleased the reporter, who believed the Prophet had hindered the passage of miners and settlers at White Bluffs, where travelers to the northeast moved away from the Columbia into the upper plateau.

Whether or not the story of the Moses-Smohalla fight is true, there certainly was bad blood between them. Each was aware of the importance of his leadership to his people, to whom the rivalry also extended, although Moses was not above marrying a Wanapam woman.[44] When attending Smohalla's services, he once invited the Prophet to drink with him. Smohalla lacked the ability of his oft-imbibing guest to hold his liquor, and he continued preaching, his usual eloquence reduced to a slur. Angered at Moses, one of Smohalla's wives stormed from the mat lodge, chasing one of Moses' wives with a pole. The latter jerked it from her attacker, whereupon Moses and his party huffily packed their gear and went home.[42] During the Nez Percé and Bannock-Paiute wars the non-aligned Moses implied to an Indian inspector that the Wanapam Prophet might cause trouble, and he threatened to take a rope and go down and hang him someday.[43]

As strong as was Smohalla's antagonism toward Moses, it was no stronger than what he felt toward the greater threat, the Americans and their government. By the same token, no thornier obstacle stood in the whites' way than Smohalla and his teachings, which pricked the Americans' consciousness like wind-blown dust-devil thorns, threatening to infest the soils of "civilization." With the typical Anglo-Saxon propensity to personalize evil, white men heaped abuse upon him. The more he felt their threatening barbs the more he was thrust into a leadership role to cope with the white-induced crisis – and the more he sharpened and uttered his creed to a stubborn, white-resisting corps of disciples. That creed is examined in the next chapter.

3
Washani: *The Creed*

> You ask me to plough the ground! Shall I take a
> knife and tear my mother's bosom? . . . You
> ask me to dig for stone! Shall I dig under her
> skin for her bones? . . . You ask me to cut
> grass and make hay and sell it, and be rich like
> white men, but how dare I cut off my mother's
> hair?
> —*Smohalla to Captain J. W. MacMurray.*

In *The Mythology of All Races,* Hartley Burr Alexander described
Smohalla as "a chieftain of the Far West . . . [from whom] comes
perhaps the most eloquent expression of the sense of Earth's
motherhood in Occidental literature."[1] The Prophet's words have
come to us as eloquently as translation will allow because they
were spoken through an interpreter in his own Shahaptian tongue,
a softer language (albeit still harsh to American ears) than that of
Salish speakers such as Skolaskin farther to the north. Even when
preaching to others of his own linguistic family, such as the Sha-
haptian-speaking Nez Percés and Klickitats, Smohalla insisted that
his words be interpreted in their languages in order that he be
clearly understood. Whenever possible, he avoided using the Chinook jargon, the lingua-franca relic of the fur trading era, which
would have rendered his thoughts less clearly.[2]

The creed that Smohalla expounded was derived from that bearing the name Washani (from a Shahaptian term meaning literally
"dancers"), which apparently was first published by anthropologist
Cora Du Bois as *The Feather Cult of the Middle Columbia* (1938). A
student of the Wanapams, L. V. McWhorter, wrote that the Washani, which Spier believed was the same as the "Prophet Dance,"
was a "graft" onto earlier native "Medicine Religion," but he cau-
tiously avoided dating the grafting. McWhorter was impressed
with the writings of Mourning Dove (Hum-ishu-ma), of Okanagon
descent, who believed the prophecy of the Okanagon Kōōms-
kooms that the coming of the whites was the source of the Pom
Pom, or Dreamer, religion among the Yakimas and others.[3] Other
informants believed that it antedated the coming of whites to the
Pacific Northwest. Prophecies of their coming certainly stimulated
either its formation or its revival.

A most important element in Washani belief was that its Prophets had "died, gone to heaven, and returned" with words from God for their followers. Important in their message was that all Indians would return to life when the world reverted to them on a "Millennial Day." More light was shed on Washani beliefs by a Simcoe agent, R. H. Milroy, in two reports of March 29 and August 15, 1884, to U.S. Indian Commissioner Hiram Price:

> [They believe that] very soon now their dead ancestors will all come to life every stone becoming a living Indian, that all the whites will be killed off, and their property go to the Indians, and further that the great Smohalla, will establish numberless great stores filled with all manner of fine goods, where all Indians can go and help themselves.
>
> They believe that if they will continue faithful to the old habits and beliefs of their ancestors, that the Great Spirit will in the near future suddenly bring to life all Indians who have died for the last thousand years or more, and will enable the Indians to at once expel or exterminate all the whites and have the whole country to themselves the same as before the white man came.[4]

The Washani found expression in the Washat dance. The early development of the Washat, like that of the Washani, is vague. There are similar Wanapam words: *washshot*, meaning "to ride," and *wahshet*, meaning "cold month" in the Wanapam calendar. The term Pom Pom, meaning "drums beating like hearts," has also been used to describe the ceremony. Informants stated that it was Wattilki who first revealed the Pom Pom. Others stated that it was a Prophet of the Yakima River country who found it.[5] Yet others stated that the Washani began "a long time back" when natives had died "like flies" during an epidemic.[6] If that was the case, the Dreamer religion possibly began no earlier than the eighteenth century, assuming that the disease mentioned was introduced by whites.

Informants also said the Washani was revived by others besides Smohalla, especially the Yakima Dreamer-Prophet Kotiakan (Kotai'aqan). A pioneer of the Yakima valley, A. J. Splawn, stated that "Ko-ti-ah-an, son of Show-a-way, whose father was We-ow-wicht, the fountain head of royalty in the Yakima tribe, practiced a religion similar to Smo-hal-la's." Close ties existed between Smohalla and Kotiakan's people, and there is a possibility that the two prophets were of the same lineage.[7] Kotiakan led a Yakima Dreamer band at Pa'kiut Village on the right bank of the Yakima River near present-day Parker and Union Gap (just below the city of Yakima). One informant stated that Kotiakan

started his religion a short time before we [the Yakimas] heard of Smo-

halla. He used to be a great gambler and a very bad man. People began
to notice that Kutaiaxen [Kotiakan] was not himself at times. He would
wander from home and lie around. While he was out some place the
Washani faith came to him. He heard a voice telling him to praise the
Lord in song and dance on Sundays. Sometimes they would find him
lying in a coma as though he were dead. He had his biggest meetings in
midwinter. People came to them from all over the reservation.[8]

Mooney stated that Kotiakan not only was Smohalla's right-hand
man, assisting him in services, but also helped originate the Smo-
hallen creed and ceremony.[9] If that seems too much, it may be said
at least that the successful enunciation and conduct of the hitherto
ill-defined Washani faith owed much to the close cooperation between the two.

We are informed of Smohalla and Kotiakan's religions from the
pens of military personnel who either visited or were aware of
them. Although with less depth than might be expected of anthropologists, their observations of native culture were recorded more
objectively than would have been expected of their missionary,
government-agent, or settler contemporaries, who frowned on Washani exponents as practitioners of a pagan cult.

Smohalla seems to have been willing to familiarize military men
with his religion, although his followers appear to have frowned on
his conversations with whites. For example, Smohalla revealed the
precepts of his faith to Captain Huggins, who rode with a cavalry
command to a valley about twelve miles distant from the P'na
Village. Huggins had been successful fighting the Sioux Indians,
and he was a keen observer of American Indian life, taking careful
note of Smohalla's creed, and of the Prophet himself. Huggins
noted that the Washani tenents and other aspects of Wanapam culture had never been put in writing, but the faith, with variations,
was passed down at second and third hand to natives even at some
distance. Those who accepted the Smohallan creed, he observed,
agreed on two of its essential precepts: that all Indians from the
east to the west coast should return immediately to observing
ancient rituals and religious dances, abandoning all appearances of
"civilization," and that soon a sudden, wonderful, irresistible supernatural intervention would destroy the whites or at least reduce
them to oblivion, if not subservience.

In answering Huggins, and, in essence, all the encroaching white
culture, Smohalla declaimed:

You ask me to plough the ground! Shall I take a knife and tear my
mother's bosom? Then when I die she will not take me to her bosom to
rest.

You ask me to dig for stone! Shall I dig under her skin for her bones?
Then when I die I can not enter her body to be born again.

You ask me to cut grass and make hay and sell it, and be rich like
white men, but how dare I cut off my mother's hair?[10]

At Huggin's suggestion that the ever-growing number of whites
could make better use of the land than could Indians, the Prophet
replied that he had learned from an Indian who had visited Washington, D.C., that whites east of the Rocky Mountains had huge
blocs of uncultivated lands and that beyond the "great sea" (the
Atlantic Ocean) they fenced off large tracts just to keep a few deer
and grouse. Moreover, he knew a man on the lower Columbia who
for years had owned a large tract of uncultivated bottomland, and
no one questioned his possession of it because he was white. Smohalla expressed to Huggins a lack of sympathy for followers of the
younger Nez Percé Chief Joseph, who, he claimed, were driven
from their lands because they had no business planting fields like
white men. Indians, he said, who emulated whites by cutting their
hair, wearing white men's clothing, and learning to sing from a
book were no better. He was alluding to the influence of early
Christian missionaries among tribes such as the Nez Percés in the
1830's and 1840's and to the agents and other officials who, three
decades later under the Peace Policy of President Ulysses S. Grant,
were authorized to administer, Christianize, and "civilize" Indians
on various reservations. An Indian inspector, E. C. Kemble, who
visited the Yakima Reservation in September, 1873, described as
follows the Peace Policy goals on that and other reservations for
the commissioner of Indian Affairs: "I thought as Peace is better
than War, so the Peace Policy which makes Christian men and
women of Indians must be better than the old policy of whiskey
alternated with whippings to keep them quiet."[11]

Huggins tried to trap Smohalla by reminding him that his own
followers worked during fishing seasons. Smohalla replied: "This
work only lasts for a few weeks. Besides, it is natural work and
does them no harm. But the work of the white man hardens soul
and body; nor is it right to tear up and multilate the earth as white
men do." To his list of earth disturbers he might have added the
Chinese, for whom he had little regard because for two decades
they had torn up Columbia shorelines searching for gold, and
because, in his words, they had worked so hard to do so. The ethnologist Albert Samuel Gatschet suggested that Smohalla's hatred
of those defacing the Earth Mother, and his belief that she would
engulf such malefactors within her bosom, stemmed possibly from
the idea that recently broken ground exhaled "miasmas deleterious
to all people dwelling near."[12]

"But you also dig roots," Huggins sparred. "Even now your people are digging camas roots in the mountains." To this Smohalla replied:

> We simply take the gifts that are freely offered. We no more harm the earth than would an infant's fingers harm its mother's breast. But the white man tears up large tracts of land, runs deep ditches, cuts down forests, and changes the whole face of the earth. You know very well this is not right. Every honest man . . . knows in his heart that this is all wrong. But the white men are so greedy they do not consider these things.[13]

Smohalla could have explained for Huggins his hexadic calendar, which revealed his people's close contact with nature. There were six seasons: the "cold month" (Wah-shet); the winter solstice (Yah-kukeelah), "when the sun 'turns around' when the sacred bird called all living things to waken"; Tzin-bick (?); the "crows coming" (Ahami); the "small insects coming" (Hish-hush); the time to "start to dig roots, make caches and move out" (Shih-tash); and "fall fishing" (Ikah-tash).[14]

Rebutting Huggins's statement that white men had given Indians many good things, including horses, Smohalla attributed the presence of such assets to the Great Spirit rather than the Spaniards or anyone else. The horses to which he referred were the fleet, sleek cayuses which over the years had come to stand about thirteen-hands high. It was bad, he said, that the cayuses were being bred with horses of the whites for draft purposes. Such animals were an anathema to him, not only because they were unsuited for riding, unlike his own pinto pony, but because their plowing etched furrows on the face of the Earth Mother. As bad as these draft horses, in Smohalla's thinking, were cattle, which had been first brought into the country by fur traders.[15] And besides cattle, the fathers at their Ahtanum Mission had several root-disturbing hogs, which they had crated at the Coeur d'Alene Mission and hauled squealing on horseback to their own establishment.[16]

Another military officer to whom we are indebted for observations of Smohalla and his creed was Major MacMurray. As incisive as Huggins, MacMurray wrote that Smohalla's Indians were called not only "Dreamers," for the dream-trances that inspired their leader, but also "Drummers," for their "ear paralyzing orchestra of seven base drums . . . a part of all their daily or more frequent services." Rather than considering his host as having invented a new faith, MacMurray characterized him as a "remodeller of several old ones."[17]

MacMurray was under orders to neutralize an explosive situation in the interior, where whites and Indians had sent numerous complaints over land to the headquarters of the military's Department of the Columbia at Vancouver Barracks on the lower Columbia. MacMurray was under orders to ascertain the Indian grievances and their progress in housing and to help them locate lands under the Indian Homestead Act of March 3, 1875 (18 Stat. 402). On July 4, 1884, at about the time of his visit with Smohalla, a second Indian Homestead Act was passed (23 Stat. 76). MacMurray called the Priest Rapids the "fountain head" of the Dreamer-Drummer religion, a term that whites rather than Indians used to describe it. MacMurray assured Smohalla and his people that by taking homesteads they would avoid trouble with settlers. To illustrate, MacMurray pointed out to the Prophet the black squares on a checkerboard, which he said represented the railroad lands, while the remaining white squares, except those reserved for schools, were for reds, whites, and blacks. He also explained how the east-west (section?) lines, again represented on the checkerboard, aligned with the sun, and those running north and south, with the north star. MacMurray's explanation had little impact on Smohalla, who believed that Indians filing for homesteads broke a fundamental law of God and would be punished by him for so doing.

The mere mention of railroads and locomotives, the *eelohksmees* (literally, "fire-built"), must have raised Smohalla's ire. He was surely aware of the passage of Northern Pacific Railroad Company survey crews between Priest Rapids and the Cascade Mountains in the early 1870's. Railroad activity had been slowed by the Panic of 1873, but was renewed during the latter part of the decade.[18] For a time Ainsworth, a Columbia–Snake River town near Smohalla's birthplace was an important link along the Northern Pacific line, which by 1883 had tied the Pacific Northwest to the upper Midwest. Smohalla's nephew Puck Hyah Toot ("Birds Feeding in a Flock"; and Johnny Buck) stated in later years that Smohalla had predicted the coming of boats and trains bringing whites in greater numbers. Certainly, Puck Hyah Toot's statement was based on the Prophet's awareness of these means of transportation. Steamers had churned to the foot of Priest Rapids as early as 1859.

An informant acquainted with Smohalla's successors in the 1930's stated that the Prophet had obtained an almanac from railroad surveyors and, in 1883, another from a station agent (most likely at Ainsworth), from whom he also obtained nails to build a bench for MacMurray. According to the informant, Smohalla's inability to secure an almanac for 1884 restricted his usual predictions of natural phenomena such as eclipses based on scientific observation. He also had a book containing alphabetlike letters which he claimed prophetically recorded events.[19]

Smohalla would have been aware of both the railroad surveyors and those in the federal government's employ on the Columbia River. In March, 1885, Indians at Priest Rapids told an employee of the United States Army Engineers, who were preparing the way for a party to establish gauges on the river near the Indian villages, that they did "not much enjoy the prospect of having the river improved," fearing it would spoil their fishing.[20] Nor would they have welcomed the steamboats that continued to navigate the river to Priest Rapids and the warehouse that white men built nearby in hopes of making that point a trade center.[21]

For MacMurray, Smohalla rendered an interpretation of law and how it came to be, placing his law higher than that of the Americans. The land, he said, was never to be marked off or divided. People were to enjoy the fruits that God planted on it and the animals that lived there and the fishes in the water. God, he said, was the father, and the earth, the mother of mankind. Nature was the law that animals, fish, and plants obeyed. "This is the old law," he declared, and those cutting up lands and signing papers for them would be defrauded of their rights and punished by an angry God. Explaining his cosmogony and the origins of man, he declaimed to MacMurray:

> Once the world was all water, and God lived alone; he was lonesome, he had no place to put his foot; so he scratched the sand up from the bottom, and made the land and he made rocks, and he made trees, and he made a man, and the man was winged and could go anywhere. The man was lonesome, and God made a woman. They ate fish from the water, and God made the deer and other animals, and he sent the man to hunt, and told the woman to cook the meat and to dress the skins. Many more men and women grew up, and they lived on the banks of the great river whose waters were full of salmon. The mountains contained much game, and there were buffalo on the plains. There were so many people that the stronger ones sometimes oppressed the weak and drove them from the best fisheries, which they claimed as their own. They fought, and nearly all were killed, and their bones are to be seen in the sand hills yet. God was very angry at this, and he took away their wings and commanded that the lands and fisheries should be common to all who lived upon them.[22]

Smohalla's beliefs about the origins of things intermingled with those of Christianity. This mix was also expressed in expositions by Kotiakan, who explained that the Great Spirit, the "High Up Chief," threw up huge handfuls of mud, creating the land, including rocks and mountains. When they were hunting and berry picking in the mountains, said Kotiakan, the people could see that their ancestors

were telling the truth about the creation of the world. He also explained that because the people quarreled, the Earth Mother
angrily threw down the mountains, damming the Columbia River
downstream (at what whites called the "Bridge of the Gods"), bury-
ing entire tribes beneath the rocks. Someday, he said, God would
expose their bones. God, he said, had fashioned the world (much
in the manner that he made the first man) from a "ball of mud," and
to assuage the first man's loneliness, he had made him a woman
companion, whom God taught to dress skins, gather berries, and
make root baskets, in which were preserved for her descendants
all the arts of design and skilled handiwork. All men, said Kotiakan, descended from one source, which was like a stick held by
white men at one end and by Indians at the other. The stick had
broken, but the pieces were to be reunited someday. The only meat
to be eaten was from natural sources such as fish and game. Thus
Kotiakan refused to accept a gift of cattle from the government, but
to inspire MacMurray's wife, he had presented MacMurray with
his own gift for her—a tiny, ancient, drum-shaped basket.[23]

When talking with the military officers, Smohalla, apparently de-
ferring to the hospitality that he extended them, did not expound
the final and most important element of his creed, the annihilation
of whites at doomsday. Perhaps the officers could have learned
more, had they, as Huggins put it, "penetrate[d] the arcanum" of the
Smohalla cult. By not doing so, they were denied knowledge of this
aspect of its eschatology. With increasing numbers of encroaching
whites in mind, Smohalla confessed that it would have been better
if his fathers had killed off the earliest ones of that race in Indian
country. Yet he knew that the rapid decline of the natives in response to the white invasion had made such a course of action impossible. The violence of his creed was thus confined to words, not
deeds.

Although MacMurray knew of Smohalla's alleged peregrinations
throughout the West (apparently not from Smohalla, but from
newspaper accounts making the rounds), he learned little of the
Prophet's heavenly travels. During long sleeplike trances, induced
by rhythmic songs and dances acting on his excited imagination,
the Prophet reportedly journeyed to heaven to see for himself
nature's overflowing bounties. There, instead of the streets of gold
on which Christianity's saints trod, he found trails over which ran
an endless supply of game. Apparently, his white visitors did not
witness the full frenzy of his followers, whom he skillfully controlled by relating his revelations and by threatening to abandon
his earthly body should they disobey his preachings. One observer,
who contacted Smohalla's survivors in 1937, claimed that skeptics
stuck needles into the Prophet's flesh during his trances, cutting

him with knives to test his sensitivity to pain, only to see no blood issuing from his body.[24]

Smohalla's visitors learned enough of his concepts of the other world to understand that it involved transporting heaven's best to earth, where the spirits of the dead would rejoin their bodies in new life. Unlike Christians, Washani worshippers had no concept of sin or of a fiery hell, believing instead that evil persons were barred from the Good Land until they had cleansed themselves from wrongdoing. This purgatorial aspect of Smohalla's creed suggests that he may have been influenced by Catholic priests in formulating it. That the whites' God could punish people with the heat of never-ending suns was inconceivable to Washani worshippers. Unlike other Indians who espoused both nativist and Christian beliefs to keep their options open for a wonderful hereafter, Smohalla remained true to his own teachings until he died. In 1873 he told a Methodist minister, the Reverend G. W. Kennedy, that he did not know the Christian doctrine (despite incorporating some of its creed and trappings into his own); and out of courtesy he permitted Kennedy to tell him about the Bible and heaven.[25] Some government agents, under the aegis of the church-oriented Peace Policy, assumed the role of preachers when dealing with Indians. One of them, Special Indian Commissioner Felix R. Brunot, explained in 1871 to the Smohalla-Kotiakan disciple Waunitta (or Weonito, and perhaps Wenatee) the basic element of Christian doctrine that at one time not only were the whites evil but the Indians as well. The remedy for their fallen state, Brunot explained, was that God in pity had sent his son to die so that humankind would not have to suffer permanent death.[26]

Unlike Brunot, most whites in the interior were less interested in saving Indian souls than in saving Indian soils for themselves, while avoiding the retaliatory attacks that they suspected Smohalla had instigated. There were exceptions, however, to the usual white anti-Smohalla posture. As reported in the July, 1886, edition of *The Northwest*, a periodical sponsored by the Northern Pacific Railroad Company, a suggestion had appeared in that month's edition of the *North Yakima Farmer* that the name Smohalla be adopted for the proposed state of Washington. The writer suggesting the name had pointed out its euphonious sound as well as the "talent and tact" of its namesake, whose features, the writer had said, expressed the "great spirituality and force" of one who would have been a leader in any civilization. No mention was made of Smohalla's sensitivity regarding the environment and its sacredness – not a burning issue in that day. Taking exception to the cognomen, the editor of *The Northwest* suggested that the name of the new state instead be Lincoln or Garfield, asking "Why honor the name of a savage whose only distinction is that he is half rascal and half fanatic and is doing all he can to hinder the civilization of the Indians under his influence?"[27] In an ironic turn, at the time of the centennial in 1989, Smohalla was selected for the state of Washington's Hall of Honor as one of the hundred persons whose contributions were influential not only in the state but nationally.

In the twentieth century serious attempts have been made to reconcile elements of the Christian faith with the lingering nativism in the Indian community, but in Smohalla's day whites believed that their Judeo-Christian religion was threatened by the likes of the Prophet. Some of them felt secure in thinking that in a Darwinian scheme of things Indians would fail the test of cultural fitness: "When settlement and civilization approach," wrote the editor of *The Northwest*, "their [the Indians'] work is done, their usefulness is past, and in the divine order of the survival of the fittest, they give place to the advancing thought so 'The old order changeth, yielding place to new, and God fulfills himself in many ways.'"

An element of Smohalla's creed that was especially suspect within the white community was the polygyny among Washani adherents. The practice was deeply engrained in Pacific Northwest native cultures, especially among leaders, such as Smohalla, who emulated those of an aristocratic stamp on the southern Columbia plateau, where heredity and wealth were important determinants of status along with leadership ability. If Smohalla indeed had contact with Mormons, it cannot be said that he adopted polygyny from them.

Like most whites and Indians of their time, Smohalla and his followers frowned on intermarriage between races. They were also contemptuous of reservation Indians who adopted white ways, calling them "whites and half-breeds." Although both white and Indian religious leaders were concerned about Indian consumption of alcohol, its optional use was apparently permitted in Smohalla's creed. The occasion when Moses persuaded him to overindulge in its use was an example.[29]

Although most whites on the plateau were not inclined to evaluate Smohalla objectively, some were making his and other nativist religious movement known. Scholars wrote, for example, about the Ghost Dance, or "Messiah Craze," of 1890–91, which was especially influential among the Sioux Indians. Such writings caused middle- and upper-class Americans to show what Charles Reagan Wilson described as the first widespread interest in mystical, idealist religions such as that of the Ghost Dancers and those of other native leaders like Smohalla.[30] The ethnologist Alice Fletcher viewed the followers of the "Messiah Craze" as suffering folk who were appealing to God to save them from their oppressors.[31] James Mooney discussed not only the Sioux but also Smohalla and his creed in *The Ghost-dance Religion and the Sioux Outbreak of 1890*, which appeared in 1896 as part two of the *Fourteenth Annual Report of the Bureau of Ethnology 1892–1893*. More recently, the Ghost Dance was analyzed by Weston La Barre in his *Ghost Dance Origins of Religion* (1979), in which he described such dances as a world-wide, age-old phenomenon. As for Smohalla, readers of an earlier day who had no access to the writings of anthropologists could learn about him in publications such as *The Overland Monthly*, in whose December, 1913, issue appeared Stella I. Crowder's article "The Dreamers." Youthful American readers found virtually no ac-curate information about the Prophet in *The Antelope Boy; or, Smo-holler, the Medicine Man* (New York, 1873), but there was excite-ment aplenty in this dime novel by George L. Aiken, which was subtitled *A Tale of Indian Adventure and Mystery*.

It remained for attendants at Smohalla's meetings to provide first-hand details of his religion and the ceremonials which animated it. We will now examine these aspects of the Washani as practiced by the Prophet and his followers.

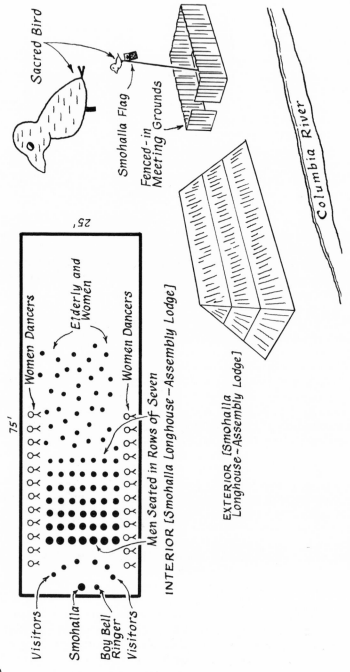

Sacred Bird

Smohalla Flag

Fenced-in
Meeting Grounds

Columbia River

75'

25'

Women Dancers

Elderly and
Women

Women Dancers

Men Seated in Rows of Seven

INTERIOR [Smohalla Longhouse–Assembly Lodge]

Visitors

Smohalla

Boy Bell
Ringer

Visitors

EXTERIOR [Smohalla
Longhouse–Assembly Lodge]

P'na Village at Priest Rapids

4

Washat: *Symbol and Ceremony*

> Much also may be learned by singing and dancing with the dreamer. . . .
> —*Smohalla to Captain E. L. Huggins.*

After explaining to Captain Eli L. Huggins the doctrines of his faith, Smohalla remarked, "Much also may be learned by singing and dancing with the dreamer. . . ." He meant the Washat dance that gave form to his Washani beliefs. The fountainhead setting in which the ceremonials were held during the captain's visit was the P'na Village at Priest Rapids, in an open space north of a large lodge that served as Smohalla's residence and the village assembly center. This layout attested to the importance that the Prophet's followers attached to him. Customarily such a ceremonial open space was enclosed by a fence, and that of P'na Village was surrounded by whitewashed boards from white settlements—driftwood from the Columbia River, which for ages had supplied natives with wood for fires, framing for their mat houses, and even palisades for marking the graves of their dead.

In the ceremonial space stood a staff atop which flew a rectangular flag that MacMurray described as having a round red path in its center, a yellow field representing the yellow grass of that arid country, a green border indicating the boundary of the world (since the hills surrounding the P'na Village were green near their tops), and a small extension of blue near the top of the flag with a white star in the center.[1] MacMurray's observations were based on his host's own explanation of this representation of his faith:

This is my flag and it represents the world. God told me to look after my people—all are my people. There are four ways in the world—north and south and east and west. I have been all those ways. This is the center, I live here; the red spot is my heart; everybody can see it. The yellow grass grows everywhere around this place. The green mountains are far away all around the world! There is only water beyond, salt water. The

41

blue (referring to the blue cloth strip) is the sky, and the star is the north star. That star never changes; it is always in the same place. I keep my heart on that star; I never change.[2]

Smohalla's flag was reminiscent of those that flew from poles in center-square enclosures of trading and military posts, presenting, in MacMurray's words, a form of "military parade." The Prophet would have been aware of such a setting at nearby Fort Nez Percés (later, Fort Walla Walla, after the merger of the North West and Hudson's Bay companies in 1821), which stood at the confluence of the Columbia and Walla Walla rivers. Another post with which he would have been familiar was the military's Fort Simcoe, established in 1856 in a beautiful oak grove at Mool Mool ("many springs") on the west in the Yakima country. During the period of Anglo-American rivalry for possession of the Pacific Northwest which terminated in the boundary settlement of 1846, nationals of both countries dispersed flags among natives, who ascribed to them the same mystical qualities that they gave to the written papers that these nationals also dispersed to impress them. Unscrupulous whites were known to have pawned playing cards off on them by telling them they had religious significance. Antecedents of Smohalla's flag may also have been the highly decorated animal skins, such as that decorated with a wolf, which hung atop poles in conspicuous places near the lodges of important chiefs.[3]

There is no record that Smohalla's flag was used by other Washani adherents, but three flags (a magical number), of solid blue, white, and yellow, flew over Kotiakan's lodge at Pa'kiut Village. The flag of another Washani leader and contemporary of Smohalla, the Klickitat Lishwailait, had red, white, and blue stars. A sacred carved-wood bird, Wowshuxkluck, the oriole, said to be a power symbol that Smohalla received on a spirit quest, stood atop his own pole, calling to birds, roots, and all other living things to awaken and bring migrating salmon to the village. Like Smohalla, Lishwailait also was said to have received messages from the bird atop his pole.

In the ceremony that MacMurray witnessed, Smohalla entered the fenced-off enclosure accompanied by a small lad with a bell. The Prophet hoisted his flags and delivered a "sort of lecture or sermon," after which what MacMurray termed "captains" or "class leaders" instructed the people. The method of instruction bore a resemblance to that of class leaders in some Christian churches. It also could be compared to the harangues that were delivered by persons who rode through Indian camps apprising the people of important events, announcing plans, or memorializing the dead. The practice of haranguing was so successful among Indians that some missionaries subsequently applied it in their ministrations.

From the enclosure the assemblage moved into Smohalla's house, which, in essence, was what was known as a "longhouse." It was about twenty-five feet by seventy-five feet and built on logs driven upright into the ground, which were covered with bark and rush matting or canvas beneath a gable roof.[4] Because ceremonials were held in such structures, the term "Longhouse Religion" came to be applied to that of the Washani. Semisedentary peoples, such as Smohalla's Wanapams and other tribes between Priest Rapids and The Dalles, retained such structures, while less-sedentary tribesmen, such as the buffalo hunters, were living in Plains-type tipis, and those influenced by whites were living in houses of logs and lumber. The Wanapams were less prone to alter their dwellings not only because they were opposed to change but also because their houses were suited to the arid climate of the region. The somber appearance inside Smohalla's house was heightened, MacMurray believed, by the smoke curling pervasively from a floor fire at the rear. To him the babel of voices and beating of drums added to the strangeness of the place, as did myriads of split salmon curing in smoke from a fire.

MacMurray did not record any explanation Smohalla may have given of the significance of his Washat, nor the occasion that inspired it. We have, however, from his Umatilla contemporary, the Washani prophet, Luls (Lals), a most articulate explanation for its observance, which reveals the dependence of Washani worshippers on the bounties of nature and their need to match that dependence with a meticulously proper worship:

> Our Creator gave us this beautiful world and the streams and the nice trees with fruit, and roots of many kinds, and fish in the waters. We must remember our Creator in these things. We must not kill these fish, gather roots nor berries, or kill deer on the Sabbath. We must honor our Creator. Whenever the first berries ripen we must pick them on week days and then eat them in our long tent. We must do the same with the first roots. Give thanks to our Creator who gave us this to live on in this world.[5]

The ceremonies which MacMurray witnessed were held not only to propitiate and seek help from the Great Spirit but to ensure the fidelity of Smohalla's followers to the Washani faith. They apparently were not the important first-root observances described by Luls, which were held in the root-digging time in spring (the Shih-tash period of Smohalla's calendar). Smohalla and his people would already have celebrated first-salmon ceremonies, since Mac-Murray observed that large quantities of that fish were drying in

Smohalla's house. The major does not give us any inkling that the ceremonials he witnessed were held on a Sunday, the whites' sabbath, though Smohalla and his followers, like Luls and his, strictly observed that special day. Some have maintained that Indians held Sundays sacred in emulation of the observance of those days by personnel of the Hudson's Bay Company. Despite the mercantilism that their tasks demanded, company officials, comprising largely Anglican, Roman Catholic, and Presbyterian adherents, attempted to set an example to natives of Sunday observance. Some Indians maintained that their ancestors had observed that day with special ceremonials antedating the coming of whites. Such observances might have resulted from Euro-American influences even before the latter appeared in the region. In any case, Sundays were strictly observed by bans against working and hunting, and special foods were reserved for eating on those days.

Inside the house the *pom pom* of the drumbeats continued as they had in the outside enclosure. Smohalla said that this was the sound of life in the world and that the drum throbs represented the trinity of the sun, the moon, and the stars.[6] His drums, which MacMurray did not describe, were possibly of the type used before the advent of white military forces, similar to those used by natives in the early nineteenth century: circular, one-faced, shallow tambourines with crossing thongs forming handgrips. Made of deer or horse skins, they figured only in the strictly religious spirit dances and were never used for amusement purposes. War drums were never used in such ceremonies. A Lishwailait disciple claimed that his leader had discovered the drum and that its round, yellow, shiny appearance symbolized the earth sound. Should the Washat drum break in some place, he believed some portion of the surface of the earth would be destroyed.[7]

In describing Smohalla's ceremony, MacMurray made no mention of the use of feathers. Smohalla, however, believed that individuals would rise from the earth on them after the world "turned over" on the Washani doomsday. They were even more efficacious for adherents of the Feather Religion, or Feather Dance, and were known in the Shahaptian languages as *waskliki* ("spin") and *waptashi* ("feather"). The Feather Dance had been revealed by its founder, Jake Hunt, a Klickitat contemporary of Smohalla, who lived on the White Salmon River in south-central Washington.

There were both similarities and differences in the Washani religions practiced by Smohalla and Hunt. In Hunt's ceremonials feathers were used more frequently; the dancers not only wore feather insignia but also waved them in the belief they had cleansing powers. Mirrors also were used by Hunt's people to represent the earth disk of his vision. They had only limited use in Smohalla's ceremonials.[8]

A most sacred color for the Feather Dancers was yellow, which symbolized the brightness of the sun's rays and the anticipated light of the afterworld. The green in the Washani ceremonials may have originated in the importance that was attached to the land. Tambourines were not regarded as particularly sacred, but drums were more so because they too symbolized the shining disk of Hunt's vision. Poles and flags were important in Feather ceremonies, as they were in those of Smohalla.[9]

Bells were important in the services of both Smohalla and Hunt. At Smohalla's services hand-picked drummers sang and drummed the Washat song: "Sound of the bell, sound of the heart. My brothers. My sisters. I am meeting you. I am meeting you at the dance." The bells, which the Prophet said would ring at the end of the world, would be heard and answered only by those of pure hearts.[10] There is no hint where Smohalla obtained his bells, but bells had long fascinated Pacific Northwest Indians from the time they first obtained them from fur traders. Silver plates and other glittering ornaments adorned Smohalla's dancers. Like other Indians, his followers put such things to uses that the fur traders had never intended. They even accoutered graves. The use of bells would have confirmed MacMurray's belief that Smohalla's Washat was reminiscent both of a military parade, and the Roman Catholic mass. Also like priests participating in the mass, Smohalla's were disciples uniformly garbed, and their chanting was a musical form deeply rooted in aboriginal worship. Later missionary priests would skillfully fuse their own traditional forms and trappings of worship with those of the natives. The segregation of the sexes observed at the mass had long been practiced by the Indians in their traditional rituals. At Fort Nez Percés, for example, soon after its founding in premissionary days, participants in scalp and slave-capturing dances had formed hundred-yard-long rows of men facing each other with women positioned inside the rows in like manner.[11]

During MacMurray's visit such a segregated alignment continued inside both the outside enclosure and the longhouse, but with a different configuration. On either side inside the house a row of twelve women stood erect with their arms crossed and their fingertips at their shoulders. Balancing on the balls of their feet with their heels slightly off the ground and their knees flexed outward, they performed what they called "standing dancing" in contrast to the "knee dancing" advocated by the early Prophet Katxot. Keeping time to the drumbeats, they chanted as they tapped their heels on the floor. Those in the righthand column were uniformly dressed in red garments, and those on the left in red and blue. They wore buckskins, as though seeking to retain some semblance of aboriginal garments. On the canvas-covered floor men and boys knelt in rows of seven.

As he had the significance of his flag, Smohalla might have explained to MacMurray the meaning of the number seven. The seven drummers in his Washat represented the points of the red star emblem on the back of his shirt, which signified seven days, of which the seventh represented the Sunday dance on the sabbath. Women in groups of seven prepared food in the Feast of the New Food, the event of invocation and thanksgiving. Among some Washani adherents, such as the Yakimas, Prophets chanted their power songs and danced to the number five, in contrast to the number seven. Their deceased were buried five days after death, an interval that was not only of ceremonial significance but also a reasonable interval to ensure against burial of persons in trances. Smohalla's successors maintained that he had taught that the number three was "bigger" than the number seven because life-making involved three important heavenly bodies: the sun, which was "life"; the moon, which was "heart beating"; and the stars, which were "like the body."[12]

In the ceremony recorded by MacMurray the males positioned their biggest dancers at the fronts of the columns immediately behind the Prophet. The other males arranged themselves in descending order of height. Elderly women and children occupied the remaining spaces. Clothed in what he called a "priest's gown," which was actually a white shirt, Smohalla sat at the front on a mattress or hassock, his left hand over his heart. At his side was a boy bell ringer. Guests sat on a mattress about ten feet from the Prophet near the back of the building and the fresh air. Those from distant villages sat on one side. Smohalla's son looked on. Yo-Yonan, the son who would in time succeed his father as the Wanapam Prophet-leader, was perhaps in his early thirties when Mac-Murray saw him. He was tall and much thinner and darker complexioned than his father, and quicker in movement. His ceremonial dress consisted of a short yellow or sometimes blue outfit ornately decorated with stars or moons cut from bright-colored cloth. His sleeves, like those of his father, were richly ornamented with beads and silver. To his left was Kotiakan. Also present were Kotiakan's brothers. The male dancers wore shirts similar to that of Smohalla.[13]

In an 1884–1885 publication, the journalist Eugene Smalley narrated the observations of an army officer whom he did not identify, but who had witnessed Smohalla's Washat at Priest Rapids.[14] From the officer's observations, it appears that visitors such as those whom MacMurray saw in Smohalla's house came with Kotiakan. The officer described the ceremony as taking place in a tent, in which Smohalla sat on a hassock, bell in hand, in front of twelve red-shirted male Indians with six white-gowned maidens on one side and six in red on the other. At Smohalla's bell signal the dancers knelt or rose. During the ceremony the Prophet's discourses were interrupted when he fell to the ground in a trance, rising after a few minutes to announce a revelation from heaven. Had the Prophet experienced a similar state during MacMurray's visit, the latter would most likely have recorded such a dramatic event.

Two years after these military officers observed Smohalla's Washat, an Indian inspector, E. D. Bannister, in a March 30, 1886, report described the ceremony among Kotiakan's people in their roughly twenty-by-ninety-foot lodge in the Pa'kiut Village. Bannister wrote that

> the men stand on one side and the women on the other, facing each other, with their right hands placed over their hearts and their eyes cast heavenward. They stand there, chanting in a low mournful tone, and occasionally, at the tap of the drum, jump up and down, until they are completely exhausted. They believe in the Great Spirit in Heaven, tell him all their troubles and ask Him to make the rain fall, the crops to grow, the fish to be plentiful in the streams . . . [Then Kotiakan said to Bannister:] "We came in here last night when the sun went down, we have been standing here ever since, without anything to eat, asking the Great Spirit to send you here today. The Great Spirit hear us poor Indians: 'Cause you are here.' He sent you as we asked him."[15]

The foregoing reveals that Kotiakan followed Smohalla closely in his ceremonials. He also followed his creed, with at least one exception: he permitted his people to raise crops and livestock, which implied a certain dependence on white culture. Smohalla eschewed the agrarian ways of whites and any aid from them that altered his traditional natural way of life.[16]

Of all aspects of the Washat ceremonial none was more important nor more strictly observed than the celebration of the Feast of the New Food. The rationale for the ceremonial was well expressed by the Umatilla Prophet Luls, quoted above. In preparing the feast, the women harvested roots and herbs, and the men speared salmon and hunted deer. Under appointed leaders, the women aligned themselves facing the sun. Timing their speech and their body movements with small hand bells, they chanted prayers of thanksgiving and supplication. Before the celebration the gatherers were forbidden to eat their harvests. The hunters were forbidden to break marrowbones. The residues of carcasses were brought to the longhouse not later than the day before the feast. Hunters circled the house three times, depositing their trophies at the far ends of the building. Women deposited their laden baskets on one side of the house, opposite that of the men who had had no part in preparing the game. Fresh roots and herbs were served in their natural state. The cooking of the fish and game was done by the women, after which many formalities were observed in serving the food on rush matting that extended around the inner court where the cooking was done. As in other phases of the ceremony, the preparations involved circling the court with arms full of dishes. Such circling, and pivoting completely around, symbolized the circular course of the sun. When asked the significance of these maneuvers, the Washani answered that in the distant past Speelyi, the Coyote, had made the rules, which had to be obeyed or something evil was certain to happen, such as failure of the salmon to return the following year or a sacrcity of deer and roots. Nothing was to be wasted from that given by the Chief Above, who would become angry should Earth and Sun be offended by such prodigality.

When the food was ready, the people, kneeling or sitting, lined both sides of the table. The host, standing near the drummers, bell in hand, signaled participants to attention. The sacred drums beat their rhythms to the accompaniment of chants. The host called out the foods to be consumed in order of their importance but first, at the word *"chesh,"* or *"chush,"* the participants sipped from cups of water, the source of life. Then they quickly partook of deer and salmon, which were followed by roots and herbs. When this phase of the ceremony had been completed, the leader-host sat down as the worshippers eagerly consumed the foods. Water was again sipped at the close of the feast, and everyone raised his right hand and uttered an "I-ah!" similar to the Christian "Amen." Filing out of the house, each pivoted, or turned around at the doorway, always from right to left. Then, in single file to the left, they circled the building, which all faced in a semicircular configuration. At the leader's signal, and with heads bared, all lifted their right arms again, uttering another "I-ah!" Revolving from right to left, they ended the ceremony. The leader-host had not eaten before the others, nor did the people drink water during the day before the close-of-the-evening ceremonies, when they began pleasure dancing and gaming.[17]

In Wishram Sunday ceremonials the leader-host commanded the people to consume water to purify their bodies before eating portions of fish, just as they were forbidden to eat other first foods such as meats and herbs until they had swallowed water first.

Feasting followed. "Cleansed" by water in a manner reminiscent of Christian baptism, the people began dancing at a bell signal. Aligned on both sides of the house, they moved their right hands in fanlike motions in front of their breasts and up to their shoulders while balancing alternately on heels and toes and singing ritual songs in cadence with the dance and the beats of the drum. Between songs, at the sound of bells, the leader summoned his "interpreter," who had positioned himself behind the leader, to stand in front of him so that others, through the interpreter, could tell of their trance visions while in the spirit world.

Ringing of bells ended the songs, most of which consisted of the seven lines. Between songs the leader rang bells in progressions of one through seven strokes. After a final ringing, the participants with raised hands uttered loud "Aihs!" or "I-ahs!" Then they sang more songs. The ceremonies ended with the men nearest the leader passing in front of him and along a line of women. Reaching the door, each man turned and bowed to the leader. Then, followed by the women, they departed, revolving to symbolize traversing the earth. As they did so, the leader rang a small bell with his right hand and a larger one with his left in single strokes, sending each worshipper on his way.[18]

Although the trappings and the rituals associated with the Washani creed and its Washat ceremonials were intricate, their purpose was simply, as one student of the phenomena observed, to provide

> a spiritual, sensual, and visual display of the life cycle. The feast recognized the gifts of Earth Mother and Nami Piap and offered them thanks, and the happy time to come in the afterworld was portrayed in the Washat. By dancing, the congregants showed that they were worthy to remain on earth when Creator punished the transgressors and helped to precipitate the time when the land would be returned to the *Nahtites* so that they could live in freedom and peace.[19]

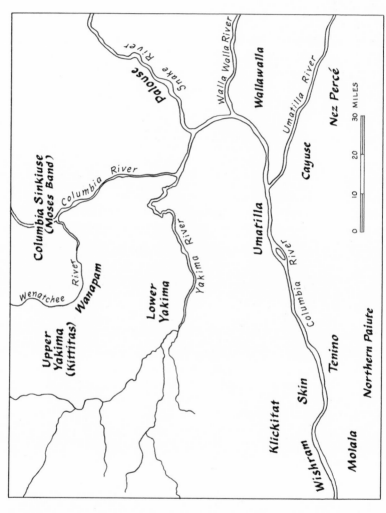

The Wanapams and Surrounding Tribes

5

Rendezvous for Renegades

Many Indians are trying to live like white men,
but it will do them no good.
— *Smohalla to Captain E. L. Huggins.*

Smohalla's creed and ceremonials matured at a time when the tribes of the Columbia plateau faced a bleak future. By combining the best of their past and future worlds, his teachings and those of Prophets like him gave wings to hopes of salvation for their cultures. Although their aspirations took them in both directions in time, Indians yet had to face the agonizing realities of the present into which their American conquerors had unleashed a host of problems for them. Establishment of the Nez Percé, the Umatilla, the Yakima, the Warm Springs, and soon the Colville reservation increased the appropriations by whites of former Indian lands. The slowness with which reservations were surveyed and bounded only aggravated the problems of establishing the Indians on them. The hesitancy or refusal of holdout Indians to abandon age-old homelands for the uncertainties of reservation life produced inevitable friction between them and white settlers. Indians were increasingly concerned about the settlers, who were breaking up traditional native holdings along stream bottoms and quickly passing local laws ensuring their possession of these appropriated holdings. Settlers, in turn, viewed roaming Indians and their reservation brothers as obstacles to progress even in such things as breeding their stock with that of whites.

One white man who attempted to ameliorate the problems arising in Indian-white relationships was former Indian agent A. J. Cain of Walla Walla. Aware of injustices to Indians, he proposed to government officials the abolition of the reservations, pronouncing the system "a great failure." He favored enactment of Indian homestead laws and fusing of Indians into American society. Such proposals, although conceived in a spirit of goodwill, would have set poorly with both the American public, and most Indians, especially those of the Smohallan persuasion. Reservation Indians preferred the "hard place" of their confines to the "rock" of American society. Nonreservation Indians preferred neither. Smohalla was among the many of his race who visited Cain seeking help, but the former agent could offer him little comfort.[1]

In the meantime the Indians remained divided between those who were forced to compromise the Earth Mother by "scratching her face" on reservation farms and those seeking to avoid such desecrations. A most important problem facing Indians both on and off reservations was that of subsistence. Meagre and often tardily received government goods drove them from their reservations to resume old subsistence patterns and, before they returned to the reservations at annuity times, to mingle with those who refused to go on reservations or with those who had escaped the prospect altogether.

Concerned with their own welfare, white settlers regarded Indians peregrinations as injurious to the interests of both races. The problem was acute not only in pockets of white settlement but also along routes of travel such as the Immigrant Road, which went through the Grande Ronde and Umatilla valleys in northeastern Oregon along the Columbia River to The Dalles, and others from there to the mines of the upper interior and along the Yakima and Walla Walla valleys. When Indian depredations occurred, whites complained to Indian agents, who, when unable to resolve the complaints, turned to the military for aid. As complaints increased, Smohalla and his cult increasingly became the targets of whites who regarded the cult as the nucleus around which gathered what one agent in 1861 called the "dissatisfied, rebellious Indians" who were disposed to resist official orders. "Smo-kol-lah," wrote the Umatilla Indian agent, "is a bad character and the peace of the country depends on the capture of him and his party in my opinion." Smohalla's homeland, wrote the agent, was "a rendezvous for thieves and outlaws"[2]—especially the area around White Bluffs, which was on the northern edge of a wide triangle bounded by the Nez Percé, Umatilla, and Yakima reservations.

The agent failed to understand that the recently established reservations were unable to prevent traditional Indian gatherings at nonreservation places. Nor could he understand that there was now even more impetus for Indians to congregate at such places since they were driven from their own lands. Even passage of Indian homestead acts to legalize land holdings for them in the manner of the whites ran counter to the communal ways of life in which they gathered in large numbers to enjoy the bounties of land and water.

Because Smohalla's homeland was relatively isolated from the reservations and had as yet an abundance of natural resources, especially salmon, it became host territory for those escaping from their agents, soldiers, and other non-Indians. They were magnetized by Smohalla's charisma and doctrines, which healed their bruised souls while his "Big River," Enchewana, provided salmon to feed their stomachs. Dreamer Indians remaining on reservations also gathered at other places isolated from agency headquarters. Among these was Thornhollow east of Pendleton, Oregon, to which were attracted elements of the Cayuse Indians and the young Chief Joseph's Nez Percés. Another place was Pa'kiut Village at the very edge of the Yakima Reservation, on the Yakima River about thirty miles northeast of the Simcoe Agency headquarters (which was at the site of the former U.S. Army Fort Simcoe). One band of "outlaws" stayed along the mouth of Almota Creek on the Snake River just outside the Nez Percé Reservation and out of reach of agency officials at Lapwai, Idaho.[3]

The Indian Office of the U.S. Interior Department euphemistically characterized Indians escaping or avoiding reservations as those who "refuse to come in and locate on permanent abodes." Lacking the decorum of the Indian Office, other whites, including Indian agents, referred to them as "renegades," a name that stuck thereafter with these Indians who avoided reservation life. Since renegades and Dreamers had much in common, Dreamer Prophets such as Smohalla were assumed to have been responsible for the renegades' behavior. The latter sometimes sought the Prophets in hopes that seers might in some way protect them from the military after they had committed crimes against whites, or even against Indians.

In response to appeals from an Indian agent to track down such offenders, the First United States Dragoons were dispatched by Major Enoch Steen from Fort Walla Walla (just east of the old Whitman Mission site) in early February, 1861. They found the Indians on the Umatilla River and nearby Willow Creek, which both enter the Columbia from the south in north-central Oregon, and on Butter Creek, an Umatilla tributary. On a similar mission, troops out of Fort Walla Walla under Lieutenant Marcus A. Reno searched out other offending Indians. After one of his men had saved his life by wresting a knife from an Indian attacker, Reno ordered his command to capture and hang two Indians from a tree. Assisting the lieutenant on his mission was the Wallawalla chief Homily, whose camp the outlaws had "cleaned out," hitting him on the head with a double-barrel shotgun. The execution of the two boded ill for Smohalla, to whose camp Reno reported he would have pushed his troops had he not run out of rations.[4]

Smohalla distrusted Homily, whom he believed advocated the

soft life of the "Greedy Ones" and whom he knew consorted with soldiers. According to a white man, Homily initially had opposed whites even to the point of contemplating drowning the crippled and elderly Indians who were unable to escape soldiers during the Indian wars. In 1860 about fifty of his tribe lived with him off the Umatilla Reservation near the confluence of the Columbia and Snake rivers. The remainder fell under leadership of the Dreamer-Prophet Waltsac (Walback, or Waltshil), who with about 150 followers roamed the Columbia from the John Day River up to Priest Rapids, subsisting largely by fishing, as did others of his tribe.[5] The Wallawallas had been torn by feuds since the killing of their head chief Peopeomoxmox. At one time, during an absence, Homily was replaced by Pierre, the whites' favorite, but he was reelected Wallawalla chief in March, 1863, while his band were itinerating back to the Umatilla.[6]

The short rations of army personnel and their reluctance to encroach on Indian Office jurisdictions helped Smohalla assume the role of protector of renegade Indians. This certainly minimized challenges from whites. A case in point was the ferry operated across the Columbia at White Bluffs by James Ritchie and Thomas Howe under a Washington territorial charter. Smohalla opposed their operations in the belief that the river at that place belonged to him and his Wanapams;[7] he wanted no interference with Indian ferrying at that place. Earlier, in 1861, a George Wilson had threatened that business by operating a ferry there.[8] Ritchie and Howe hoped that officials would act against the Prophet, and apparently seeking to intimidate him, they spread word of a tragic event that had occurred in mid-August, 1862, in the Grande Ronde valley. A confrontation had occurred between the Dreamer Tenounis, who opposed white settlement in his Grande Ronde homeland, and Captain George B. Currey of the First Oregon Cavalry. When the confrontation ended, Tenounis and three of his followers lay dead.[9]

Although forces were at work to weaken or destroy Smohalla's leadership, certain events helped him escape removal to the nearby Yakima Reservation and its Simcoe Agency jurisdiction. That agency was rocked by dissension and shifting of personnel at a time of low government morale while the spoils system ran unchecked. Among changes occurring on the reservation was the removal of the Simcoe agent, Dr. Richard H. Lansdale, in 1861. He was replaced by Wesley B. Gosnell, who in turn was followed by Charles Hutchins and by Ashley A. Bancroft. Bancroft was replaced by the Methodist Reverend James H. ("Father") Wilbur, appointed in June, 1864. These rapid changes worked to Smohalla's advantage. The Dreamers were emboldened to abandon their

former secrecy and come out in the open to hold meetings on Toppenish Creek, only four miles from agency headquarters.[10] The
measure of stability that subsequently permitted Wilbur to advance the Peace Policy of "The Plow and the Bible" only strengthened Smohalla's resolve to accept neither. During this turbulent
time the Prophet spurned an invitation to meet with Captain Amos
Harris, who was leading a twenty-five-man First Cavalry detail that
arrived at Simcoe Agency headquarters on March 16, 1863.[11]

Smohalla's growing influence among the Indian tribes caused
government personnel great concern at this time. One who came
under his influence was a rising young Tyigh Dreamer, Queahpahmah. In November, 1865, Oregon Superintendent of Indian Affairs
J. W. Perit Huntington directed the famed Indian scout Donald
McKay (whose numerous clan pronounced their name "McEye")️ to
lead a posse to return Queahpahmah and his followers, who
numbered about eighty, to the Warm Springs Reservation. The
superintendent in frustration described the band as "lazy, thievish,
and vile," living a "vagabond life."[12] The editor of the The Dalles,
Oregon, *Weekly Mountaineer* noted that Queahpahmah was wintering during 1865 and 1866 in the Yakima country, where the editor
wrote, he would "probably never be cured of his vagaries until he
gets a bullet through the head, which has so far been the only way
to abate the hostility of the 'dreamers.'" The editor urged the Tyigh's
immediate arrest and return to the Warm Springs.[13]

The two hundred Queahpahmah followers remaining on the
Warm Springs Reservation refused annuity goods in order not to
obligate themselves to the government. They and other Indians in
the area believed the goods were given in exchange for their lands.
In March, 1870, Queahpahmah again left the reservation, taking
several families with him. Officials feared their departure would
have a bad effect on those remaining. They chose to spend their
summers fishing rather than farming on acreage which government officials had broken for them to plant. As true Smohallans
they sought livelihoods in what the Dreamer-Prophet called "natural work." Fear of the Northern Paiutes, who continued raiding
the Warm Springs Indians as they had the lower-interior natives
from early times, also kept Indians away from the Warm Springs
Reservation.

Aware that many Oregon Indians had escaped into neighboring
Washington Territory, the Oregon Superintendent of Indian Affairs, A. B. Meacham, sought to return them. In February, 1870,
Smohalla was visited by Meacham, who tried to break up what he
called "a grand scheme of rascality being hatched under leadership
of a head man of the Walla Walla tribe who is also known as the
Great Dreamer, alias 'Big-talk on Four Mountains' alias Smokeller."

Meacham believed that Smohalla's influence extended as far as Nevada. Such information, he wrote, was from Dr. William C. McKay (of the McKay clan), who had visited the "Snake" (Paiute?) country the previous winter.[14] Meacham's plan to visit Smohalla was conceived in the erroneous belief that he was a Wallawalla and thus, under the terms of the Walla Walla treaty, belonged on the Umatilla Reservation in Oregon. Meacham's error is understandable, for at that time Smohalla's Wanapams apparently were not listed in official reports as a separate tribal entity and were associated with the Wallawallas.

Smohalla sent a messenger to Meacham when the latter and his party, which included Homily and a half-dozen other men, were within fifteen miles of Priest Rapids at a point where their northerly advance was blocked by high bluffs. The messenger told them to advance no farther because Smohalla, perhaps in deference to the Sunday Washat, had said he could not meet them until Monday. On that day the party was ferried to the Columbia right bank and moved on up to P'na Village at the foot of Priest Rapids. The party's interpreter, Andrew Pambrun, who had a reputation for highly coloring his accounts, recorded an incident on their journey to Smohalla. When Meacham complained of a severe headache, another member of the party, acting Umatilla Agent, Lieutenant W. H. Boyle, jokingly attributed it to Smohalla's incantations and supernatural power. The pronouncement evoked a round of laughter from the group, but not from Meacham, whom Pambrun believed to be afraid of the Dreamer and his immediate followers. Boyle numbered the latter at 350 souls.

Meacham's attitude toward Smohalla was one not of fear but of tolerance. He believed that Indians, like other people, should freely practice their own religions, and he even proposed establishing for Smohalla a reservation at the confluence of the Columbia and Yakima rivers. Pambrun's description of the nearly four-hour meeting with Smohalla reveals the different attitudes toward the Prophet of Meacham and himself:

> We were introduced at one end and marched through an opening in the entire centre, shaking hands right and left with bucks, squaws and babes. It must have . . . occupied us fully one hour before we reached the end of the pavilion, which was carpeted and furnished with some chairs, bunting and a United States flag was hung around, and other ornaments strewed about, exhibiting the rude taste of this great fraud. Well, the upshot of the affair, was a short and unavailing speech by Meacham, wherein he explained the object of our visit, which was responded to in a short and evasive speech by Smokalie, other talk by the Umatillas [in the party], were more to the point but of no avail, so

we returned as we came, having disbursed a few thousands of Uncle Sam's surplus.[15]

A tragic incident that occurred in Idaho Territory in 1872 revealed Smohalla's reciprocal affinity for Meacham. When the superintendent's brother, H. J. Meacham, was killed by a falling tree, Smohalla dispatched a delegation to a native root-gathering grounds near Grangeville to offer solace to the grieving family. The delegation used the occasion to express what they believed to be the superiority of their religion to that of the Meacham family.[16]

After his visit to Smohalla, Meacham traveled down to the Warm Springs Reservation, which he regarded as "a great fraud upon the Indians," who failed to advance there as rapidly as he thought they should. The Indians, he claimed, had wanted to become like whites, except, of course, for the Dreamers of that confine.[17] Of Queahpahmah he wrote: "I confess much charity for him when I realize how he and his have been swindled at Warm Springs Reservation. They giving up good homes for paltry consideration of money and a miserable, bleak, sterile, devil's garden." Meacham suggested to General George Crook, commander of the Department of the Columbia, that he delay sending an expedition to arrest Queahpahmah until his whereabouts were known.[18]

The military had to be cautious not to overstep its bounds in the conduct of Indian affairs. Occasionally conflict occurred between it and the Indian Office. When these two arms of the government failed to settle conflicts involving whites and Indian renegades, the Indian Office sent special inspectors from the East to attempt to resolve the problem. Had Inspector Felix Brunot been unaware of it before, he would discover conflict not only between whites and Indians but also among the Indians themselves. For example, in his meeting with Yakima chiefs in council in July, 1871, one of them attributed the divisions on the Yakima Reservation to three of its groups: Roman Catholics; Agent Wilbur's followers, which included Methodists; and lastly, the Drummers, or Dreamers.[19] It was at this time that Brunot made his Christian beliefs known, as did Waunitta his Dreamer beliefs.[20]

In 1871, the year of Brunot's visit, white settlers in the Yakima country feared that religious strife on the reservation would spill over into an all-out Indian war.[21] Despite Agent Wilbur's efforts to prevent it, religious factionalism continued. Fifteen years later the Indian inspector, E. D. Bannister, identified the factions on the Yakima Reservation as the Methodist, composed of Klickitats; the "Simcoes" (those near agency headquarters), composed of Catholics; and lastly, the Yakimas and the "Toppenishes" (those living on Toppenish Creek), composed of Catholics and Drummers. The last faction, in Bannister's words, was headed by "Chief Cotiackan."[22]

On the Umatilla Reservation, Brunot, as had Meacham, found similar ill feelings festering between Catholic and "heathen" Indians. Such conflicts, he believed, had prevented the advancement of the latter. Among the factors dividing Catholic Indians from their "heathen" fellows, especially those of the Umatilla tribe, was the Catholic Indians' previous life-style, in which, as horse-riding huntsmen, they had ranged between their western homelands and the Rocky Mountains and Great Plains. The more sedentary tribes had followed age-old subsistence patterns along the Columbia River, where they were drawn to the renegade ranks.[23]

White settlers were naturally more concerned with their conflicts with Indians than with those among the tribesmen themselves. Area newspapers made much of the troubles breaking out between renegade Indians and whites over land. One editor charged that those wishing to keep settlers out of the fertile Yakima valley had circulated stories that Indians at Priest Rapids were about to break out and cause trouble.[24]

In 1871 and 1872 the war between the Modocs and American forces in the Lava Beds of southern Oregon and northern California was covered by the expanding regional press, and the conflict sent repercussions northward affecting Smohalla and his followers. The year after visiting Smohalla, Meacham was appointed to a commission to effect a peace with the Modoc leader Captain Jack, and during a council the Indian superintendent was seriously wounded by his Modoc attackers. After the Modoc War, Meacham appeared less charitable toward Smohalla and his kind. Curley Headed Doctor, a shaman-Prophet like Smohalla, had inspired the Modocs to war.[25] In 1875, with memories of the unfortunate confrontation still fresh in his mind, Meacham described his feelings and experiences in his *Wigwam and Warpath; or, The Royal Chief in Chains*. Nevertheless, he refrained from attributing evil to Smohalla and stated that any lack of "progress" on the Umatilla Reservation was due to the enervation of its natives rather than any pernicious Smohallan influence. His book caused a stir in Pacific Northwest white communities, which believed he had taken too soft a line against the Indians.

After the Modoc War, many whites feared a general Indian uprising under Smohalla. One of the places where they believed his influence was harmful was the Siletz Reservation in western Oregon. Its agent, J. W. Fairchild, on January 4, 1875, reported to the commissioner of Indian affairs that during the Modoc War the "Smohallow dance" had come to his and other reservations, where medicine men and women had adjured their people to keep dancing so that whites would be driven from their country and their properties returned to the Indians. The ceremonies held on the Siletz resembled those of Smohalla and the Feather Dancers. Participants waved and lowered feather clusters and beat drums as Prophets foretold the return of the victorious dead. A white man, T. M. Ramsdell, stated that on nearby Yaquinna Bay he had attended such dances, which he claimed were held to rouse all Indians to a "united slaughter of all whites which scheme originated from Smohalla, a medicine man of the Snake Indians."[26] That whites ascribed such dances to Smohalla, who lived far away, attests to the notoriety he had achieved at that time. At the end of the Nez Percé War the Siletz agent reported to General Oliver O. Howard, commander of the Department of Columbia, that Indians of his agency were embracing what he called the "Warm House or Drummer Religion." The agent tried to dissuade, rather than force them to stop their dances.[27]

In the West hysterical whites were little inclined to probe the source of dances such as were held on the Siletz and elsewhere in southern Oregon and northern California. Possibly they were unaware that they may have derived more directly from the Ghost Dances out of Nevada than from Smohalla. The first surge of the Ghost Dance between 1862 and 1872 was attributed to preachments of the Paiute Wodziwob.[28] Leslie Spier was so certain that the Ghost Dances derived from the Prophet Dance that his *Prophet Dance of the Northwest and Its Derivatives* bears the subtitle *The Source of the Ghost Dance.* Tracing the physical association between Smohalla and the Paiute prophet Wovoka, the leader of the second Ghost Dance (1889–1892), is more plausible, since Wovoka was said to have gained knowledge of Smohalla's teachings when he worked two seasons in Oregon hopfields, and he had ties with Paiutes of the Warm Springs Reservation.[29] Besides spreading to the Sioux Indians, the second Ghost Dance, like the first, spread westward among the Indians of the Siletz and other reservations in southern Oregon and northern California.[30]

Several hundred miles from the Modoc War, in the interior of northern Oregon and Washington Territory, most whites were unconvinced of Smohalla's peaceful intentions. From the beginning of the Modoc troubles, rumors had raced through the white communities that Indians at Priest Rapids were about to go to war.[31] The rumors apparently were spread for financial reasons, to keep settlers in more established white settlements such as The Dalles, or to keep them out of places like the Yakima valley, where their farming could interfere with cattle-raising operations already underway.

That Smohalla meant no harm to whites in that time of tension was revealed in his confrontation in the Yakima country with two of them, F. Mortimer Thorp and his son. With about eighty painted and mounted men he bore down on the two in what an early fur trader, Alexander Ross, would have called a "sudden and unexpected rencontre." The elder Thorp cocked his rifle with one hand and seized Smohalla's bridle reins with the other. Smohalla laughed, offered his hand in friendship, and explained that he wished to dispel rumors that a thousand Indians were about to raid the settlements. The smallness of his force, he assured them, proved his peaceful intent. Accounts of the Smohalla-Thorp confrontation became enlarged with the telling. According to the Yakima-country pioneer Jack Splawn, Thorp jerked Smohalla from his horse and beat him until he cried for mercy.[32]

Attempting to ascertain the truth of the rumors, military authorities in May, 1871, dispatched "Doug" Ballard with an interpreter to Priest Rapids to investigate reports of Indian earthwork fortifications that were presumed to be in preparation for war. Ballard returned in mid-May to report that the Indians at the rapids were peaceable and well disposed toward whites. He reported good treatment by his hosts with "all kindness and consideration," including his attendance at Smohalla's Sunday services. Smohalla, reported Ballard, admitted the presence of "outlaw" Indians but made no claim to them. The only "fortifications," Ballard reported, were ditches and tailraces that Chinese had dug along the Columbia a few miles above Priest Rapids in searching for gold.[33] Further evidence of Smohalla's peaceable disposition came from Mr. Cooncy (Coonce), a white settler near White Bluffs, who stated that Smohalla had assured him that although he did not want to go to a reservation, he and his Indians were peaceful and meant no harm to whites. Cooncy stated the report of a thousand Indians at White Bluffs was ridiculous. In their fear, whites failed to realize that, if there were a "thousand" Indians of Smohallan persuasion, they would not all be in his immediate presence at one time and ready for war. Pacific Northwest historian Frances Fuller Victor at that time suggested that Smohalla's preachments about restoring Indians was but a "forlorn hope." She suggested that perhaps that was why the Prophet and his followers were called Dreamers.[34]

The Reverend G. W. Kennedy, who visited Smohalla in the Kittitas valley in May, 1873, in the root-digging time of *Shih-tash*, was unconvinced of the peaceful disposition of the one he called the "war leader of the Columbia."[35] Smohalla and two hundred followers met with Kennedy and three other men of his party, who approached the Prophet's lodge nervously. Inside, Smohalla permitted his guest to state the reason for his visit. In the Chinook jargon Kennedy stated his wish to preach to Smohalla and his people a sermon from the "white man's book of heaven," as Kennedy described the Bible. "For the space of half an hour," wrote the minister, "not a muscle moved; not an eyelid quivered. Rigid attention."

Breaking the silence, Kennedy assured them that they were all brothers whom the Great Father wanted to live together as friends, not foes, Smohalla replied: "Why has the white man taken our lands from us? Has the white man any rights here in Kittitas that the Indian has any right to respect. The Indian came first." Composing himself after such an "unanswerable" argument, Kennedy could only say that Smohalla and his people could hunt and fish there while whites plowed and planted. The conversation ended with handshaking and a benedictory pipe smoking. Smohalla bade his guest a Chinook jargon farewell, *Klose tillacum mika* ("Good be with you, my friends"). The sternness of his countenance softened. He had won his point and had kept his own religion intact.[35] His conversation, however, had revealed a concession to white settlement in the Kittitas valley and a willingness to coexist with white men. A white Kittitas-valley resident had reported 150 voters in the previous year and about twelve thousand head of cattle there and, in the month before Kennedy's visit, the laying out of the town of Kittitas.[36]

The Indians in the Kittitas valley included, besides Smohalla's band, the native Upper Yakima peoples, and Wenatchee Indians who had fled to safer grounds there during the aftershocks of a severe earthquake that rocked the Pacific Northwest on the night of December 14, 1872.[37] Indians believed that the Earth Mother was shaking the land in anger at whites and those Indians who were desecrating her face, and at Indians who would let them do this. Among the reports of quake damage was the killing of Indians near White Bluffs by rocks shaking loose and rolling down on their camp.[38] Smohalla, who reportedly had predicted the quake, became host to frightened Indians fleeing to P'na Village to dance the Washat to appease the angry Spirit. Among them was Moses, some of whose people also had fled to Patoi, the mysterious Dreamer-Prophet of a Wenatchee band. Native prophets such as Patoi and Smohalla used the quake to warn their people that the Great Spirit was displeased with them for lying, gambling, stealing, and drinking. Drinking could certainly have been a problem for Smohalla and his followers if there was truth to the report coming out of the Kittitas valley that one of the two saloons in Yakima County was at Priest Rapids.[39]

When the aftershocks died down, Indian life continued much as before. Returning hunger-driven to reservations to accept annuity goods, some renegades surrendered the independence that Smohalla and his followers still retained. Agents constantly feared that, were annuity good withdrawn, their erstwhile recipients would drift from the reservation to join, or rejoin, the renegade ranks. Among those continuing to avoid confinement and annuity goods was Waltsac, who had absented himself from Oregon's Umatilla Reservation since 1869, spending considerable time in Washington Territory across from the Celilo Falls on the Columbia, near The Dalles, where he reportedly came under the influence of a Smohallan Dreamer. Oregon Superintendent of Indian Affairs T. B. Odeneal had assumed Meacham's task of confining the Indians (who themselves had invited him to meet with them), and on September 19, 1872, he reported that four hundred belonged on the Umatilla Reservation and one hundred on the Warm Springs in Oregon.[40] Odeneal was especially alarmed by reports from the Umatilla agent, Narcisse Cornoyer, that Smohalla had sought to keep renegade numbers high by going from reservation to reservation seeking Indians to join his following.[41] Even so, Odeneal's statistics were more accurate than those appearing in a local newspaper, which reported three thousand to four thousand off-reservation Indians congregated at Priest Rapids. The white penchant for numbering people and things was not shared by the Indians, who often responded to census takers by saying that, since God knew their numbers, no one else needed to know them. Refusal to give their numbers also made it easier to deny having children to send away to government schools. Under orders to record Indian numbers, agents were frustrated by their itinerancy and intertribal mingling, which made the task of these officials most difficult.

Another Dreamer-Prophet was the Smohallan disciple, Hackney (Hehaney, Hiachenie) of the John Day (or Dockspus) Tenino band. Hackney, who had about eighty followers, had escaped from the Warm Springs Reservation by filing off his chains, only to be rearrested. When he made "fair promises," he was released and reportedly joined Queahpahmah. In 1873 he and his band fled to White Bluffs, which, especially with the establishment of the Umatilla Reservation, had replaced the area around Wallula as a major rendezvous for renegades. Wallula was closer to that confine than were the bluffs. Hackney was repeatedly arrested and released throughout most of the 1870's. As late as 1878–79, at the close of the Bannock-Paiute War, he left the Warm Springs only to be rearrested and confined under military guard at Vancouver Barracks.[42]

In the meantime, Queahpahmah returned to the Umatilla with his followers in 1873. His return stirred excitement among the reservation's Indians and hope among agency officials that his people would resume their lives in harmony with the other Indians there. They had fled in the first place, reported one official, because Queahpahmah had taken offense at "some discourtesy" by an agent when the Warm Springs was administered by military authorities.

According to Indian sources, the offense against him was no mere discourtesy but physical abuse inflicted on him. Queahpahmah's granddaughter claimed that Wasco Indians on the reservation who had espoused Christianity told some soldiers to make him stop his Washat dancing, and that when he refused, the soldiers cut his drum into pieces and threw them into the fire. Then, mounted, they dragged him behind their horses and clapped him into a vermin-infested cellarlike jail. Despite his unsavory surroundings, he defiantly sang his song, bereft of one braid which the soldiers had cut off.[43] At Queahpahmah's request, Hackney was returned to the Warm Springs, where he was reincarcerated, but after further pleadings with officials by Queahpahmah, he was released to remove with some John Day Indians to the Yakima Reservation. When one of that reservation's Indians told Hackney and his people that on the Yakima they could follow the old ways unhampered, seven of his men and their families abandoned the Warm Springs without obtaining the passes needed for leaving. The Warm Springs agent, Captain John Smith, believed that they would do Yakima Reservation Indians no good and was glad to see them go.

Since Smohalla did not lead a war against whites in emulation of the Modoc Captain Jack, a white resident of the Kittitas valley in 1873 tried to calm fears of whites there that the Dreamer-Prophet had lost control even of his own Priest Rapids people and, like the Yakima chief Kamiakin after the Indian wars of 1855–56, had taken the trail to oblivion.[44] Smohalla had not taken that trail, but had avoided meeting with the special Indian inspector E. C. Kemble, who was sent to the Pacific Northwest to assess the "renegade problem" and hear their grievances. On August 19, 1873, Kemble dispatched from the Umatilla Agency a notice to Smohalla, the Wallawalla dreamer Homily, and other Dreamers to meet him between September 10 and 13 at council grounds at Wallula. A short while later Homily and some lesser chiefs sent the inspector a message from Wallula to postpone the council until September 22. When Kemble arrived there, he was both regretful and annoyed – and Homily appeared to be ashamed – because Smohalla and other leading Dreamers were not on the grounds. Also absent were the Dreamers Pascappa (Paskapum) and Luni representing 130 souls at the mouth of Willow Creek. Among those present were ten or twelve Dreamers representing most of the renegades living along the Columbia and lower Snake rivers. It would appear that Smohalla and the others absented themselves from the council because they feared pressure to remove to reservations. It would also appear that Smohalla stayed away because he did not wish to be associated with Homily and other Dreamers of the Pacific

Northwest lower interior whom government officials were eager to plant permanently on the Umatilla Reservation. Some Dreamers absented themselves simply from fear of white men. Representing about 250 followers, Skimiah, whom Kemble described as one of the most "obstinate" of the Dreamer chiefs, sent a telegram from his "dwelling place . . . among the rocks at Celilo" requesting the inspector to pay passage for himself and his band by steamer to Wallula. Kemble denied the request.

Unwilling to be in the dark about what might transpire at the council, Smohalla did condescend to dispatch two representatives to it. Because of his absence, Smohalla knew far less about Kemble than the inspector knew about this one whom he called a "little withered, decrepid, 'medicine man' who . . . practices the same species of enchantment which a class of white men and women employ in the dark and disreputable business of the fortune teller, the spirtualist, juggler, and the trance medium, a kind of 'religion' as old as the days of Pharoah's magicians." Kemble discerned that Smohalla had borrowed some practices from the Christian faith, and he learned from his envoys that it was the Dreamer-Prophet's belief that he had received messages from heaven. To Kemble it appeared that Smohalla's Christian-like beliefs were combined with pantheism and spiritualism. He also divined that the Prophet's followers, emulating their forefathers in their dress and foods (primarily fish and roots), conceded to live peacefully with whites while awaiting the day of deliverance from them. He estimated their numbers at 1,860, a more precise figure than the well-rounded 2,000 appearing in government reports at the time.

First to speak in council was Homily, whose followers now numbered sixty-two. The inspector's assessment of him as "the most intelligent and influential" chief among the Dreamers may have been influenced by Homily's cooperation with government officials and his susceptibility to manipulation by them. Nevertheless, the Wallawalla Dreamer cited government nonfulfillment of certain portions of the Walla Walla treaty of 1855 and his failure to receive a $100 annuity that he claimed was due him under the treaty as the successor to the slain Peopeomoxmox. He said that white men had ended his predecessor's life with violent suddenness and were slowly ending his by appropriating his people's root grounds. "Those things which we have had for food," he lamented, "are dear to us—we were raised on them. . . . I see the whites have good houses and homes but they wont let me live." The Umatilla Prophet Luls, representing about 133 followers, declaimed in a more mystical vain that the "Big Water running" (the Columbia River) spoke for the Indians—that like the earth, it listened to them because it belonged to the Creator. Because the Creator placed it there for the Indians, Luls vowed to remain along it.

Homily expressed willingness to yield his claim on the Umatilla Reservation in favor of a strip sixty miles long and five or ten miles wide along the Columbia west bank between Priest Rapids and Wallula, which was to be a reserve for those avoiding the already established confines. Evaluating this tract as a fox would the rabbit's briarpatch, the inspector believed that, save for a small space around the mouth of the Yakima River and good fisheries and climate, it was a land in which "the horned frog could scarcely subsist," and there was no better place "to dispatch the Indian to his Happy hunting ground, without assistance from the whites." Making it less suitable for Indian occupation, he believed, was the withdrawal of most of it from the public domain by the Northern Pacific Railroad. He believed its fisheries might be opened to Indians for seasonal use as a means of adjusting difficulties and gradually reconciling the Dreamers to the reservation system.

Perhaps Homily was willing to remove to this proposed reservation because it bordered on the ancient sacred waterway of the Columbia. Also, the chief complained of neglect by the Umatilla agent and persecution by the reservation priest and the Catholic Indians there, whom he claimed had driven those like him from the Umatilla. He also complained of the manner in which annuity goods were dispensed, explaining that renegades would not accept them on the Umatilla, Yakima, and Nez Percé reservations.

The renegade Dreamers at the Wallula council were sufficiently aware of the bureaucratic nature of American government to know that Kemble could make no definite promises to satisfy their grievances. They agreed to meet with other government representatives about six months later. Kemble apparently believed the renegade problem would solve itself in time. "They are," he wrote, "certainly not increasing in strength, and there is pretty good reason to believe that a work of disintegration has begun among them which is diminishing their numbers every month." The major hindrance on their trail to peaceful relations with whites, he believed, was the presence of evil white men telling them that the government had no right to confine them on reservations, whose lands, those whites said, should be appropriated.[45]

On adjournment of the September, 1873, council Kemble conferred with Skimiah and Waltsac. The latter promised to return to the Umatilla Reservation and abandon his "wandering habits." Skimiah's "teeth [were] . . . drawn," reported Kemble, by Agent Wilbur's brash entry into his lodge. The agent had captured him in front of his peers and imprisoned him at Simcoe. The absence from the council of the influential thirty-year-old Palouse Dreamer Hush-hushcote (or Husishusiskote; also known as The Bald, or

Table 1. Renegade Dreamers, 1873

Name	Rank	Number of Followers	Reservation	Present Home
Homli	Chief	62	Umatilla	Umatilla Agency
Smohalla	Medicine man	300	Colville	Priest Rapids
Qui panna (Queahpahmah)	Chief	80	Warm Springs	Near Priest Rapids
Thomas	Medicine man	150		Snake River below the Palouse
Skamaya (Skimiah)	Medicine man	250	Yakima	Celilo, on north side of the Columbia
Luls	Medicine man	133	Umatilla	Umatilla Reservation
Paskapum (Pascappa) and Luni	Medicine men	130	Yakima (one half)	Mouth of Willow Creek
Hosekiuwet (Hush-hushcote)	Chief	575	Nez Percé	Snake River above the Palouse
Walsack	Chief	100	Umatilla	
Haihuny (Hackney)	Chief	80	Warm Springs	
Total:		1,860		

Source: E. C. Kemble to Commissioner E. P. Smith, October 3, 1873, Secretary of the Interior, Indian Division, Letters Received, 1873, RG 48, box 82.

Shorn Head) did not disturb the inspector, who had recently heard good accounts of that Dreamer's "behavior and progress." Hush-hushcote lived peacefully at the mouth of the Penawawa, a Snake tributary. Smohalla's absence did nothing to enhance him in the eyes of the inspector, who evaluated the Dreamer religion as follows:

> Among the Indians about Ft. Colville [to whose Colville Agency, Kemble erroneously believed Smohalla belonged] he is either not known or regarded as a person of small influence and standing. He has evidently borrowed some of his doctrines and practices from the Christian religion. His followers claim to be led by a Paper (or Book), and to receive messages from Heaven. Briefly, their belief would appear to be a mixture of Pantheism, Spiritualism & Christianity. The strongest bond of

fellowship among them is the doctrine that they must be Indians as their fathers were before them, that they must dress & hunt, dig roots and catch the salmon, live at peace with the whites and wait for the day of deliverance. They are not adverse to being taught to read and write – some of them profess to be able to do so already. I think much of their disaffection towards Christian instruction, and remaining on the Reservations, comes from injudicious attempts to proselyte among them, and the oppositions which have been Kindled by the spirit of religious partizanship among men professing to be Christians. . . .[46]

During his tour of inspection Kemble visited the Warm Springs Agency, which was then under the control of the United Presbyterian Church, in keeping with President Ulysses S. Grant's Peace Policy in effect at that time. The Peace Policy precipitated intense competition among religious demoninations. Had Kemble not learned of such competition for Indian souls before he had learned of it from those at the Wallula council, where Homily complained of persecution of non-Christians by Catholics and other church people on the Umatilla Reservation. After the council Kemble wrote the Umatilla agent Narcisse Cornoyer, warning that the Indians had complained of "interference and discrimination." He said that he believed that the refusal of the renegades to accept instruction, as well as their flights from reservations, were due to "injudicious attempts to proselyte among them."[47]

Kemble believed the problem on the Warm Springs Reservation to be of less moment than that on the Umatilla. After touring a renegade camp with its agent, Captain John Smith, whose efforts greatly impressed him, he attended a Sunday service in a schoolhouse. In the absence of a preacher, Smith spoke from the biblical text "Blessed are the meek." That he numbered his charges among the meek, because they had laid down their arms to white men, must have set poorly with Dreamers of the Smohalla faith, who in Kemble's words, stood at the back of the room in blankets and grotesque attire. They sought to reinherit the earth on their own terms without the religious formulas of Smith or any of his "praying" Indians. It would have been of little concern to them that Smith likened their religion to that of Mormons and others who, he said, worked on "evil passions," allowing the plurality of wives and "immunity for punishment for law-breaking."[48] As the meeting adjourned, Kemble could only say, "Our hearts yearned for them."[49]

The Indian Office likewise could do little more than wring its hands in condemnation of the Dreamers and their leaders. Citizens continued petitioning with complaints against Smohalla. Attempts by Indian agents to have him, Homily, and other Dreamers come on the reservations to parley with them ended in failure. Kemble had accomplished little in his mission, and another inspector, William Vandiver, did no better in 1874. In his November 20 report of that year, Vandiver explained that the Indians objected to removal because, as they said, they refused to cultivate the soil and become as white men, preferring instead to live along rivers, where fish, their principal food, was still plentiful. The pasturage of their horses and their few cattle, he reported, caused great concern among white settlers of the region and threatened its peace and quiet. Vandiver wrote:

> These renegade Indians claim the whole country as theirs and seem to cherish a superstitious belief that it will in some way be restored to them at no very distant day. One old chief called Smohalla who is regarded as a sort of prophet exercises great influence among the indians. He counsels them not to settle upon reservations nor to receive assistance from the government . . . His teachings are pernicious, for he inspires a belief among his followers, that white people will soon disappear from the country, and that the indians will then have it to themselves again. The welfare of the various indians and the security of the settlers requires that this man should be restrained.[50]

In his annual report for 1875, the commissioner of Indian affairs singled out Smohalla for special indictment:

> About 2,000 Indians are roaming on the Columbia River, in Washington Territory and Oregon, under the leadership of a self-constituted chief, Smohalla by name, whose followers represent nearly all the tribes in the Territory and State, and whose influence extends even into Idaho. He has been able to inspire in his adherents veneration toward himself, and by his teachings, which are received with implicit faith, superstition is fostered, unbridled license is granted to passion, civilization is despised, and reservation Indians are looked upon with contempt and disdain. These Indians, in their present unsettled and unrestricted [l]ife, have no earthly mission beyond that of annoyance to settlers and hindrance to the opening of the country, and are a positive detriment to all other Indians who are gathered upon reservations, many of whom are unable to refuse the inducements offered for a free vagabond life among these renegades.[51]

Yet, although the white community greatly feared Smohalla during the early and middle 1870's, it was much more frightened by him later in the decade. In 1877 and 1878 the Dreamers and the Dreamer-influenced Nez Percés, Palouses, and Bannock-Paiutes were provoked to open resistence to the United States. Despite fears of American settlers and the military that Smohalla would be involved in the conflict, he was only indirectly so. He was far away from it in his desert homeland, which was unfit for white settlement, unlike Nez Percé Joseph's coveted Wallowa country. Yet the struggle was his as much as it was Joseph's, who, in fleeing American troops at this time, had to resort to the way of war to save a way of life.

6

The Dreamer and the General

> Those who cut up the lands or sign papers for
> lands will be defrauded of their rights, and will
> be punished by God's anger.
> — *Smohalla to Captain J. W. MacMurray.*

Officials such as the commissioner of Indian affairs and other
whites had little understanding of the sacredness to the Dreamers
of natural resources, especially the land. The preservation of the
land in its natural state and its eventual restoration to them, both
essential parts of their religion, were regarded by government officials and other whites as far-fetched dreams or forlorn hopes. Typical of the official response was that of Oregon Superintendent of
Indian Affairs T. B. Odeneal, who reported to the commissioner
that

> a new and peculiar religion by the doctrines of which, they are taught
> that a new God is coming to their scene, that all the Indians who have
> died heretofore and shall die hereafter, are to be resurrected; that as
> they will then be very numerous and powerful, they will be able to con-
> quer the whites near their lands and live as free and unrestricted as
> their fathers. Their model of a man is an Indian; they aspire to be In-
> dians and nothing else.[1]

Whites believed the Dreamer religion to be a root cause of Indian
discontent and an ever-present danger to the advancement of both
whites and Indians. Although the gatherings of renegades followed
traditional patterns, whites viewed such assemblages as seedbeds
from which an Indian confederation might emerge all readied for
war. In reality, renegades represented but scattered pieces of pan-
Indianism. Whites failed to see the highly individualized nature of
Indian societies—that for every Dreamer like Smohalla there were
more like Moses who made their painful peace with the whites.
Even the reservation populations were patchworks of tribespeople
shunning the renegades, those sympathizing with them, and the

70

renegades themselves who might be avoiding reservations or itinerating between them and their old haunts, not to make trouble but
merely to subsist.

Because of a gathering of renegades at White Bluffs in the summer of 1873, rumors floated throughout the lower Columbia plateau that an Indian war was about to break out. Some whites fled
the country, secured forts, or applied to the government for arms to
protect themselves from what they believed to be imminent attacks. With five Simcoe Agency Indians, Wilbur visited White
Bluffs and other suspected trouble spots, only to discover that the
rumors were spread by what he termed "a class of irresponsible
whites [who] were quite anxious to have a war, that the treaty
might be broken up and the land of the [Yakima] reservation
opened for white settlements."[2] Such an eventuality was an anathema to Wilbur, who believed the Yakima was a model of the
white efforts to Christianize and "civilize" the Indians. Despite his
calming words, rumors continued appearing in newspapers such
as the Portland, Oregon, *Pacific Christian Advocate*, which reported
on October 1, 1874, that three hundred painted and feathered
braves were holding war dances under Smohalla.

Smohalla's words were heeded by Indians who were escaping
reservations to join other bands along the Columbia down to The
Dalles who were avoiding the reservations altogether. Among the
more numerous of these bands there was a strong corps of
Dreamers. For example, during the Indian wars of the 1850's no
tribe had opposed American forces more doggedly than did the Palouses. During that decade miners en route to the northern interior
goldfields had tramped across their lower Snake River lands. In
1855 the Palouse chief Kahlotus had signed the Walla Walla treaty
under Kamiakin's Yakima standard, but their inclusion with his
followers was a strategy of American negotiators to expedite the
treaty-making process. When subsequently the Palouses were
scheduled to remove to the Yakima Reservation,[3] they remembered the treaty, which they claimed had left muddled the matter
of compensation for the properties that they had yielded under it.
An Indian inspector reported that the government's failure to pay
them for their improvements was the main reason why they refused to remove to the Yakima Reservation. Eight hundred
Palouses did not remove despite petitions from whites to government officials to have them settle on area reservations.[4] Stubbornly
clinging to their lands, they and their Nez Percé neighbors of like
persuasion comprised a substantial portion of the approximately
two thousand Dreamers in the area. Smohalla, who inspired them,
believed that a revival of the Washani had saved them from extinction.[5] The threat of loss of their lands at the hands of cattlemen and

other settlers strengthened the Palouses' Dreamer faith, which promised them hope for the future. Not understanding their fierce independence in the face of these threats, the commissioner of Indian affairs in 1870 branded them "a wild, lawless race."[6]

Prominent among those gathering around Smohalla was the Upper Palouse Hush-hushcote, who was often found at White Bluffs where Smohalla held forth. Agent Wilbur's protective attitude and the absence of any hostilities emanating from that place had kept the military from nearby Fort Walla Walla away from the bluffs, giving Smohalla a platform from which to preach his religion. Hush-hushcote came to White Bluffs to strengthen the Dreamer faith that he had initially received from his Prophet Father at their village at Wawawai on the Snake River about twenty-five miles downstream from Lewiston, Idaho. Also coming under Smohalla's influence was the Middle Palouse Hatalekin (Nehtalekin, Taktsoukt; Red Echo), who was three years Hush-hushcote's junior, and Thomas (Thomash, or Tomas), the leader of a Palouse Dreamer band farther down the Snake.

The stimuli that drew the Palouses to Smohalla were also present among the Nez Percés, whose middle Snake-watershed lands abutted those of the Palouses on the west. During the 1860's miners had swarmed eastward across the Palouse lands to those of the Nez Percés, on which gold was discovered. On the miners' heels came the usual hangers-on and cattlemen. Treaties with the United States in 1855 and 1863 reduced the Nez Percé lands and precipitated ill feeling not only toward whites but also between treaty and nontreaty tribesmen. The latter were opposed to accepting white ways and, especially, to yielding their lands to them, which was in opposition to their traditionalist religious beliefs.

Edward S. Curtis observed that the Nez Percés seem to have been "the highest priests" of the religion of the Earth Mother in their adherence to the "invisible law," the Holahholah-tamaluit, which, holding the earth sacred, was basic to the Dreamer faith. In the Holahholah-tamaluit, as in Smohalla's Washani ceremonies, there were dream-prophecy elements in songs and dances, of which Curtis recorded words and tunes.[7] Another early twentieth-century scholar, Herbert Joseph Spinden, observed that the Dreamer religion nurtured by Smohalla was a natural outgrowth of religious ideas of the Nez Percés and other Shahaptian peoples.[8] While her people were under pressure from white encroachments on their lands, the Nez Percé Dreamer-Prophetess Wiskaynatónmay told of her "death," her visions, and her return to earth. On the basis of these experiences, she instructed her people how to worship and how to have pure lives, leading them in their traditional circling and spinning dances.[9]

By the 1870's the Nez Percés were aware that the whites wanted more concessions from them than those that they had already granted under the treaties. Even President Ulysses S. Grant's June, 1873, agreement under his Peace Policy to reserve the Wallowa country of northeastern Oregon for the Dreamer-oriented Young Joseph and his people would prove to be short-lived. When asked if he wanted schools and churches at an August 2, 1873, meeting with a commission headed by John P. C. Shanks, Joseph answered that he did not. Even his father, Old Joseph, an early convert to Christianity, had abandoned that religion for the old ways because of the differences between the preachments and the practices of the whites. Aware of the divisions among praying and nonpraying, and Protestant and Catholic Nez Percés, Young Joseph observed that churches would only teach his people "to quarrel about God." He thought that schools would teach his people to want churches.[10] The school that the commission proposed for his people never materialized, since a June 10, 1875, order put his Wallowa Reservation into the public domain. The order was calculated not only to open the Wallowa lands to whites but also to force its tenants onto the Nez Percé Reservation under the pro-American chief Lawyer. This sudden shattering development enhanced the Dreamer cause because it dismayed even traditionalist Nez Percé chiefs such as Looking Glass and Eagle from the Light.

Under orders of the secretary of the interior, a commission was instructed to lose no time in sending for the nontreaty Nez Percés, especially Young Joseph, to get them out of the Wallowa country and onto the reservation. Besides David H. Jerome, A. C. Barstow, and William Stickney, the commission consisted of General Oliver Otis Howard, commanding the Military Department of the Columbia, and his aide Major C. E. S. Wood. The commission met with the Nez Percés at Lapwai on November 13, 1876.

Recognizing the Nez Percé Dreamers as the immediate stumbling block to the removal of Young Joseph and his band, the commissioners recommended that, should they refuse to go on the reservation, they be removed by "immediate transportation to the Indian Territory [Oklahoma]." Although they met with the commissioners, Joseph and his nontreaty tribesmen refused to enter into negotiations with them. The commissioners believed that they failed to obtain Joseph's agreement to remove from the Wallowa because of Dreamer "fanatics."[11]

In January, 1877, the Nez Percé agent, John B. Monteith, received an official order to implement the commission's recommendations by issuing Joseph and his band an ultimatum to remove to the reservation. To reinforce the order, Monteith asked General Howard to dispatch troops into the Wallowa valley, and the agent

ordered its Indians to be on the Nez Percé Reservation by April 1.
In response, Joseph declaimed that the country where he and his
people lived had belonged to his father, who had passed it on to
them. "I will not leave until I am compelled to," he retorted.[12] He
asked for another Lapwai council. It is unclear if his request for a
council with the whites was to address the problem of removal, to
forestall it, or to talk his way into remaining in the Wallowa
country.

Having suspected a link between the Upper Palouse–Nez Percé
Dreamers and those of the Columbia River, Howard, en route to
Lapwai to council with the Nez Percés, met a delegation of
Dreamers at a steamboat landing at Wallula on April 18, 1877.
Speaking for the Dreamers, as he also had in council with Inspector Kemble, the Wallawalla chief, Homily, begged Howard to remain to confer with Smohalla and a large number of renegades
who were camped across from Wallula on the Columbia right
bank. Unaware of the serious conflict that he was soon to face in
the Nez Percé country, the general brushed Homily aside with a re-
minder that he had not come to see them and, that moreoever, they
were required to remove to reservations. When Homily suggested
that they would move into the mountains if he did not meet with
them, the general replied, "Let them go."[13]

At that time Homily was playing a double role, sometimes seeking the favor of government officials by residing on the Umatilla
Reservation and sometimes remaining in his old Wallula homelands, where he held Washani meetings and kept his children out
of school.[14] He was also in council with Howard shortly thereafter
at the military's crumbling Fort Walla Walla. There the general, re-
suming his easterly journey, met three hundred painted and
feathered Indians, to whom he made it clear that he would send
troops very soon to occupy the Wallowa. Among those at the council was Thomas, who, Howard believed, was the most "wild and
fierce" of all the Indians there and was contemplating war against
the Americans. Had Thomas taken such action, Howard believed
Thomas would have been annihilated without the support of tribes
such as the Nez Percés, whom the general was seeking to keep
under surveillance. Young Chief, another Umatilla Reservation
Dreamer, was also in attendance, along with the Umatilla agent,
Cornoyer. The agent's explanation of the benefits of reservation life
was of less concern to Thomas than was Howard's plan to send
troops to the Wallowa, and the chief stormed out of the council.
Howard's interpreter, Andrew Pambrun, wanted Thomas arrested
on the spot, but the general refused, using the occasion of Skimiah's
confinement in the Vancouver Barracks guardhouse to warn Smo-

halla and Young Chief that, should they not conform to government regulations, they would suffer the same fate.[15]

Finding increased dissatisfaction among the Indians in council,
especially those of Dreamer bands, Howard hurried back to Wallula on April 23 more willing than previously to hold council with
the Columbia renegade Dreamers. Fearing an attack against himself, he spurned the invitation that Smohalla sent by messenger on
April 24 to cross the Columbia to meet with him, masking his ap-
prehension by giving the impression that he cared little whether he
met with Smohalla or not. To the messenger he replied that, should
Smohalla have anything to tell him, it would have to be said at Wallula.

That afternoon Smohalla, with about 250 men and 50 or more
women and children, crossed the river to meet the general and his
party which included Agent Cornoyer, Homily, and Pambrun.
Howard recalled that Smohalla, with "great parade" but seemingly
"with fierceness," declared his peoples' intent to remain free of reservations. In keeping with his neutral posture, Homily evaded the
inevitable subject of removal to reservations. Writing of a conversation with Homily, Howard later recalled how the chief, wishing
to offend neither whites nor Indians, once had told him at a meeting at his lodge: "Yes, Smohally's my friend, my priest. He dreams
great dreams, and he tells all the Columbia Indians, miles and
miles up and down the great river, about the Great Spirit; and often
what's coming. He cures sick folks by good medicine and drumming. He's a great Indian—Homili's friend. . . ." At the April meeting with Howard, when Smohalla inquired of the general about the
"Washington [D.C.] law," Agent Cornoyer, desirous of gathering
renegade Indians onto the Umatilla, explained that it was the law
that all Indians go on reservations. Less definite about the U.S.
government's position in the matter, Howard promised to write the
president on Smohalla's behalf.[16]

We have no record of Smohalla's appraisal of Howard. He would
have been aware of the general's mental traits, which included a
strong sense of duty, that at times clashed with his humanitarian
sentiments, and of his physical traits, which included a missing
arm, a casualty of the Civil War. From Howard's pen we have a description of Smohalla, whom he said was the author of the
Dreamer religion and the cause of restlessness among the renegades (Howard's term), keeping alive their hopes that supernatural
aid somehow would come to them through a general Indian uprising. As though scanning a battlefield, Howard assayed the individual before him: "a large-headed, hump-shouldered, odd little wiz-
ard of an Indian . . . a strange mixture of timidity and daring, of

superstition and intelligence." Howard observed of Smohalla that he was "short and shapeless . . . scarcely any neck; bandy legs, rather long for his body. . . ." He further noted that although Smohalla was deformed and was the strangest-looking human being that he had ever seen, the Dreamer had a finely formed head and clear, expressive, magnetic eyes that contrasted with his head covering, two corners of which were tied under his chin. Wind blowing through cracks of the warehouse where the council was held kept his bandana handkerchief moving at all times. The Prophet's suit was coarse and gray, somewhat ragged and soiled. Howard's assessment was written several years later when any animosity he might have had would have had time to cool.[17]

Howard agreed to hold a council at Lapwai to hear Joseph out, and on Thursday, May 3, the opening day of the eleven-day event, Joseph and about fifty nontreaty Dreamer and Dreamer-influenced Nez Percés arrived at Lapwai. Their warriors were in traditional garb, faces painted and hair braided. Their women wore bright-colored shawls and skirts. The council got underway with the arrival on the following day of the Nez Percé Dreamer White Bird and his band, who were closely allied with Joseph and his followers. With the disposition of Joseph and his people uppermost in his mind, Howard asked that they vacate the Wallowa and move to the Nez Percé Reservation.

If Howard anticipated Joseph as his main antagonist in council, he would have been surprised to learn that the loudest voices of opposition were those of the Nez Percé Dreamer-Prophet Toohoolsote and his Palouse counterpart Hush-hushcote. Howard described Toohoolsote as an "ugly, obstinate savage of the worst type." Later he recalled that he was "broad-shouldered, deep-chested, thick necked" with a "deep guttural voice . . . [that] betrayed in every word a strong and settled hatred of all Caucasians."[18] The general had less regard only for Hush-huscote, whom he described as an "oily, wily, bright-eyed young chief who could be smooth-tongued or saucy as the mood seized him." Toohoolsote's dominance in the deliberations denied the Palouses as much time as they wished to voice their beliefs. Howard would not forget Toohoolsote's pivotal influence in the proceedings, recalling that the Indians "appeared at one time almost on the point of yielding, but bad advice intervened to renew the Dreamer Sophistry."[19] Toohoolsote continued his declamations with Joseph and White Bird concurring in them.

On Sunday, May 6, differences between the worship of the Nez Percés and that of the whites were revealed when, in the words of Howard, a preacher in his own right, Joseph's warriors "went through with a weird dance, accompanied by the incessant beating of tom-toms, and other ceremonies characteristic of their heathen worship." When on the next day the verbal clashing resumed with neither the general nor the Dreamer yielding ground, Toohoolsote delivered his fiercest rejoinder: "What person pretends to divide the land and put me on it?" To which Howard answered that he did, for the president.[20] The Dreamer responded that his own authority came from the "Great Spirit Chief," whose authority was greater than Howard's because it was he who "made the world as it is, and as he wanted it, and he made a part of it for us to live upon." Seeking to have the last word, Toohoolsote countered, "I do not see where you get authority to say that we shall not live where he placed us."[21]

After a week of wearisome bitter debate the General lost his composure. "Shut up!" he shouted to his adversary, warning that he wanted no more of his talk. Toohoolsote would not be silenced. "Who are you," he asked, "that you ask us to talk, and then tell me I sha'n't talk? Are you the Great Spirit? Did you make the world? Did you make the sun? Did you make the rivers to run for us to drink? Did you make the grass to grow? Did you make all these things, that you talk to us though we were boys? If you did, then you have the right to talk as you do."[22] His boast that Howard did not frighten him was the last straw for the general. With troops at his command and the acquiescence of treaty-reservation Nez Percés, he felt safe to order the Nez Percé Dreamer incarcerated for five days in the guardhouse, not so much to protect as to silence him.

Howard took advantage of Toohoolsote's incarceration to escort Joseph, White Bird, Looking Glass, and others, including Hush-hushcote, on a tour of the reservation, attempting to entice them into taking lands on it. This was to no avail. His reiteration of the usual promises of schools, teachers, and so on only angered Joseph, who said that such were the very things his people did not want. Moreover, he told Howard that he would not take lands on the reservation because they did not belong to him. "I have never taken what did not belong to me," he declaimed. "I will not now."[23]

Returning from touring the reservation, Howard released his prisoner, whose promise to give his people "good advice" was but a truce in the ideological war between the general and the Dreamer, who were in cultural worlds apart. At this time Howard issued an order for Joseph to return to the Wallowa, collect his people and properties, and move to the reservation within thirty days. "If you are not here in that time," he warned, "I shall consider that you want to fight, and will send my soldiers to drive you on."[24] Joseph gave no indication that he would disobey the general's order. Too-hoolsote would never concede to removal, but Hush-hushcote agreed to it, although the Walla Walla treaty had stated that he should move to the Yakima Reservation. The turbulent council ended May 14.

The centerpiece of the Lapwai council, the Howard-Toohoolsote confrontation, was less a clash of personalities than of differing views of life. While Howard worshiped his Judeo-Christian God, Toohoolsote honored the Great Spirit and the Earth Mother. Howard was loyal to his nation, while Toohoolsote was loyal to his band within the tribe. Howard wanted to develop the land for human purposes, while Toohoolsote lived in harmony with nature. The two leaders also had differing concepts of time. Howard declared, "Let us hear it no more, but come to business at once." Toohoolsote said, "We want to talk a long time, many days, about the earth, about our land." "The Earth is our mother," he often declaimed. Finally, the two leaders had different goals in mind: American Manifest Destiny opposed to Indian resurrection and revitalization.[25]

In an article, "The True Story of the Wallowa Campaign" (the campaign that preceded the Nez Percé War), appearing in the *North American Review* of July, 1879, Howard responded to Joseph's article, "An Indian's Views of Indian Affairs," which had appeared the previous April in that periodical.[26] The general's article revealed that he had retained his hostile views of the Dreamer religion. He included in his article the following description of it by a special commission, as much to justify his actions as to inform the public about a most vital aspect of Indian culture:

> The Dreamers, among other pernicious doctrines, teach that the earth being created by God complete, should not be disturbed by man; and that any cultivation of the soil or other improvements to interfere with its natural productions; any voluntary submission to the control of the Government; any improvement in the way of schools, churches, etc., are crimes from which they shrink. This fanaticism is kept alive by the superstition of these Dreamers, who industriously teach that if they continue steadfast in their present belief a leader will be raised up (in the East) who will restore all the dead Indians to life, who will unite with them in expelling the whites from their country, when they will again enter upon and repossess the lands of their ancestors.[27]

On May 31 the general set out from Portland for the interior because he had received a May 4 report from Pambrun that, if fighting were to erupt in the trouble-torn Wallowa valley, the "Columbia River renegades" were prepared to cause trouble along the Columbia and Snake rivers and they posed a personal danger to Pambrun.[28] From The Dalles, Howard moved north overland to Simcoe to hold a council with Dreamer chiefs and the non-

Dreamer chief Moses, who also had not yet signed a treaty. Accompanying him was Skimiah, who had asked Howard to release him from confinement.

The Simcoe council opened June 9 under oaks that sheltered the participants from a hot sun. Among those whom the general met was Thomas, "trembling wild and fierce" (from a nervous ailment). He had fled the April Wallula council with his people because he feared incarceration in the Vancouver Barracks guardhouse, despite his boast to whites that his power would prevent them from holding him in irons. He had been induced to attend the Simcoe council by Pambrun and the Yakima chief, the Klickitat Joe Stwyre. Sitting next to the tall, spare Thomas was the portly Colwash, a "rump Dreamer chief" of a Columbia band near The Dalles whom Wilbur had whisked from his homeland to Simcoe. Lesser chiefs were also in attendance.[29]

After an opening prayer, the chiefs and their assembled people received Indian Inspector E. C. Watkin's warning that the United States required them to remove to the Yakima and Umatilla reservations and that they had best do so because Howard would enforce the requirement. On the following day, a Sunday, the chiefs presented their points of view. In response, Howard was careful to project a picture of harmony between the war and interior departments in the conduct of Indian affairs. It was thus arranged that the keynote speech should be delivered by Wilbur, who sought to impress those present with the success of his "Plow and Bible" program on the Yakima Reservation. Unlike white men attending the council, the Dreamer renegades there were unimpressed with the program and with Wilbur's exhortations to them to remove to the established reservations "for their own good."

The concept of a reservation might not have been distasteful to Smohalla if it were to serve as a sanctuary where he and his followers could be left alone. We do not know, however, how he responded to Meacham's suggestion that a reservation be established for him and his followers near the confluence of the Columbia and Yakima rivers, or to Homily's proposal of a reservation five to ten miles wide running for sixty miles along the Columbia west bank from Priest Rapids down to Wallula. On Monday, June 11, Moses expressed willingness at the Simcoe council to lead scattered upper-Columbia-River Indians to a reservation that he wished to see established for them in his ancestral homeland on the Columbia plateau. The lower, southern portions of his requested reservation, which lay close to that suggested by Meacham and Homily, would have set poorly with Smohalla, as would any dealings Moses might have with the government.

The council did little to improve Howard's assessment of Smohalla, whom he called "the author of the 'dreamer religion,'" which he termed "the cause of the restlessness of the Columbia River tribes, for it keeps alive the hope of supernatural aid, somehow, to come through a general Indian resurrection."[30] When the council ended, Howard turned his attention to the troubled Nez Percé country.[31]

Corresponding with Howard after the council, Wilbur continued stressing the peaceful disposition of the Indians, not only of his agency but along the Columbia River. He did so at least partly because he wanted no intervention of the military in the area, believing that it exerted a negative influence on the Indians. He was quoted as saying he wanted soldiers no nearer than the Rocky Mountains. Even Skimiah and his band, he stated exuberantly, had joined the church (Methodist) and were "praying and singing."[32]

Pambrun did not share Howard's favorable assessment of the council. Writing about it in later years, he recalled that Agent Wilbur, after conferring with Watkins and Howard, decided to leave the matter up to him. "I called Smokalie up," wrote Pambrun, "[I] wanted no prevarications . . . [but] a direct and positive yes or no." To that he said Smohalla replied, "I will come into the reservation as soon as the white salmon fishing is over" (around August). He also recorded a surprise follow-up visit to Smohalla's village about a month later. On entering the Dreamer's lodge, he found him seated in silence, with his head beneath his knees, as though sleeping. To waken him, Pambrun called him a squaw, a dog, and a liar and threatened to write Washington, D.C., about his conduct. Responding to Pambrun's verbal blast, Smohalla, "shamming," rose to shake the interpreter's hand, ordered his people to do likewise, and reiterated his pledge to remove to the reservation at the end of the white-salmon season. Pambrun believed he had succeeded in inducing an Indian of an anti-Smohalla faction to defect from the Dreamer, taking with him all the women, save the elderly. This he said would impoverish Smohalla, weaken his "medicine," and break his influence in general. He proudly recalled that he had accomplished much in conversing with Smohalla and also, had gained the upper hand on Thomas after Howard had given him carte blanche to do what he pleased with him. Pambrun boasted of placing Thomas in irons and breaking the power of his "dream spirit . . . unacquainted with handcuffs."[33]

While his interpreter was en route to Smohalla's village, Howard made his way to Nez Percé country. There, after the second Lapwai council, Joseph's Indians held one of their own, at which they decided to move out and onto the reservation. Toohoolsote, angered and in no way penitent from his confinement, talked war and gathered a following of young warriors ready to fight. They bought up ammunition, and under the old Dreamer's guidance, organized a war party.[34] In the meantime Hush-hushcote went around, with little success, attempting to recruit warriors from other tribes to join Joseph in his growing anti-American cause. Some of Hush-hushcote's fellow Palouse Dreamers were in the north among the Coeur d'Alenes at their Catholic mission. The Catholic priests were strongly opposed to the Dreamers, and remembering that Palouses had enticed the Coeur d'Alenes into a humiliating defeat two decades earlier at the hands of Colonel George Wright, U.S.A., the missionaries did not want another such rebellion led by "pagans" among them. From Lapwai to Spokane Falls rumors spread like wildfire among the white communities of atrocities committed against them. Petitions went flying to American civil and military authorities for aid, in the absence of which, volunteer militia outfits were formed to meet the threat of the "hostiles."

Unlike Hush-hushcote, for whom hostilities were a means of unifying the Indians in a crusade against the whites, Smohalla, like Thomas, seems to have opposed conflict in the belief that the Great Spirit, not war, would free them in his own good time. Smohalla's teachings inspired Joseph's people, but they guaranteed them no protection from whites in the here and now as they stumbled into a fight with American troops. In mid-July, 1877, Hush-hushcote and other Palouses joined Joseph's band at Wieppe Prairie in Idaho where they sought not war but escape from American troops. Hush-hushcote comforted the Nez Percés and Palouses with his Dreamer preachings throughout their retreat, defeat, and eventual incarceration in the Indian Territory.[35] Hatalekin also joined Joseph after Captain Stephen G. Whipple, U.S.A., attacked the camp of Looking Glass, to whom some of Hatalekin's Middle Palouses were related. Hatalekin was killed at the battle of Big Hole, and Toohoolsote died in the final fight at Bear Paw Mountain.

The capture of Joseph's decimated, war-weary band in Montana Territory and their incarceration in Kansas and finally in the Indian Territory did not lessen their belief that they would escape their dilemma by supernatural intervention. The June, 1878, issue of the magazine *Council Fire and Arbitrator* stated that the captives, under the continuing influence of the "Walla Walla Dreamer" (the Palouse Hush-hushcote), clung to the belief that a "deliverer . . . would come" who would save the Indians so "that they need not labor and adopt the white man's laws." Back home in the Far West, at about the same time, the Nez Percé Dreamer Stoke Kiyi was preaching that a messiah would come and return the land to the Indians.[36] It is difficult to ascertain how widely his prophecy was believed among the treaty Nez Percés. Presbyterian and Catholic missionaries had taught them about a coming Christian messiah. One of their number, Chief Utesinmalecum, admitted that some of his people were interested in Dreamers who accoutered themselves in feathers and other trappings, but confessed his inability to discern the rightness or wrongness of their religion.[37]

Languishing in a hot southern land far from their beloved Wallowa country, Joseph and his band could only hope that the Dreamer prophecies would be speedily fulfilled. He blamed the events that had sent him and his people into exile on the short notice given them to remove to the Nez Percé Reservation and the high-handed, humiliating treatment given to Toohoolsote,[38] who, more than any other Dreamer, had led the Nez Percés and their Palouse allies into conflict with the United States. The oft-told story of Joseph's War, or more properly, Joseph's flight, needs no retelling here.

Joseph's capture by the United States Army did not end the fears of the white community and of Howard himself that the Columbia renegades would go to war. There were repercussions along the Columbia River during the following year. Conflict broke out in another quarter when resistive Northern Paiutes joined Bannocks in a war against American forces. The Indians believed that the time had come for the long-promised resurrection of Indians and that a victory was possible, not only because their coalition seemed more powerful to them than Joseph's had, but also because the self-styled "medicine-man" and Paiute Dreamer-Prophet Oytes had assured and excited them with the following claims: "I can defeat all my enemies! No bullet can hurt me. I have the power to kill any of you! It is wrong to dig up the face of the earth, – the earth is our mother; we must live upon what grows of itself." Oytes refused an offer of three hundred dollars from the Malheur agent, Sam B. Parrish, to aim a rifle at his chest.[39] Beginning in Idaho Territory, the war spread north into the Oregon interior as the Bannocks and Paiutes skirmished American forces to the Umatilla Reservation and beyond. A "hostile" Umatilla remnant fought and escaped from the reservation across the Columbia River.

General Howard was too concerned with bringing the wars to a successful conclusion to heed the views of a fellow minister, the Reverend W. H. Gray. After visiting the Nez Percés in June, 1878, Gray wrote that the wars originated "in the sectarian sentiments inculcated during the occasional visits of Jesuit Priests, and by the supersticious [sic] worship of images extended to their medicine men, now called *dreamers*, including the impression that it was of no use to them to go upon the reservation, for if they did, they would not be allowed to keep their homes or improvements, as the heretic (Americans) would steal them from them."[40]

Howard's overriding objective was to prevent Smohalla's Columbia River renegades and Moses's people from joining the Bannock-Paiutes, or at least to quiet them in order not to have a two-front war on his hands. Thus he dispatched Lieutenant M. C. Wilkinson in early May, 1878, to meet with the two chiefs, whom he found in the Kittitas valley, where their people were gathering roots. Wilkinson soon learned that an Indian coalition under the two leaders was unlikely when Moses used the meeting to denounce Smohalla's drumming and dreaming and promised "to take the nonsense out of him" should Smohalla wish to join the Columbia Sinkiuse chief for any reason. Moses' words indicated that Smohalla may have sought a temporary alliance with his rival, who had more influence on Howard than he did. To Charles McKay, whom Howard dispatched to him early in July, Moses projected a peaceful image in relation to whites, unlike that of his youthful warrior days. Moses voiced to McKay not only annoyance with Smohalla but outright animosity towards him for the serious trouble that he said the Dreamer-Prophet might cause.[41] In Howard's thinking, Smohalla posed a far greater threat to the peace of the interior than did Moses. After all, it was his Dreamer-Prophet teachings that had stirred the Nez Percés to fight with the American forces, causing the general so much trouble.

Although Moses persuaded Howard of his peaceful intent, he certainly did not reassure the tense, rumor-riddled white communities. A tragic footnote to the Bannock-Paiute War began on July 10, 1878, in some lonely hills near Snipes Mountain, between the Columbia and Yakima valleys, when hostile Umatilla renegades, fleeing north from the war, killed a white couple, Mr. and Mrs. Alonzo Perkins. The whites pointed the finger of blame at Moses and Smohalla, and legal indictments were written out against them as the murderers. In that day of poor communications and a lack of accurate information, whites imagined fictitious scenarios in which Smohalla and other Dreamers were invited by Bannock-Paiutes to share in their war booty.[42] Other Dreamer chiefs, such as the former hostile Colwash, were included in the scenarios. Colwash had made his peace with whites, in the words of Agent Wilbur, "singing and praying" on the Yakima Reservation. Forty of his warriors were said to have been sent to guard the Naches Pass in the Cascade Mountains while Smohalla's men were said to have guarded another pass farther north in that range. Bannocks and Okanagons were said to have been dispatched to block other routes on the east and south.[43] Settlers believed deployment of Indian braves to mountain passes and other strategic points was calculated to prevent whites from escaping the Indians. Rather than involve himself in such plans, however, Smohalla tried to keep out of trouble.

Under an arrest warrant, and warned of possible capture by whites, he moved his people out of the path of the advancing Umatilla renegades, while some of his followers fled to Moses for protection. Smohalla's move prompted Indian-haters to speculate that he had been "quietly disposed of." Rumor also had it that he had given up his Dreamer faith.[44] Moses, likewise, wished to stay clear of the troublesome Umatillas. He warned a party of them to turn back from his camp in the Wenatchee country, fearing that they would cause trouble and jeopardize his already shaky position with whites. The Umatillas may have formed the party of twenty or thirty, under a Chief Umassit, who moved on north to the mouth of the Okanogan River, where in March, 1879, they were reported camping.[45]

The deployment of the military to strategic points was real, unlike the supposed movement of Indian braves to those places. Fearing trouble in the Okanogan valley from Indians who might be joining those on the south, General Howard ordered Lieutenant W. R. Parnell, First Cavalry, out of Camp Coeur d'Alene (on Coeur d'Alene Lake in Idaho) to undertake a reconnaissance along the Canadian border. Deep snows in February and March, 1879, would prove more troublesome to his expedition than would the unfriendly Indians, who Parnell reported were farther south.[46] Howard, however, did not dispatch troops to the south to corral Smohalla, although many whites believed he should have. On August 30, 1878, the editor of the *Tacoma (W.T.) Herald*, described the Prophet as probably the most dangerous Indian in the country, roaming through the Yakima valley at will, ready at any moment to give the signal for "murder, rapine and pillage." Rumor also had it that Smohalla and his men had killed two hundred head of stockmen's cattle.

Such stories were trouble enough for Smohalla and Moses, but even more cutting were those emanating from members of their own race who capitalized on the ill-feeling of the white community toward them. In early May, 1878, the Okanagon chief Tonasket reported to the commandant of Fort Colville (near present-day Colville, Washington) that Moses' Indians, with those of Smohalla and Thomas, were planning to attack Howard when he came their way.[47] Among the Indians empathizing with Moses in his time of trouble was the Klickitat-Yakima chief Joe Stwyre, who said that Moses had a good "tum-tum" (heart) and that, were anyone to fight, it would be Smohalla, whose efforts he said would be feeble, as he had but few braves.[48]

His hands full with the Bannock-Paiute War, General Howard was happy that Moses, whose followers included a number of malcontents, reiterated his peaceful intentions, which Moses expressed to the general at the "Steamboat Council" held aboard the *Spokane* at the foot of Priest Rapids in early September, 1878. This council was between Howard and his party and the Indian "friendlies," including Homily. Smohalla absented himself from the council, although it was held within sight of his P'na Village at the head of steamboat navigation on the Columbia. At the council Moses delineated for Howard his requested reservation. The general promised to pass on Moses' request, but warned that he was unable to assure the establishment of the reservation. He believed that a reservation for Moses would go far toward easing tensions in the interior. Under Howard's order of September 9, the vaguely defined reservation lay within a line running from White Bluffs northeast to the Spokane River near its mouth, and crossing the Columbia, north along its right bank for eight miles. From there the line ran west, parallel to the Columbia River and twelve miles distant from it, to a ridge near the crest of the Cascade Mountains. From there the line ran southeast to the falls of the Yakima River, then along that river fifteen miles to its confluence with the Columbia, and up the Columbia to the place where it began.[49]

For cattlemen, some of whom attended the council, Howard's proclamation was like a flag waved in front of a bull in one of their herds. These ranchers cast covetous eyes on rich plateau bunchgrass in the proposed reservation to range their livestock. They hoped to appropriate these lands by linking Moses with the Perkins murders. Consequently, in December he was tracked down by a citizen posse and incarcerated in the Yakima City jail.[50] In the same month, and in the previous October, a relative of Moses, the shaman Weat-tatatum, talked, as had Smohalla, with Indian advocate A. J. Cain. Weat-tatatum inquired about deliberations in the council at Priest Rapids and affirmed that Moses and his men were not on the warpath as rumored.[51]

The posse searched not only for Moses but also for Smohalla and any weapons that he might have. They found that the Prophet and his people had abandoned his P'na Village, leaving no weapons. Wilbur triumphantly reported to Commissioner E. A. Hayt on December 31 that 250 Smohalla and Moses people had come on the Yakima Reservation. The previous week a Lieutenant E. B. Rheem, Twenty-first Infantry, had written Howard that, if Columbia River renegades had wanted to go on the warpath, Moses' jailing would have dissuaded them. Aided and encouraged by Wilbur, many were rapidly coming to the reservation, according to Rheem.[52] Despite the optimistic tenor of official reports, Wilbur must have known that many Moses and Smohalla people had no intention of remaining on the reservation and that they had gone there only to keep out of harm's way.

In the same month, March, 1879, Wilbur sent an Indian, Hahah-sawuni, accompanied by Captain W. H. Winters, to incarceration at Vancouver Barracks for sowing "seeds of discord" among the Indians, urging them to leave the reservation, Moses was released to journey to Washington, D.C., where he projected the picture of a modern cooperative Indian who had abandoned the old ways. "All of those customs," he told a reporter, "are now left mostly to the 'dreamers'," who rarely lived on reservations. "Civilized and converted" Indians, he assured him, had abandoned the old religion to Dreamers and Drummers, along with their "ceremonies and incantations . . . invariably accompanied by drumming."[53] Moses' public-relations campaign with government officials paid off, for he was promised a reservation extending from Lake Chelan to the Canadian border, but it was later to be taken from him by the executive orders opening the way for his removal to the nearby Colville Reservation. On August 8, 1879, Howard wrote Washington Territorial Governor Elisha P. Ferry that he believed the governor would concur with him that it was now best that proceedings against Moses and Smohalla be discontinued.[54] In the following month Indians from Priest Rapids, unsure of their status, appeared at Camp Winfield Scott (about six miles north of present-day Ellensburg, Washington) to ask its commandant, Major John Green of the First Cavalry, if he had been apprised of the coming of soldiers to compel them to remove to a reservation.[55]

At the time the military did not wish to alarm Indians by threatening them with confinement, but such was not the case with Indian Office personnel, especially agents such as Cornoyer who wanted Indians confined not only for what the agents believed was their own good but also to keep the white community from harassing agents about the presence of renegade Dreamers. On August 10, 1880, Cornoyer reported to the commissioner that the only way to deal with the Indian "problem" was to remove their leaders and their followers to reservations and keep them there by force, if necessary. Hitherto this treatment usually had been reserved for uncooperative chieftains. Typical of those whom Cornoyer would confine now were the Dreamers Waltsac and Suitz (Stock Sweetzh) and their 150 people, who refused lands on the Umatilla Reservation and elsewhere as they continued roaming the hundred miles up and down the Columbia between Wallula and the mouth of the John Day River. Cornoyer found less troublesome Thomas and John Cluah, who wished to retain lands above the mouth of The Snake River, where they lived with about fifty followers and had made considerable improvements.[56]

In the meantime, those factors that had helped assure Smohalla's escape from confinement were still at work. Because of accidents of location and events, his colleague in drumming and dreaming Kotiakan did not enjoy the same good fortune. Since James H. Wilbur's tenure as agent was ending, and the Moses' problem had been settled for him, Wilbur had tended to let things take their course with regard to removing renegades to the Yakima Reservation. His replacement, R. H. Milroy, however, sought to gather the renegades with considerably more vigor. Milroy's determination to bring them under the "civilizing" arm of the Simcoe Agency would bring about a most unpleasant chapter not only in Dreamer-government relations but in the history of the Indian agencies themselves. While caught up in these conflicts, Kotiakan and his people epitomized the resistance and vitality of Dreamers trying to save their threatened way of life.

7
The Demise of Smohalla

> God told me to look after my people – all are
> my people.
> — *Smohalla to Captain J. W. MacMurray.*

After the Nez Percé and Bannock-Paiute wars, increasing white settlement in the interior brought increasing turmoil not only between whites and Indians but also between the Indian Office and the U.S. Army. The delineation of the military and the civilian roles in the conduct of Indian affairs on the Pacific Northwest frontier had been hazy and troublesome. On April 10, 1884, General Nelson A. Miles, commanding the Department of the Columbia at Vancouver Barracks, fired a round in the intensified conflict by seeking instructions from his superiors at the Division of the Pacific headquarters in San Francisco about what powers military authorities had, according to the division circular of July 30, 1883, to protect roaming Indians, not only on the Columbia River but throughout Miles's department.[1]

On the Indian Office side, R. H. Milroy, replacing the Reverend Wilbur as Simcoe agent, fired a round for his department in an April 13, 1883, letter informing Colonel C. Grover, the commander of Fort Walla Walla, that numerous complaints and petitions from settlers about nonreservation Indians had caused him to seek their removal to the Yakima Reservation. Their removal, he wrote, would not only help their children "rise above the ignorance of their parents" but also allay the clamor among whites to open the reservation to white settlement.[2]

The American public watched through its newspapers as the two arms of the government struggled with the problems of dealing with both nonreservation and reservation Indians. The news accounts, often based on rumor, made the officials' conduct of Indian affairs appear bumbling and ineffective. For example, the Portland *Oregonian* of March 28, 1883, carried an article entitled "An Indian Scare: Four Hundred Umatillas Reported Having Left the Reservation and Being on the War Path." By the next day things had cooled down in the interior, and the same newspaper called the situation "the most ridiculous scare that ever originated on any frontier," citing nervous whites along Willow Creek as the laughing stock of the whole country. The *Oregonian* did not acknowledge that its contradictory stories, following each other so closely, were equally laughable. At that time stories of the army running down "troublemaking" Indians in both the Southwest and Pacific Northwest made exciting reading back East and even in larger western urban areas such as San Francisco and Portland. Frontier journals, nearer the scene of the troubles, viewed the Indian presence with much more concern, although there were exceptions, such as the *Yakima Record* (Yakima City, W.T.), whose editor in an April 21, 1883, edition felt a special need to minimize news that might tend to frighten settlers away.

In late March, 1883, at Fort Walla Walla, Captain Thomas McGregor, First Cavalry, and his companion, Lieutenant Robert Wainwright, visited the tension-filled settlement at Willows, Oregon, which was a small railroad station two miles down the Columbia from the mouth of Willow Creek. During their tour, the two officers visited the Dreamer Chiefs Pascappa and Suitz and their people, who roamed the Columbia down to John Day River, and they also heard from Waltsac and Hackney. During his councils with the Indians, McGregor met two men, named Williams and McCredy, whom the captain reported as the most active in spreading false reports about the red men.

Pascappa and Suitz assured McGregor that they had no thought of causing trouble – no Umatilla, Yakima, Warm Springs, or Paiute Indians had ever been among them – and they expressed surprise that white settlers had been so alarmed as to flee their homes. When questioned, Williams admitted that an Indian (perhaps the one named Salmon Man) had warned him to keep off lands on Long Island on the Columbia River, a short distance above the mouth of Willow Creek. McGregor tried to quiet the Indians by assuring them he knew of no orders for their removal, but he warned them to leave whites alone and keep their ponies out of white lands. He also assured settlers that it was safe for them to return to their homes. In summing up his report, he located the sources of the excitement as Williams and another Long Island settler, Mr. Fernard. Wanting Indian lands on the island, Fernard had taken a petition to Milroy stating that warlike tribesmen had warned Williams and him to leave the island. As lands on the Washington side of the Columbia were, in McGregor's words, fit only for grazing, he recommended that Indians be allowed to remain there and that citizens of the Willows area be so informed and an officer sent to communicate with them. Like other officials, he knew the risks of moving Indians without prior approval of the Indian Office.[3]

On another journey to the Willows area in mid-April, McGregor met with Pascappa, Suitz, Callapoo, Hackney, Skimiah, and their people. He also met Thomas Simpson, captain of the Yakima Agency Indian police, and four others. They had been dispatched by Milroy to order the Dreamer leaders and their people to come on the Yakima Reservation, under threat of being put in irons should they resist. McGregor believed the police force served only to frighten the Indians and reported that the only instruction Milroy had given his police was to tell the Indians that the military were coming to compel them to come on the reservation.[4]

Many, if not most, of the Indians whom McGregor met were under Smohalla's influence. More of them might have been under his influence if some, in the worlds of Indian Inspector Robert S. Gardner, had not abandoned the "Smohalla doctrine" to affiliate with the Presbyterian Church on the Warm Springs Reservation.[5] Verification of Smohalla's influence came from the pen of Captain F. N. Upham, First Cavalry out of Fort Walla Walla, who reported on March 18, 1884, that about four hundred "bucks" . . . known as Drummers and Dreamers" lived along the Columbia River and that he had urged them to take Indian homesteads while they were still available.[6] Because of their religion, reported Upham, they wanted no part of homesteads. To pay even the small filing fee to the land office to obtain one, they maintained, would have denied a basic tenet of their religion.[7] Even had they wanted to take homesteads, they would have found it difficult to obtain them. To file for lands, they would have had to journey to one of four offices in Vancouver, Walla Walla, Yakima, or Spokane and make affidavits supported by the testimony of two disinterested white men – a procedure that was required only of Indians, who were unfamiliar with such legalities in the first place.[8] Meanwhile, the quickened pace of white settlement on the many unsurveyed lands of the interior threatened to narrow their choice of homesteads.

Not the least troublesome problem for government and Indians was the latter's right, as guaranteed by the June, 1855, Walla Walla treaty, to fish in their "usual and accustomed places." Milroy admitted to the Indian commissioner that the treaty had given Indians the right to fish, hunt, dig roots, and gather berries, even though he said that the law denied them the right to reside off the reservation. They must, he asserted, be brought on the confine, a task that he grudgingly admitted the military was mandated to carry out. His zeal in gathering off-reservation Indians to destroy their "barbarism" became a crusade that he believed humanity demanded.[9] To the commissioner, he described renegade Dreamers as avoiding reservation life to lead "an idle, and vicious life" getting drunk and gambling all night and racing horses all day. He said that they obtained the means "to gratify" their "evil propensities" by prostituting their women to whites more degraded than they. Especially troublesome to him were the twenty or more saloons at The Dalles and elsewhere on the Oregon side of the Columbia River.[10]

Milroy characterized what he called "drummers, dreamers, or pumpummers" as not only "barbarous" but "savage," "vicious," and most demeaning of all, "animal."[11] Attempting to halt their practices, he ordered all medicine men and women of the Yakima Reservation to attend a council scheduled for May 1, 1884, at which he planned to use arguments from "the Bible, and History, Reason &c, to try to get them to stuff up this barbarism." He also proposed offering them one hundred dollars in gold to reveal some of what he called their "Tamaniwus" powers. He did not record how well he carried out his strategy, stating only that he gave the Indian doctors "strong talk." His task must have been difficult for him, since he believed that it was as impossible to change the beliefs of adult "uncivilized" Indians as it was to remove "their color from their hides."[12]

One Indian Office representative at that time approached the problem firmly but more calmly and more optimistically than did Milroy. "Conflict of authority," wrote Special Agent Cyrus Beede to Indian Commissioner Hiram Price, "should not interfere with settling the Indians." Beede had just returned that summer of 1884 from a council with Indians in The Dalles area where he had encouraged those on both sides of the Columbia River to pay for surveys and apply to the land office to file on lands as soon as possible. At an August 2, 1884, council he listened to a lengthy discourse from Skimiah, who stated that a military inspector, Arthur Chapman, had told the Indians to stay where they were—that it was understood that they were to keep their lands. Beede reported that, if he had had with him a surveyor to show the Indians the appropriate boundary lines, they would have taken lands then and there.

On August 24 two Indians reported to Beede that military men (MacMurray and Chapman?) "not a month ago" had met in council with the Indians and that in another month General Miles would come up to confirm their ownership of the Columbia River. Beede naturally regarded such statements as evidence of the heavy hand of the military in the conduct of Indian affairs. To soften the pressure from that quarter, he suggested that in November, when the Indians returned from gathering subsistence in the mountains, an interpreter, surveyor, and military force send to proper reservations by proper transport all Indians refusing or neglecting to take homesteads.[13]

Although Milroy would have wanted these Indians on reservations, especially his, he believed that only their children could rise to a "civilized" level—and only by means of formal education. Earlier, in 1884, General Miles had anticipated the Indians' strong opposition to this and other Indian Office policies. "The burden of their complaint," he wrote, "is, that their children are taken from them against their wishes, to be sent to school; that efforts are being made to force upon them a religion against their will, and that they are not allowed to wear their own hair in the way they desire."[14]

To implement his educational policies, Milroy on September 19 dispatched his police captain, Simpson, and his first sergeant, Dave, to go the thirty miles down to Kotiakan's Pa'kiut Village to induce its Indians to send their children to the agency school.[15] Simpson told Kotiakan's people that they had come to tell them that their children would be given a vacation on the condition that their parents return them to the school in six weeks. Speaking for the Indians, Waunitta replied:

> Now I will answer you. We are not making the stand we do without good reason. We keep our children from school in consequence of what Major McMurray told us at the Council. After we received one letter from him we wrote to him to tell us when he would be here to hold another council as he promised. We expect his answer today. When we get it we will know when he will be here to hold the council and we will all be there. We wont send our children till we hear from him. Don't you have a bad heart toward us. On this account, for we have reason to act thus. We are waiting till Maj. McMurray comes to learn whether the soldiers are to have permanent charge of the reservation. If they do we will send our children to school.[16]

Milroy was uncertain if the Indians' impression of receiving help from the military stemmed from MacMurray's words or from their own misinterpretation of them. He admitted that the problem was moot by that time, since their belief in MacMurray's help was deeply engrained in their thinking.[17]

When the Indian police returned to Simcoe Agency headquarters and reported their failure to induce Pa'kiut elders to send their children to school, Milroy, accompanied by an interpreter, two police, and the influential and tractable Joe Stwyre and his fellow Klickitat Eneas, went down on September 23 to Pa'kiut Village to induce the people to change their minds. Responding to Milroy's statement of the advantages of schooling for their children, they said that

MacMurray had told them that they no longer needed to regard his authority as agent, since from then on the military was their authorized custodian. Further increasing Milroy's anxiety, they said they were expecting to hold another council with MacMurray in about twenty days. Their spokesman, Waunitta, responded with moderation but said that MacMurray had made him chief in charge of all the Indians and had told him to keep the children away from school. Should anything go wrong, said Waunitta, MacMurray had told him to report to him.

Waunitta refused to return to the agency with Milroy. Then followed what the agent called "a scene of indescribable confusion." As he reported it, forty or fifty Indians hiding in the brush rushed him and his party, with three to five Indians springing on each of his men. His police were quickly overpowered, their clothing was torn from them, and some were quite seriously injured. Fearing that his police might fire their guns, Milroy quickly disengaged from the fracas, ordering his men to retreat. As they did, the Indians, in Milroy's words, "loaded us with abuse," and their women rushed to the council tent with rifles and pistols for their friends, saying that they were ready to commence shooting.[18]

It would appear that the cause of the Indian resentment against Milroy and his party lay deeper than his order to send their children to the school where he admitted they had been mistreated. Possibly elderly ones at the village still smarted from the defeat there of Indian forces by American troops in October, 1855, and, according to Indian accounts, the hanging there of seven Indians after the 1855 killing of an Indian agent, which had helped precipitate the Yakima War.[19] Milroy speculated that the villagers were also angry that, to establish his authority at his Simcoe Agency, he had used the more conforming Klickitats on the Yakima Reservation rather than members of the less cooperative Yakima tribe to which most the villagers belonged.

After the Pa'kiut incident, Milroy hurried a dispatch to General Miles asking for troops to preserve order and prevent further bloodshed. As requested by the commissioner, Milroy also sought clarification from Miles about the authority of the general to inquire into the agent's official conduct. Milroy was alluding to the MacMurray-Chapman visit to ascertain the Indians' grievances and explain to them their options under the March 3, 1875, Indian Homestead law. Milroy described that legislation as "a mistaken and pernicious policy," because, he claimed, there remained for Indians nonreservation lands superior to their own improperly farmed homesteads. Moreover, he believed Indian homesteaders were more vulnerable to rapacious whites than were reservation Indians, who were guaranteed protection by the government for themselves and education for their children. He believed MacMurray's visit to Kotiakan's Pa'kiut Village had inflamed its people, precipitating their attack on his own party. Also rankling him was his initial ignorance of MacMurray's visit, which he claimed had "intensified lawlessness among the wilder portions of the Indians." Most galling of all was the Indians' word that the captain allegedly had assured them that they no longer needed to submit to agent's authority, since the military was their authorized custodian.[20]

Milroy believed the source of the renegades' resistance was with their Dreamer-Prophets, and he believed it necessary to destroy what he believed was their malign influence. Believing that the leadership of Smohalla and Kotiakan inhibited the advancement of their followers, the agent regarded their villages as fortresses preventing the forces of progress from occupying the fertile valleys of potential "civilization." Basing his understanding of the Dreamer-Prophets and their teachings on Milroy's reports, the commissioner of Indian affairs wrote:

> The greater portion of the Indians belonging to this agency [the Simcoe] who are non-residents of this reservation [the Yakima] are wild anti-civilization Indians. They nearly all are known as drummer, dreamers, or pumpummers who have a wild superstitious belief, in which they are very fanatical, that renders them unalterably opposed to the white man's ways. They believe that if they will continue faithful to the old habits and beliefs of their ancestors, that the Great Spirit will in the near future suddenly bring to life all Indians who have died for the last thousand years or more, and will enable the Indians to at once expel or exterminate all the whites and have the whole country to themselves the same as before the white man came. They have rude drums and meet in crowds on Sundays and indulge in drumming and wild, fanatical dances, and the old men make speeches to them, telling them of the good old times of long ago, and of the good time coming if they will continue faithful to the ways of their ancestors.[21]

In a lengthy letter to the assistant adjutant general, MacMurray narrated the events of his inspection tour which had precipitated the troubles. It all began, he stated, when he went in search of Smohalla, "the Prophet of Dreamers," to explain to him the Indian homestead laws and to encourage him and his followers to take homesteads. Not finding Smohalla, the Captain sent word to Smohalla to come meet him in Yakima City (present-day Union Gap). Leaving Fort Simcoe on his way to Yakima City, MacMurray stopped off to meet with Kotiakan at Pa'kiut Village as he had promised Kotiakan at Fort Simcoe he would do. At the Pa'kiut Village, on learning of the recent death of Kotiakan's child, MacMurray decided to move on to his destination. Late that evening several Indians came to MacMurray and informed him that Smohalla had come in. The captain sent word he was retiring for the night and would see him the next morning. In the continuing jockeying between MacMurray and the Indians, the latter countered that he should come to meet Smohalla then or not at all. MacMurray countered that Smohalla should wait for him, not the reverse, and that he would see the Dreamer-Prophet the next day at noon at Kotiakan's village. MacMurray returned there about noon the next day and talked at length with Smohalla. He was also invited into Kotiakan's church lodge, where a large number of Indians attended the funeral of that Dreamer's child.

Taking advantage of the presence of so many of Smohalla's "religious confrères" on the grounds, MacMurray pronounced to Smohalla the realities of the advancing white civilization and the need for him and his people to cultivate the soil, to comply with reservation laws, to be sober and industrious, and so on. Smohalla was appreciative but noncommittal. Having observed the Prophet, and aware of his creed and ceremonials, MacMurray appointed the day on which he met him at Priest Rapids to exhort him further. Perhaps because of the psychological jockeying over when they would meet, MacMurray apparently had made little impression on Smohalla at Pa'Kiut Village. His visit to Smohalla's P'na Village may have been to help atone for his apparent snubbing of the Prophet at Pa'kiut.

On hearing complaints from the Smohalla-Kotiakan people of "tyrannical and brutal" actions by Milroy, such as having their people shackled and imprisoned on bread and water for failing to send their children to school, MacMurray exhorted them to go to this agent, Milroy, whom Washington, D.C., had sent to help them. In response, the Indians claimed that Milroy had turned a deaf ear to their complaints, angrily cursing them. According to MacMurray, when Milroy leveled accusations against Kotiakan, the agent asked that the Dreamer be brought to the agency headquarters so that he could accuse him in person. MacMurray had him brought in to confirm through an agency interpreter the truth of the charges. At that time, still smarting from his confrontation with Kotiakan's people, the agent struck his fist on the table and angrily declaimed:

My word is law. I will punish any man on the Reservation as I see fit to do, when he breaks the law. They must obey me. They must understand that I never punish except for a breach of the law. Making complaints to the military will do no good, as they are only punished when

they do wrong. When they do well I treat them well. I am going to do
my duty to the best of my ability, as the Government directs me, and as
God lets me.[22]

On Feburary 28, 1885, MacMurray reported to the adjutant general at Vancouver Barracks that Kotiakan had sent two Indians
there seeking General Miles to complain that Milroy had arrested
some Indians and placed them in the Simcoe guardhouse for failing
to send their children to school. The captain reported that Kotiakan
had also instructed the two runners to have the general report the
plight of his people to officials in Washington, D.C., and had sent
word to his people at Pa'kiut Village to keep the peace and return to
their farms. Kotiakan also wanted the military to help him seek redress for Milroy's recent sending of twenty armed Indian police to
arrest himself, Waunitta, and Walasset. Waunitta was released
after ten days' confinement. Walasset was held in irons and released after three weeks. Kotiakan was handcuffed and leg-ironed
and given little food or water for nearly a week, during which time
he was taken out to saw wood. Then he was confined in like manner for six more weeks, uncuffed only to saw wood. During his
confinement Milroy ordered him to send his children to school or
remain in irons. The two runners to Vancouver told Miles that Kotiakan and Waunitta were arrested without charge because they
were leading men. In other words, Kotiakan's severe punishment
was evidence of his religious influence.[23]

It also came to light through MacMurray that runners had gone
to the Colville Reservation to relate to Chief Moses the wrongs per-
petrated on the Dreamer leaders and to seek his support for their
cause. Moses was anti-Dreamer, but diplomat that he was, he advised them to contact Miles to seek redress from Washington, D.C.
It also came to light through MacMurray that Indians in the Kittitas
and Wenatchee areas had advocated attacking Fort Simcoe, despite
Kotiakan's admonition to them to keep the peace.[24] Smohalla and
Kotiakan's people had ties with the Upper Yakima, or Kittitas, Indians, who also had ties with the Wenatchees. Like the Dreamer-
Prophets, none of these tribes relished the prospect of going on a
reservation.

Much correspondence circulated within military circles relative
to the injustices done to Kotiakan's followers. During his incarceration among them about twenty-five families abandoned their
sheep, goats, hogs, plows, harnesses, wagons, and other farming
appurtenances to escape to Priest Rapids and Smohalla's enclave
there.[25]

MacMurray believed the Indians' dislocations and their other
troubles had been aggravated by Milroy, whom he believed incap-

able of governing or comprehending his Indian charges.[26] The secretary of war recommended Milroy's transfer to another agency,
and Major General John Pope, commanding the Division of the
Pacific, recommended his immediate suspension.[27]

On March 19, 1885, Kotiakan broke through the floor of his cell
and escaped. Four Indian policemen failed to track him down to return him to the agency.[28] Suffering from a heart condition, the age-
ing Milroy found it increasingly difficult to achieve his goal of rescuing the likes of Kotiakan from "barbarism." The rigors and frustrations of his task hastened his death in March, 1890. Kotiakan
died on January 3, 1890, in his forty-fifth year.[29]

Kotiakan's people continued to follow a subsistence pattern
that he had delineated for them. Their willingness to meet "civilization" halfway was limited to performing agricultural chores at
or near their village. Most of his people worked for nearby white
farmers and had orchards and domestic animals to supplement
the fish that they caught in the rivers. Apparently, Kotiakan's
priestly successors were more permissive than he was in allowing their people to pursue occupations of white men. Their deference to farming, unlike Smohalla's opposition to it, was based
as much on environment as it was on religion; their lands around
Pa'kiut Village adapted more readily to farming than did the unir-
rigated desert lands around Smohalla's Priest Rapids home.
Moreover, they lived in closer proximity to whites than did Smohalla, and they followed their example in farming.

Kotiakan's immediate successor, his stepson Tianani (Teanana),
or Many Wounds,[30] leading about three hundred people, cooperated with later Simcoe Agency officials, who followed a softer line
against the Dreamer-Prophets than did Milroy. Shortly before Tianani's death, reportedly at the hands of two drunken Indians, he invited the Simcoe agent, Jay Lynch, to a meeting at Pa'kiut Village in
1893. During a ceremonial, Tianani explained for the agent the
principles of the Dreamer religion, referring to the Creator as the
father who lived beyond the sun and who provided his children
with fish in bright, clear rivers. In olden times, said Tianani, there
were many prophets, who lived so close to the Great Father above
that they were able to foretell the future, having long foreseen the
coming of the whites, whom they advised their people to treat as
brothers.

At the close of the ceremonials, Lynch's "conductor" (Tianani?)
said to him, "I will shake hands with you, Indian fashion," which
involved placing his hand over his heart and directing the agent to
do likewise. He then extended his hand to Lynch, palm upward,
and the agent, following his example, raised his hand in like manner. Tianani then clasped Lynch's raised hand and elevated it three

times, as high as before. The two then unclasped their hands, and placed them again on their hearts. The Indians believed that the first placement of the hands signified a "good heart," and the extension of the palm upward above the head showed willingness to share whenever and whatever the occasion required. The greeting was reminiscent of that of the Blowers, who appeared among the Yakimas in the 1880's. On meeting strangers, instead of shaking hands with them, the Blowers first waved their hands gently like fans in front of the faces of those whom they greeted, to "blow" away the "madness" from them. In their ceremonials they made the sign of the cross and used candles and a variety of other Christian trappings. They emphasized shaking and curing, much in the manner of Indian Shakers. Their blowing greetings possibly stemmed from the practice of native doctors blowing on the patients to remove evil spirits from them. The day following Tianani and Lynch's meeting, a Sunday, was given to songs, prayers, exhortations, and fasting. Eventually Tianani was succeeded in his priestly role by one of Kotiakan's younger sons, Showaway, while a Dreamer known to whites as Billy John or Dr. Billie supervised priestly functions.[31]

Bernice E. Newell, a journalist who traveled through the Yakima country at a time when Indian Inspector Province McCormick was visiting its Indians (perhaps in 1894), was struck by the independent spirit of Dr. Billie and his people, who she reported were able to "snap their fingers at the 'tyhee,' or agent, and all his tries to induce them to enter into a more civilized life." To this guest the Yakimas appeared a handful of "desperate, determined savages" who held what she termed variously as "sun," "ghost," "war," and "root" ceremonials while clinging tenaciously to traditions of their fathers and to belief in their mother the Earth. With three other visitors, Newell attended what she learned was the Pom Pom dance, which she described from a vantage point atop a pile of blankets:

> The dance amounted to little more than a spring, Shaker-like movement, which gradually increased with time and energy, becoming a frenzy of excitement as the climax of each stanza was reached, and the assembly stretched hands toward the noonday sun streaming through the open peak of the roof. There were withered old squaws, the very incarnation of ugliness; there were young girls and women and children and they all wore their black hair in two thick braids, parted from forehead to neck, the part dyed a brilliant vermillion, with patches of white on either side of the head. There were braves in splendid attire, and there were babies that cried and had to be strapped on the 'skinth' which the mother carries on her back by means of a strap across the forehead.[32]

For a time a "half-blood" Yakima, Charles Ike (Charley Snyder),
explained for white visitors the Smohalla ritual as practiced at
Pa'kiut Village.[33] By 1893 the eight or ten families remaining there
had been outnumbered by worshippers from other places. In June,
1893, Agent Lynch, trying to overcome, or at least minimize,
Charles Ike's influence, wrote letters to off-reservation Indians
such as those at Pa'kiut Village telling them to seek allotments on
the Yakima Reservation and citing a statement signed on July 6,
1893, by Yakima headmen that they would welcome them there.[34]
In the general area of Pa'kiut, however, the Indians continued to
fence sizeable tracts and earn money by selling hay and horses.
Newell noted that they held a portion of their land in common. In
1894, Kotiakan's successors, unwilling to surrender their Indianness, asked Inspector McCormick to set aside for them a separate
tract as a reservation. When he told them that he had no authority
to do so, they asked him to leave.[35] They also refused annuities and
blankets at the Simcoe Agency headquarters and spurned the invitation to allot on that reservation. Indian Office personnel hoped
that the allotting process under the Dawes Indian Severalty Act of
February 8, 1887 (24 Stat. 388), would lure holdout Indians onto
the Yakima, and certain Indians of that reservation wanted those
outside it to allot before all its good lands were taken.

In December, 1891, Umatilla agent John Crawford went to the
Oregon town of Umatilla on the Columbia River to talk with about
twenty-seven men and women, seeking to have them allot on the
Umatilla Reservation. Some renegade Indians living below Umatilla, some of whom were scheduled to remove to the Warm
Springs Reservation, feared that because all of the good lands on
that confine would be appropriated, they would have to take allotments on its poorer mountainous areas. The Indians told Crawford
that they would take allotments only if Smohalla told them to,
since it would be difficult for them to do so without horses and
farm equipment. They appeared anxious to have Crawford visit
Smohalla. Unwilling to make the last part of a journey to Priest
Rapids, as he put it, "on the hurricane deck of a cayuse" in that
winter time, Crawford declined the invitation.[36]

A half-dozen years after passage of the Dawes Indian Severalty
Act on February 8, 1887 (24 Stat. 388), about two hundred "wild"
renegades still refused to take allotments on the Yakima Reservation. By 1897, a decade after the act's passage, these practitioners of
the Pom Pom, or Seven Drums, Dance – the modern form of the
Washat of the Washani religion – were attending two large
churches on the reservation.[38] On the Umatilla Reservation, Agent
Crawford forbade such dances, and in 1892 he went so far as to
cancel the reservation's Fourth of July celebration. His Indian

policemen also gathered up children and, in the manner of Milroy, punished their elders for refusing to let them be taken to the agency school. In early December, 1893, accompanied by two policemen, Crawford brought to the school four children from a Dreamer camp at Wallula that was the target of complaining whites. Homily's death two years before had left the Wallula Dreamers without a spokesperson to intercede with whites in such matters.[39]

Smohalla, who exerted so much influence in the latter half of the nineteenth century, never lived to see the twentieth. Perhaps more saddening to him than his advanced years and blindness were the defections of his followers to reservations. Many of them became disillusioned, no longer believing as strongly as formerly that the dead would return and every stone become an Indian. Nor did they believe that the whites would be killed off and their properties dispersed among the Indians. The stores never materialized that they once believed Smohalla would fill with all manner of fine goods from which they could help themselves.[40]

Until his death in 1895, Smohalla remained resolute in his religious faith. As was his people's custom, their wailing women daubed his dead body with paint, covered him with matting and Washat flags, and let him lie as though in state in a longhouse, which, ironically, was on the Satus Creek, in the lower Yakima Reservation, not in his Wallula or Priest Rapids homelands of his earlier years. Mourners encircled his grave throwing handsful of dirt on his body to properly return it to the Earth Mother and his spirit to the Creator.[41] It remained to be seen if his survivors could muster enough of his faith to practice it under pressure that he and they knew would threaten them and their religion with change, if not with extinction.

As it happened, the erosion of Smohalla's religion, which set in before his death, increased in the twentieth century. The Prophet did not live to see how many more of his followers were driven by starvation to remove from white-appropriated root and fishing grounds to reservations.[42] The promise had become empty words that an unnamed American "general" had made to some Wanapams during the 1855–56 Indian war that they could remain at Priest Rapids,[43] although as late as the mid-twentieth century the tule-mat-covered longhouse in which Pom Pom ceremonials were held was still standing.

The surviving longhouse attested to the attempts of the faithful to cling to Smohalla's Dreamer-Prophet beachhead. As late as the 1980's, modern-day Smohallan disciples of the So-Happy family defied Washington and Oregon state laws regulating salmon fishing and rationalized their actions on the grounds that such fishing was an irrevocable right given them by the Great Spirit. In the early twentieth century, at Priest Rapids and on the Yakima, Umatilla, and Nez Percé reservations, and along the Columbia to The Dalles, braided Pom Pom dancers still held hopes that Smohalla's fading dream would be revived by some supernatural intervention. In December, 1917, the year that Smohalla's last surviving son and successor, Yo-Yonan (Yu-yunne), died on a hunting trip in the mountains north of the Kittitas River,[44] an event far to the southeast on the Duck Valley Reservation in Nevada and Utah gave a glimmer of hope for revitalization in the future. Two Paiute woodcutters claimed to have seen six men and women dressed in the old buckskin clothing, who identified themselves as the "Animal People" and said that they had come to warn Paiutes that the end of the world was drawing near. With the warning that should the people not worship every day and prepare for the catastrophe they would be lost, the twelve visitors "changed" into as many wolves and slipped away.[45]

Although the world did not end, two decades later there was evidence of continuing efforts to retain the Pom Pom on the Yakima Reservation. Approximately one-third of its Indians held worship services and feasts in three longhouses near White Swan, Wapato, and Toppenish.[46] At the same time participants kept their religious options open by membership in Methodist, Roman Catholic, Pentecostal, and Indian Shaker churches.[47] Whereas at the height of Smohalla's ministrations the government found native dances such as the Pom Pom intolerable, the official position was more favorable toward them, beginning in the 1930's. The change in attitude was brought about by not only a growing tolerance of such ceremonials but also the knowledge that they no longer threatened American civilization. The government had come full circle. Section Four of the rules establishing the Court of Indian Offenses in *Regulations of the Indian Department* (April 10, 1883) had read:

> The "sun-dance," the "scalp-dance," the "war-dance," and all other so-called feasts assimilating thereto, shall be considered "Indian offenses," and any Indian found guilty of being a participant in any one or more of these "offenses" shall, for the first offense committed, be punished by withholding from the person or persons so found guilty by the court his or their rations for a period not exceeding ten days; and if found guilty of any subsequent offense under this rule, shall be punished by withholding his or their rations for a period not less than fifteen days, nor more than thirty days, or by incarceration in the agency prison for a period not exceeding thirty days.

Commissioner John Collier's circular 2970 (January, 1934) read:

No interference with Indian religious life or expression will hereafter be
tolerated. The cultural history of Indians is in all respects to be considered equal to that of any non-Indian group. And it is desireable that Indians be bilingual-fluent and literate in the English language, and fluent
in their vital, beautiful, and efficient native languages. . . . . The Indian
arts are to be prized, nourished, and honored.

Under the dominance of white culture, Pom Pom, or Seven
Drum, practitioners no longer seek to avoid or destroy that Euro-
American culture as they did in Smohalla's day. Ceremonials, although surviving, appear to be paying homage to a fading Indianness. First-roots feasts, for example, were continued by Puck Hyah
Toot with as much fidelity as the passage of time would permit.
One participant told a white visitor: "This is one day of the year
when they [the children] can be Indians." When a young lad was
caught reading a comic book during the ceremonial, his mother
quickly snatched it from him.[48]

Among those who today follow Smohalla with more ceremony
than creed and more caution than conviction, will a leader of his
calibre arise to inspire a new belief in revitalization? Or have concessions and resignation to the Americanization that he eschewed
prevented such a possibility? Do Smohalla's survivors sense a loss
of control over their destiny? Or are they overwhelmed by the
technology that created monolithic Columbia River dams in ironic
fulfillment of Smohalla's prophecy of the flooding of the sacred island, Chalwash Chilni? Has the unlocking of atomic power at the
Atomic Energy Reservation at Hanford, on what was once Wanapam land, superseded for them the quest for the powers with
which he unlocked the spirit within the Washani? The greater
question remains: Which triumphs in the world, the power of matter or the power of the spirit? In their rush to master the physical
world, human beings may live to regret that they did not heed what
spiritual leaders such as Smohalla, the Dreamer-Prophet Yantcha,
were saying.[49]

The Priest Rapids at high water: Smohalla and his followers settled here on the right bank of the Columbia after migrating from the Wallula area farther south. Seven rapids stretched over nine miles, according to Lieutenant Thomas William Symons of the U.S. Corps of Engineers, who explored the river in 1881. Before the Columbia was dammed here, there was an eighty-foot drop from the upper to the lower rapids where the Wanapams had their fisheries. Photograph by Asahel Curtis, courtesy of the Washington State Historical Society, Tacoma.

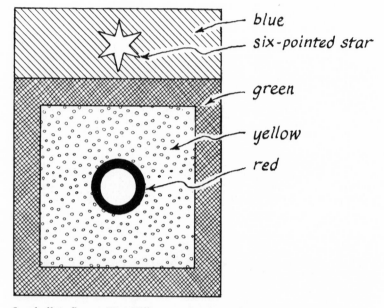

blue

six-pointed star

green

yellow

red

Smohalla's flag at P'na Village at the time of Major J. W. MacMurray's visit in 1884. The Prophet told MacMurray: "This is my flag and it represents the world. God told me to look after my people – all are my people. There are four ways in the world – north and south and east and west. I have been all those ways. This is the center, I live here; the red spot is my heart; everybody can see it. The yellow grass grows everywhere around this place. The green mountains are far away all around the world! There is only water beyond, salt water. The blue ... is the sky, and the star is the north star. That star never changes; it is always in the same place. I keep my heart on that star; I never change" (MacMurray, "The 'Dreamers' of the Columbia River Valley," 245).

A sketch entitled "Smohalla and His Priests" was made from this photograph to illustrate James Mooney's *The Ghost-dance Religion and the Sioux Outbreak of 1890*. Courtesy of Smithsonian Institution, Washington, D.C. (negative 2903A).

Sketch of the "Interior of Smohalla's Church," drawn from a photograph of poor quality taken for James Mooney's *The Ghost-dance Religion and the Sioux Outbreak of 1890*. Courtesy of Smithsonian Institution, Washington, D.C. (negative 2903C).

On the left is Jake Hunt, a Klickitat Indian contemporary of Smohalla and the founder of the Feather Dance Religion, a revitalization movement. On the right is Martin Spedis, a Wishram follower of Hunt. Besides feathers, the members of the sect used mirrors, which they believed represented the earth disk of Hunt's vision. Courtesy of Oregon Historical Society, Portland (negative 4351).

Yo-Yonan, the last surviving son of Smohalla, with his family. Yo-Yonan, who assumed leadership of the Wanapams after Smohalla's death, died in 1917, while on a hunting trip in the mountains north of the Kittitas valley, and was succeeded by his cousin Puck Hyah Toot. Smohalla's successors tried to retain the purity of the original Prophet's religion, but were forced to make concessions to modernity in their ceremonies. Courtesy of Washington State University, Pullman (McWhorter Papers).

Bell-ringing Wishram Shakers at The Dalles on the Columbia River, far away from their sect's origins on southern Puget Sound. The Indian Shaker religion was a revitalization effort to restore native lands and products to the Indians. The followers stressed curings and moral precepts. Shaker churches are still found in the Pacific Northwest over a century after the sect's founding. Courtesy of the University of Oregon, Eugene.

These Nez Percé Dreamers were photographed before their 1877 flight from American troops. Their leader, Toohoolsote, was a disciple of Smohalla. The Nez Percés' resistance to changes imposed by the United States government caused them to flee, hoping to find asylum in Canada. An important cause of the Nez Percé War was the government's closing of their reservation in the Wallowa country in northeast Oregon and its insistence that they remove to the Nez Percé Reservation. Courtesy of Washington State University, Pullman (no. 82-026).

This wooden building was moved from the nearby Hanford Atomic Works to the Wanapams' P'na Village at Priest Rapids shortly after 1950. In it the Indians held their sacred Washat dances and other festivities which had formerly taken place in mat longhouses. After it burned, it was replaced in the 1960's by a Quonset-type longhouse. Photograph in the authors' possession.

Puck Hyah Toot ("Birds Feeding in a Flock"), who replaced his cousin Yo-Yonan as the leading Priest Rapids Prophet. When Puck Hyah Toot died in 1956, he was succeeded by Rex Buck, whose son, Rex Jr., succeeded him on his death in 1975. Courtesy of Washington State University, Pullman (McWhorter Papers).

A first-roots feast held in the 1960's, presided over by Puck Hyah Toot, Smohalla's nephew. The first-roots ceremony preceded the Washat dance. The mats on which the feast was served were laid in a serpentine fashion back and forth across the large floor area, and participants sat on the floor around the mats. Besides freshly dug roots, berries, venison, cooked salmon, and black eels—which were the usual fare in Smohalla's time—doughnuts, colored eggs (when the ceremony occurred around Easter), canned milk, oranges, and sweet rolls were added in later decades. Photograph in the authors' possession.

The setting here is the Priest Rapids longhouse about 1960. Although photographs of the Washat dance as a rule have not been permitted, because of the sacred character of the ceremony, Clifford ("Click") Relander, a Yakima, Washington, newspaperman and recorder of Wanapam history, was permitted to photograph the assembled dancers before the dance on a couple of occasions as he did here. Relander did not explain why there were only three drummers instead of the usual seven. Courtesy Public Utility District of Grant County, Ephrata, Washington.

Puck Hyah Toot conducting a Washat dance in the 1960's. Courtesy of Public Utility District of Grant County, Ephrata, Washington.

This rare photograph of the Washat dance, taken in 1975 before restrictions were imposed on the photographers, shows men and boys holding ancient swan wings as they sit between songs. The Quonset-type longhouse, erected for the Wanapams by the Grant County, Washington, Public Utility District, is still used for ceremonies today. Bids were let in 1987 to enlarge it. Photograph in the authors' possession.

At the same 1975 Washat shown in the photograph above, the men and boys are dancing on the left, and the women, each holding an eagle feather, are on the right. The two lines of dancers are separated by a center aisle of dirt. Photograph in the authors' possession.

This huge granite rock, known as Whitestone, on the left bank of the Columbia River between the mouths of the Spokane and Sanpoil rivers, was a natural monument to Skolaskin and his people. Their village on the other side of the Columbia bore its name. Since 1939 the 500-foot landmark has been covered by the waters of Lake Roosevelt behind Grand Coulee Dam. Photograph courtesy of National Archives, Washington, D.C.

This photograph of Skolaskin was taken some years after he returned from his incarceration in the military prison at Alcatraz. His contracted and shortened left leg is tied at the side of his saddle. Like his other leg, it did not fit in the stirrups of a regular saddle. He was said to have mounted his horse by standing on stumps, or other elevated objects, and swinging from them onto his horse. The photograph, taken on June 30, 1905, by Frank Avery, superintendent of the Colville Agency schools, is in the authors' possession.

Skolaskin's church after its restoration. Originally built at Whitestone Village, it was moved to the Colville Agency near Nespelem, Washington, so that it would not be inundated by water behind Grand Coulee Dam. Photograph in the authors' possession.

The Reverend Urban Grassi, S.J., of Saint Mary's Mission near Omak, Washington, in Southern Okanagon Indian country on the Colville Reservation. Standing with her hand on his shoulder is the first Wenatchee Indian whom Grassi baptized. Although the priest persuaded the Wenatchee Prophet Patoi to let him preach to that tribe, he could not bring Skolaskin and his followers into the Roman Catholic fold. Grassi's successors would be more successful. Photograph courtesy of the Museum of Native American Cultures, Spokane, Washington.

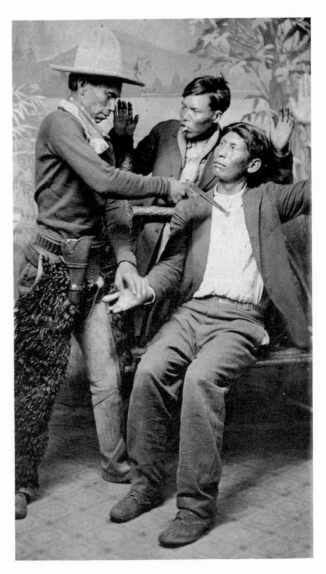

On the left, holding the pistol in this posed photograph, is Billy Skolaskin, the Dreamer's son, who froze to death during incarceration in a jail. Seated are Charlie Black and, in the back, Pete Marchand. Photograph in the authors' possession.

These Sanpoil women in 1897 had spent money that they earned picking hops on clothing and high-buttoned shoes in the style of white women. The Sanpoils were among several tribes that traveled annually to work in the Yakima valley hop fields in the late-nineteenth and early-twentieth centuries. Photograph in the authors' possession.

Henry Covington in 1958. As a young man he interpreted for Skolaskin on their journey to Washington, D.C., early in 1911. Covington was a valuable informant about the Sanpoils and their close neighbors the Nespelems. Photograph in the authors' possession.

In this sketch in the April 10, 1891, *San Francisco Chronicle*, Skolaskin is shown wearing braids. At that time he was incarcerated at Alcatraz, charged with being a disturbing element on the Colville Indian Reservation. In fact, he was being punished for opposing government policies on the reservation.

Skolaskin reveals his short gray hair, indicating a final concession to the whites. Like other Dreamers, he had worn his hair long as a symbol both of traditionalism and defiance of American influence. Photograph in the authors' possession.

Part Two
Skolaskin of the
Sanpoils and Nespelems

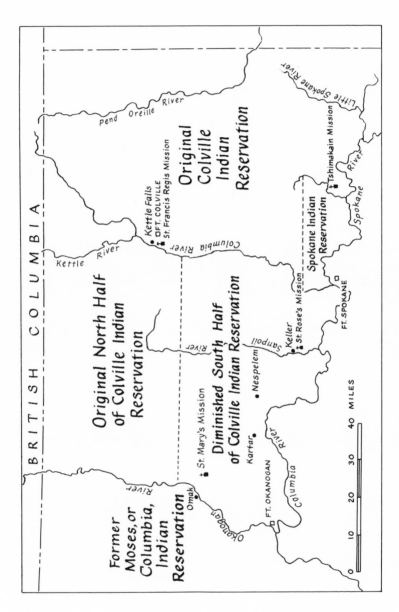

Reservations and Other Places Affecting Smohalla's Ministrations

8
Skolaskin's Sanpoil Heritage

> Our medicine men prophesied to our fore-
> fathers of the coming of a new race with white
> faces like snow. . . . This land was the home
> of the San Poils from the beginning (and shall
> be to the end) when all the country from there
> to the rising sun was a big sea.
> — *Skolaskin to Major R. G. Gwydir.*

Like his counterpart and contemporary the Wanapam Dreamer-
Prophet Smohalla, Skolaskin (or Kolaskin), who was born about
1839, a generation later, was of a Columbia River people, the Sanpoils. The tribal name derived from their own word *snpui'luxu.*
Among the many renditions of their name was that of an early
North West Company fur man, Alexander Henry, who claimed
that they rendered it Spoil-Ehiehs.[1] Whites erroneously assumed
that it stemmed from the French words meaning "without bristles"
or "hairless." Like Smohalla's Wanapams, the Sanpoils were a small
tribe, as were their close neighbors and allies on the west, the Nespelems, whose name derived from their word *snspi'lem,* meaning
"barren hill."[2] Both the Sanpoils and the Nespelems were in the Salishan linguistic group.

During most of the nineteenth century the Sanpoils scarcely ex-
ceeded two hundred souls. Because of their peaceful disposition,
their lands, like those of the Nespelems, had been encroached on
by other tribes: the Senijextees (Lake Indians) on the north; the
Spokanes and the Blackfeet on the east; the Nez Percés, the Yakimas, and other Shahaptian peoples on the south; and the Columbia
Sinkiuses on the west. All of these peoples at sundry times ran off
Sanpoil horses and attacked Sanpoil women, children, and elderly
when the men were away. On one occasion raiders tied thongs to
Sanpoil children and threw them over salmon racks to die.[3] Yet,
after suffering such predations, a Sanpoil chief lamented: "Our children are dead and our property is destroyed. We are sad. But can
we bring our children back to life or restore our property by killing
other people? It is better not to fight. It can do no good."[4]

Like Smohalla's Wanapams on the lower Columbia, the Sanpoils'
peaceful disposition contrasted sharply with that river, which they

127

called Entwakaitqua, as it rushed by their lands. On the river's left
bank stood Whitestone, a huge gray granite landmark known to
the Sanpoils as Kula'lst or Quel-lelst, "mountain at the edge of the
water." Downstream the river churned through the turbulent Hell
Gate rapids. Today these landmarks lie beneath the waters of Roosevelt Lake behind Grand Coulee Dam, which was completed in
1939.

Partly because of the obstacles to canoe transport, the Sanpoils,
like the Nespelems, were more isolated than their neighbors. This,
however, did not prevent them from trading, mostly with Salishan
peoples at the mouths of the streams that entered the Columbia
right bank like their own Sanpoil River: the Okanogan, the
Methow, and the Wenatchee on the west; the Spokane on the east;
and the Kettle on the north. Near the mouth of the Kettle on the
Columbia roared the mighty Kettle Falls, where hundreds of natives from miles around netted the salmon seeking to escape that
cataract.[5]

Along the Sanpoil River lived the most numerous branch of the
Sanpoils, the Enparailik, whose name meant "something growing"
or "light in color as leaves of cottonwood trees."[6] Many tribesmen of
other Sanpoil villages joined them to catch salmon in weirs constructed across the river. Not only was there ample food along the
Sanpoil River but shelter from the winter cold and deep snows of
the surrounding highlands. The Sanpoils also depended for subsistence on deer and antelope, which they hunted most successfully
on level ground such as that across the Columbia atop the Columbia plateau. From twenty to sixty villagers would surround and dispatch their quarry with flint-headed arrows. With the iron-headed
ones acquired in the nineteenth century, they killed game more effectively than with guns, which frightened the animals away. Like
other area natives, the Sanpoils traveled to root grounds such as
those surrounding Grand Coulee on the south.

The scarcity of horses (the horses had reached upper-interior
natives shortly before the mideighteenth century) and a tendency
to isolation and avoidance of confrontations with Plains tribes prevented the Sanpoils from going "to buffalo" to the extent that their
Salishan neighbors did.[7] Sanpoil women married to men of other
Salishan tribes did travel onto the plains and risk attacks of Blackfeet and other Plains Indians who resented their presence on lands
that they claimed as their own. One such was the Sanpoil woman
Camilla, whose death from a rifle ball through the throat orphaned
two daughters who were raised by the Flathead chief Ambrose.[8]

Among the Sanpoils' rich heritage of legends were stories involving the Columbia River. They believed that its rapids were created
by the animal figure Coyote, who brought the migrating salmon

upstream through them. Among the other animals in their legen-
dry was Rattlesnake. He and Coyote threw Skunk into the river to
float downstream, where a shaman fitted the latter with his well-
known apparatus which enabled him to chase his two rivals from
the top of Whitestone.[9] The Sanpoils believed that long-armed Evil
Ones at Hell Gate pulled canoes and their occupants beneath the
river. Later stories told of the whites' treachery at Hell Gate in their
lust for gold.[10] The Sanpoils and other natives gave those rapids a
wide berth on the well-traveled trail that ran west from the Sanpoil
villages, such as Whitestone to those along the Sanpoil River
farther west. The legends involving Whitestone and Hell Gate reveal, among other things, the Sanpoil belief in the presence of good
and evil forces in the world.

Winter was the Sanpoil time for story telling and religious ceremonials, including that which Leslie Spier called the Prophet
Dance. Edward S. Curtis wrote that the "dreamer cult . . . was
strongest, or at least survived longest, among the Nespilim and the
Sanpoel."[11] An elderly Sanpoil informant told of a famine that had
found his people without prayers. During that earlier time an
elderly man had recounted his "dream," in which he said he had
been commanded to assemble the people in a circle to dance in
worship, not in merriment, as he sang the song given him. The
Dreamer had then ordered them to hold their hands open level
with their heads. Afterwards, the elderly Sanpoil explained, the
spirit transformed each person. The dancing continued all winter,
preempting other activities. Then, with the approaching of spring,
the Dreamer warned the people to resist the temptation to eat instead of dancing. He said that roots and berries would drop from
their hands should they try to eat them. His prophetic warning
came true that spring as roots spilled from hands of unheeding
ones and berry baskets tipped over. Afterwards no one gathered
foods, which they believed were possessed of evil spirits. Finally,
the Dreamer commanded that all foods and anything associated
with them be placed on robes and thanksgiving prayers offered for
each one.[12]

Because no written records were left, it is difficult for latter-day
informants to pinpoint the times of such prehistoric events. Two
catastrophes, however, stimulated the San Poils and Nespelems to
religious fervor in dances to propitiate and appease the wrath of the
Great Spirit. One was near the beginning of the protohistoric
period at the close of the eighteenth century, and the other occurred two decades later at its end. The first event was the smallpox
epidemic of 1782–83, which swept away an estimated one-third to
one-half of the Sanpoils and Nespelems.[13]The second event was
the ash fall from Mount Saint Helens in southwest Washington

state in 1802. Alarmed at the swirling ash covering the ground, the people held "praying" dances nearly every night and day, imploring the "Dry Snow," which they also called "Chief" and "Mystery," to explain its presence. Dancing continually all summer, they neglected to gather food, and their elderly starved to death the following winter.[14]

The Sanpoil and Nespelems' neighbors on the west, the Sinkaietks, or Southern Okanagons, responded to such cataclysms with what Spier has termed the "Southern Okanagon Complex." For these Indians falling stars, earthquakes, and other natural convulsions portended the destruction of the earth.[15] As a result, Okanagon Dreamer-Prophets, especially during troublesome times, communicated with the Great White Chief, or Creator, in dreams and "journeyed to the land of the dead to rejoin the living," in what the anthropologist Walter Cline has termed the "Dream Dance."[16]

Okanagon informants told of Dreamer-Prophets who wore no special clothing and used no drums, dance poles, or other paraphernalia such as the Washani and Feather Dancers had. They also told of a strange-looking goose, similar to the bird in Washani and Feather Dance worship, which appeared after the "Dry Snow" to signal the beginning of dancing. Throughout the ceremonial participants held their places and took no food. Some of them uttered prophecies and joined the Dreamer in the center of the formation, exhorting the people to righteous living as the Washani and Feather Dance leaders did. The people were so impressed with these exhortations at the time of the ash fall that they kept their children in after dark lest they commit some evil act. After a few days, when the world did not end, the people resumed routine tasks until some other crisis interrupted them. During such times their dances did not combine with nor replace traditional winter guardian-spirit ceremonies conducted by shamans.

The Southern Okanagons' fear of natural disasters, which portended for them the end of the world, stimulated them to perform a "confession dance" during which young and old alike gathered in a house for two or three days and nights for ceremonies in which they swayed rhythmically around the Dreamer-Prophets, confessing sins and dancing until panics subsided. Such dances were also held among Washani-adhering Teninos and other lower-Columbia peoples.[17] It is unclear if the Dreamer dances that arose among the Sanpoils were indigenous or were borrowed from others such as the Southern Okanagons. The Sanpoils and Nespelems had close ties with the Okanagons and could easily have adopted elements of their culture. Later the Okanagons would claim the Sanpoil Skolaskin as one of their own.[18]

With the coming of white fur traders – first the Nor'Westers, who established Spokane House among the Spokanes in 1810, and then the Astorians, who in 1812 established Fort Spokane adjacent to Spokane House – information about the natives' religious life and other aspects of their culture came firsthand rather than from later native informants. The Nor'Wester David Thompson is believed to be the first white man to enter Sanpoil country, on his "Journey of a Summer Moon" to the lower Columbia River seeking new trade opportunities for his company. His observations of the Sanpoils, two of whom were his guides, as well as his observations of the Nespelems, reveal their strong religious orientation, which apparently had diminished but little since the revival of religious fervor following the eruption of Mount Saint Helens a decade earlier. Wrote Thompson: "They seemed to acknowledge a Great Spirit who dwelled in the clouds to be the master of everything, and when they died their Souls went to him; the Sun, Moon and Stars were all divinities, but the Sun above all; and that he made the Lightning, Thunder and Rain. Their worship was in dancing, and the last dance they gave me was for a safe voyage and return to them."

Thompson found his hosts to be mild, friendly people whose religion, composed of songs, dances, and prayers, was "simple and rational, without sacrifices or superstition." How the Sanpoils and Nespelems arrived at their spiritual state he was unable to tell, tersely recording, "I had no time to learn much." In meeting these two and other Columbia River peoples, he evinced a practicality and mundaneness in contrast to their exuberance, although they received him somewhat as if they were welcoming a returning culture hero.[19]

Sanpoil isolationist tendencies were observed by Thompson's colleague Alexander Henry, who wrote; "The Simpoils seldom leave their own country, and, like their neighbors, the Spokanes, live upon the produce of their lands and the vast quantities of fat, well-favored salmon which they take in their river."[20] Yet another Nor'Wester, Ross Cox, attributed their isolation to the remoteness of their lands, which lay between two of his company's posts, Spokane House at the mouth of the Little Spokane River and Fort Okanogan at the mouth of the Okanogan River. He believed that the tribe's distance from those two posts also forced them to commit depredations. He attributed their "poverty of spirit" to a paucity of weapons, mistakenly assuming that they were jealous of others who, unlike them, had obtained guns and other trade goods from his firm. He interpreted their democratic spirit and absence of strong chieftains as "insubordination, local feuds and love of thieving."[21]

The Sanpoil tribal leadership came from chiefs who conducted peaceful religious and managerial functions, such as those involved in the harvests of salmon. In their democratic society the leaders were not drawn from an aristocracy such as existed in tribes of the southern Columbia plateau. Despite Cox's assessment, we know that the Sanpoils exhibited fewer warlike traits than did some of their Salish neighbors, who from journeys after buffalo had adopted dances and trappings of aggressive Plains tribes just as Shahaptian and Shoshonean buffalo hunters did. The losses among such hunters, especially their men, were heavy. The Sanpoils' avoidance of conflict on the plains may have been one reason why they had preserved their adult males, as revealed in an 1827 census by a clerk at the Hudson's Bay Company's Fort Colvile on the Columbia, who reported ninety-one men, seventy-seven women, twenty-four boys, and twenty-six girls among the Sanpoils.[22]

Although trading but little with fur men, the Sanpoils absorbed mercantilist-Christian ideas from the neighboring tribes with whom they traded, fished, and socialized. Like their neighbors, they had contacts with Christian Iroquois Indians who circulated among them as employees of fur companies. In the late 1830's and early 1840's, they came under the influence of Christian missionaries. The latter arrived in time for Skolaskin to incorporate elements in their faith into his religion – which under his leadership became neither nativist nor Christian.

Just as his people, the Sanpoils, were known for their isolationist spirit and independence, there was in Skolaskin's personality an insularity and a uniqueness of mind and spirit that would prepare him for the dramatic life-changing events that made him a Prophet.

9

The Crippling

> I was dead. I died. I went so far to where dead
> people go. . . . They told me, "You have to go
> back and preach." . . . Well I'm alive. I came
> to life. I'm going to get well and I will keep on
> what I saw when I was in a trance.
> —*Skolaskin to his people.*

Upriver from the Sanpoils' Whitestone Village stood a smaller settlement, Snuke'ilt, or Sinakialt ("brush spring"), on the Columbia's
right bank about a half-mile north of its confluence with the Spokane River. The Sanpoil Dreamer-Prophet Skolaskin was born in
this village in about 1839 in a mat house occupied by four or five
families, most of whom were relatives of his father, Kichteamakan,
or Swi'laken. The Prophet was said to have had three younger half-
brothers, a full brother, and a sister. His mother, Qatsipitsa, or Kat-
ceapeetsa, was his father's only wife. He also was said to have acquired a benign guardian spirit in his youth and to have participated in normal activities such as gathering subsistence and playing games.[1] The most important event of his young manhood was a
crippling malady that was to shape the rest of his life, as well as the
lives of his people.[2]

His crippling, which in no way reduced his mental capacity,
forced him to use a staff or place his hands on his knees when
walking. When he mounted a horse, his weakened and contracted
legs fell short of the stirrups, although his powerful arms enabled
him to swing with lightening speed into the saddle. Some informants said that he also used a crutch, or any available stump, to help
him mount his horse.

That Skolaskin was crippled was obvious; less so were the circumstances of the onset of his malady. Accounts of its cause were
numerous and conflicting. Prominent among them were falls from
horses and other horse-related accidents. Some accounts attributed
his disability to rheumatism or infections after exposure to the elements. Other alleged causes included retribution in kind from a
crippled man whom Skolaskin had struck in a gambling game[3] to
an injury inflicted on him by a group of vengeful husbands who cut

133

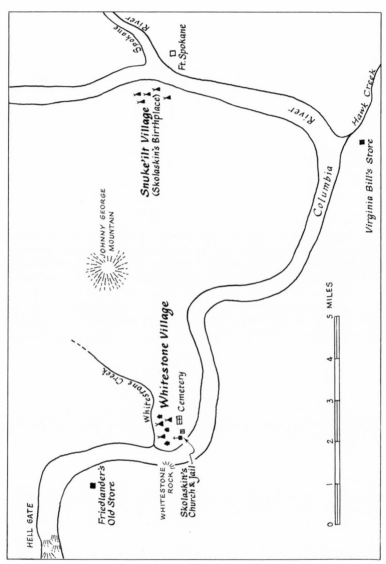

Whitestone Village and Its Environs

his leg tendons for using their women. An Indian agent who knew him well claimed that one of his legs was much more constricted than the other.[4]

Sifting through the confusing accounts of his crippling, one cannot, with only the available information and no medical reports, pinpoint it as the result of a certain illness or injury. Since this Prophet rose to prominence with the great earthquake of 1872, that made it much too easy for informants and recorders to associate the onset of the disability with the earthquake. According to Verne Ray, an authority of the Sanpoils and Nespelems, Skolaskin was crippled in his twentieth year, which would place the cause of his disability about a dozen years before the quake.[5] His convalescence appears to have been extensive, possibly as long as two years, and this is a point on which all accounts agree. The malady also appears to have struck when Skolaskin was away from home.[6] Although some informants claim it happened in Sanpoil country, there is evidence that it occurred when he was visiting a Lower Spokane Indian village near present-day Detillion, Washington[7] This is a viable possibility, as the Sanpoils' lands bordered on those of that Spokane group, with which they had close ties, and into which Skolaskins's sister Quielt (or Que-elt) had married.[8] Whatever the extent of the Prophet's relationships with the Spokanes, they exhibited toward him a cool neutrality, if not outright skepticism, when he began his ministrations. Their attitude stemmed most likely from the presence among them between 1838 and 1847 of the Reverends Elkanah Walker and Cushing Eells and their wives at their American Board Tshimakain Mission. From an examination of letters and diaries of these missionaries, it would appear that the Sanpoils and Nespelems did not visit the Tshimakain Mission, nor were they visited by its workers.[9]

There is evidence that Skolaskin used his close encounter with death and his recovery to claim that he had visited the other world and had returned with injunctions from the deity Quilentsuten (or Quilinsutin), "the Spirit who made us" or "the Maker," to teach the people.[10] A group of elderly Sanpoil panelists narrated Skolaskin's experiences in the heavens as follows:

I was on my way some place. I came to the gate to go through and there was a man standing there watching that gate. When I got there this man says "where are you going?" I says; "I'm going someplace." And this man told him, "you can't go through the gate, your [sic] have to go back. Go back where you started from." So he turned around and come back. He come back to where his body laid. Thats the time he woke up. That was his story. And then on he recovered and got well. His sores was all healed up. It drawed up his legs [believed by some scholars to be partial ankylosis of the knee joints or contracture of the tendons]. He couldn't walk but he could hold his hand on his knees when he walked around. He started in the same teachings that this Michel did. He preached his religion – his dream.[11]

The Michel to whom the Sanpoil panelists alluded was a former resident among the Sanpoils who claimed, "years after the Dry Snow," to have talked with God, who he said gave him supernatural powers, including the ability to prophesy the coming of whites.[12] According to the panelists, some soldiers gave Michel a piece of paper on which a hymn or song was written. This he sang in his own language, which was an astounding feat because he had never attended school, much less studied music, which was "all in his mind and head." Later, at the confluence of the Columbia and Okanogan rivers, Michel preached to a white family. Encouraged by their amazement at his powers, he undertook his ministrations among the Sanpoils and Nespelems, who learned from his prayers and songs a revived Dreamer religion.[13]

Skolaskin developed a control over the people, especially over the women, who were drawn to him less by love than by fear. Later, he empathized with the Sanpoil Dick Cilpetsa (or Silpteetsa), who, deformed and ugly, was spurned by a beautiful girl whom Skolaskin ordered to marry Cilpetsa.[14] Women paid homage to the Prophet as if hypnotized. They were both enamored of him and wanting to go with him to heaven and the angels, they were fearful of his warnings that they and their families would go to hell if they did not come and live with him.[15]

About half of the stories about Skolaskin tell of his relations with women. Like other Prophets, he was said to have taken advantage of maidens. The first of his marital conquests was believed to have been a woman who poured love and sympathy over him when he was in the death trance in which he claimed to have gone to heaven. When he awoke, he was said to have grabbed her, saying that he had had a vision from God that he was to marry six virgins. Of his reported half-dozen wives, his first was Suzanne, or Chisheetqua, a daughter of Nespelem chief Quequetas.[16] It was reported that "all of the women were crazy about Kolaskin and it went to his head."[17] Suzanne had previously been sold for flour, beans, and bacon as a reported slave wife to stockman John ("Portugese Joe") Enos. Shortly afterwards she ran off to live with an uncle, Wiltstakia, and later married an Okanagan, Twizliken. Skolaskin's other wives, approximately in the succession that spanned more than a quarter-century, included Ceeapeetsa, Cheezet, Skoqwaele, Harriet Swimptkin, and Quinspeetsa.[18]

Skolaskin's experiences, marital and otherwise, real or imagined, gave him a sense of power as well as insight, and a notoriety among his peers. These attributes alone would not have elevated him to a leadership role had his people not suffered malaise from their fear of natural catastrophes and the ever-increasing American presence in the lower interior of the Washington Territory. The white settlers were beginning to spread northward, threatening the independence that the Sanpoils cherished with a passion. The natives' fear prepared the way for Skolaskin to preach escape and salvation from the clutches of the encroaching whites. Fortified by his experiences, he believed that he had the necessary spiritual credentials and personal magnetism to calm them with his message of hope.

10

The Encroaching Whites
and the Shaking Earth

> The cougar, the wolf and the bear will fight for
> their young, and why not the Indian?
> —*Skolaskin to Major R. G. Gwydir.*

During the 1857 lull in the 1855–58 Indian war a government
agent, Ben Yantis, met with several tribes of Washington's northern interior. The Sanpoils treated him coldly because he expressed
the government's wish to send them tools and teachers to help
them farm; they wanted no such help, which they regarded as
threatening to their way of life.[1] Yet, despite their wish to live in
peaceful independence, after the midnineteenth century Skolaskin's tribe was seldom able to isolate itself from the actions of the
American government. Like most of their Salishan neighbors, the
Sanpoils had not been party to the 1855 Walla Walla treaty, which
the United States was slow to ratify in any event; and miners, traversing the interior searching for gold, were embroiling the factions of most of the interior tribes in the war. Aware of the possible
consequences of an American victory, the Sanpoils and other
northern tribesmen met with the Washington territorial governor
and superintendent of Indian affairs, Isaac I. Stevens, in December, 1855, "all highly excited" at the prospect of American troops
crossing the Snake River and extending their conquests northward
into their lands. When the war shifted north in 1858, the Sanpoils
shunned the attempts of a Spokane war chief (Polatkin?) to entice
them into the hostilities, in which the Spokanes, Coeur d'Alenes,
and other Salishan peoples became embroiled. At that time the
peace-loving Sanpoil chief Quetalikin (Qualitikun) kept his men at
home, forbidding them on pain of punishment from going to war.[2]
A correspondent of the *Weekly* (Portland) *Oregonian* reported on
October 9, 1858, that after the collapse of the Indian war coalition
the Sanpoils were among 107 Indians seeking to make peace with
the vengeful Colonel George A. Wright, U.S.A., who had led the
American forces against the northern Indians.

The Indian defeat implied the end of Sanpoil isolation, for it opened the way for the government to deal with nontreaty tribes of the Colville Agency and to establish reservations for them as it had for tribes of the lower Washington interior after treaty making there. The respite that time and space had allowed the Sanpoils was to be short-lived. They would have been even more aware and fearful of American inroads had they known of an 1858 recommendation by the Oregon-Washington superintendent of Indian affairs, Edward R. Geary, to move them to the Yakima Reservation.[3] Fortunately for them, the recommendation was never carried out. After the 1860's, Colville Agency officials tried to coax the Sanpoils into cooperating with them, but the tribe kept its distance, unable to shake off fears that government aid was merely a ploy to take their lands. After 1871 the government was better able to impose its will on Indians by executive orders that established, altered, and even eliminated reservations.

The 1870's began ominously for the Sanpoils with the late June visit of Colville Agent W. P. ("Park") Winans to the main Sanpoil village near the mouth of the Sanpoil River. When he arrived, the Indians began powwowing. Wrote Winans: "They seem to be suspicious of something, they don't know what. They fear their lands will be taken and they not know it; they think that they are the most civilized, independent and happy people in the world, and don't want any interference from the whites. They are decidedly opposed to being in any manner under obligations to the government." Winans attributed the Sanpoils' fear that their lands would be taken to the presence of a few "worthless" whites living in their country with native women, a practice carried out from the fur-trading era. Winans feared that these "squawmen," as the white community contemptuously called them, believed that a treaty might prevent them from living among the Indians, with whom they lived for reasons that varied from escaping the law to raising cattle. There were, indeed, scalawags among them. Some took advantage of the informality of Indian marriage bonds to break them with the same ease with which they were consummated, although other unions were stable, such as that of the white merchant, John C. ("Virginia Bill") Covington and the Sanpoil woman Smillkeen. The offspring of such a union, the "bloods," experienced some alienation from living in two cultural worlds; at the same time their dual heritage linked them to both races, and it was from their ranks that many interpreters were recruited.

Explaining his wish to ascertain the Sanpoil needs and numbers, Winans urged them to file land claims in the manner of white men. Such practices were alien to them, for like other Salish speakers, they held lands in common and permitted others to fish in their waters. The only favorable response to the agent's advice was from Polpolkin (Popokin), or William Wilson, who said that he wanted the government to establish among his people churches and schools with Protestant instructors. Polpolkin was mistrusted by many of his tribe because of the pro-white leanings that he had acquired when he was taken to the East by whites. His granddaughter claimed that he once rescued some American soldiers during the Indian wars. On returning from the East in his twenty-first year, he had settled in the Sanpoil country on upper Wilson Creek, which bears his name. He had a farm and had also built a church.[4]

Speaking for the majority of the Sanpoils, Chief Quetalikin told Winans:

> I am a child in knowledge. I have listened to what you have said. There are three things you have spoken of. First you want our numbers: second you desire to know if we have any religious instructions or wish to have any; and third you want to know what our wants and wishes are. The first I understand; the second I poorly understand, but the third, I don't understand at all. The Chief of us all God has numbered us and no man shall number us.[5]

George W. Harvey, the farmer employed to teach farming to the Indians on the Colville Reservation, sought to wrest the agency leadership from Winans. Using the occasion of a May 7, 1871, gathering of over a thousand Indians at the Rock Creek root grounds, which were about thirty miles southeast of the mouth of the Spokane River, he warned them to have nothing to do with Winans, who would allow the encroaching whites to overrun their country.[6] Under government orders, Winans, whom Harvey failed to unseat, would have much to do with the Indians. In late June, 1872, two Sanpoil chiefs attended a council, near the site of the present-day city of Spokane, at which Winans informed headmen of several tribes that the first Colville Reservation had been set aside (without the approval of the Indians and without his recommendation) by an executive order on April 9, 1872.[7] The order had been issued under pressure from white settlers and squatters in the lush Colville River valley. Among the Salish-speaking tribes scheduled to occupy the reservation were the Colvilles, the Kalispels, the Spokanes, the Coeur d'Alenes, and the Sanpoils. The reservation lay within a boundary drawn from the mouth of the Spokane River north along the Columbia River to the Canadian border, then east along that border to the Pend Oreille River, south along the Pend Oreille to the Washington-Idaho territorial border, and from there southwest along the Little Spokane River to the place of beginning.

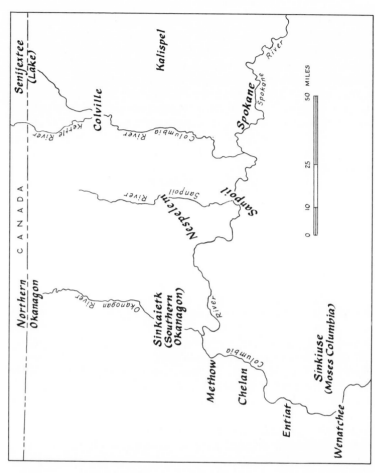

The Sanpoils, the Nespelems, and Surrounding Tribes

With much anger and not a little irony, a Sanpoil spokesman declaimed that his people did not want their men "to be branded or driven like cattle from where. . . . [they] were born." "This country, is ours," he maintained, "and instead of the whites giving it to us, we have given to them what they now occupy."[8]

On June 27, 1872, when Winans was ill, his interpreter, S. F. Sherwood, visited the Sanpoils on their own grounds to discuss the new reservation. Speaking for his people, one of the chiefs, Komotalakia, scolded Sherwood:

> I want to know if you thought the President was God Almighty that he should make a Reservation for us. Our God has given us the land we live on, the laws we live under, he made all men equal, so that they could think for themselves. We do not want the whites to think for us. We can think for ourselves. We do not want anything to do with your President or any of his Agents. God is our agent and is all the one we want, and all the one we will listen to. We will not obey the laws of the United States.

When Sherwood replied that Komotalakia's words amounted to a declaration of war, the chief blustered, "If war is the President's heart it is ours, we won't go on the Reserve, we will stay right here, where we were born in our country."[9]

Winans believed that the revocation of the executive order of April 9, 1872, and the establishment of the second Colville Reservation by a similar order on July 2, 1872, would prevent conflict such as that threatened by Komotalakia, whom the agent described as a chief of the "most intractable and independent of all Indians of this Territory." This second Colville Reservation was on Sanpoil-Nespelem lands west and north of the Columbia River and east of the Okanogan. Winans also believed that, because the Sanpoils loved their homeland, they would have fought before removing to the first Colville Reservation. Then, on November 20, 1872, Winans was replaced under the Federal government's Peace Policy, by the Roman Catholic John A. Simms. Simms reported to the superintendent of Indians affairs in Washington that the Sanpoils were of a "haughty and independent spirit" and that they now unhesitatingly declared their opposition to the reservation in which their own lands lay.[10]

In treaty making with Indians, the government sought to deal with selected head chiefs, but the crisis facing the Sanpoils at this time, severe as it was, did not produce an aggressive leader to do battle with the government. Quetalikin, who was best qualified to be the head chief, could not have assumed that role effectively because of his increasing age and debility. Besides in punishing malefactors, his leadership was as much religious as it was political. Unlike American officials, Indian chiefs supervised religious, moral, and political matters, all of which were inexorably combined. For example, in his role as a moral leader, Quetalikin had a tribesman tied to a tree and severely whipped for stealing a calf that belonged to a white man. He then forced the miscreant to make restitution to the agency for the theft.[11] Quetalikin said grace before meals and was the first of his people to have a Bible, which he received from one François. Quetalikin could not read it, but he held prayers and preached sermons over it.[12]

The Sanpoils' strong democratic spirit, which did not tolerate powerful chieftain control, by the same token encouraged factionalism, especially in the tribe's all-important religious life. Those such as Quetalikin and Mr. Wilson who favored Protestant teachers were opposed by those following in Michel's footsteps who were keeping the Dreamer faith. Important in the latter group, and apparently more important at this time than Skolaskin, were Umtosoolow (Umatosoolow) and Suiepkine, the Standing Bear. A Southern Okanagon, Suiepkine exerted an especially strong Dreamer influence among his people not only in the Kartar valley but also on the east among the Sanpoil-Nespelems. He and his followers resisted the Catholic priests who would have shaken their Dreamer faith and the officials who attempted to bring them under government control. In the summer of 1870, Suiepkine said to an Indian agent, "There is one thing I desire which is the breath of life. . . . I don't want the Government to give me any farming implements. I was born without them. There is but one Chief of the Universe and he is 'God.'"

Although even as late as 1872 no mention of Skolaskin appears in government records, this would soon change. Earlier in Sanpoil history cataclysms of nature had propelled Dreamers to the forefront, nudging traditional leaders aside. Now a repetition of natural events was to bring Skolaskin to the fore as a Dreamer-Prophet. Never in the future would he go unacknowledged by the American policy makers and implementers or by his own people, who may yet have believed that his twisted limbs fitted him poorly for leading them into the future.

The 1872 Earthquake

It was in what the Sanpoils called the season of *kumikuten*, the "time that it snows," on the night of December 14, 1872, in the whites' measure of time, that a severe earthquake shook the Pacific Northwest. In few places was the evidence of the shaking more visible than in the Sanpoil-Nespelem, Okanagon, and Chelan Indian lands. Below the mouth of the Chelan River a crumbling cliff tumbled into the Columbia, damming it for a few hours. According to Sanpoil-Nespelem accounts, the quake opened cracks in pit houses, filling them with water as people huddled and prayed in fear. Those familiar with Christian prayers repeated them over and over and tore off their clothing. Some tribal members lost their minds and ran around the hills or across the Columbia onto the Columbia plateau. One Sanpoil girl ran off in fright never to be heard of again. During the spring of 1873 hunger stalked the land because instead of gathering food, the natives continually prayed to the Great Spirit to withhold his wrath. He seemed unmindful of their petitions, as the earth continued shaking, reminding them of their sins.[14] They had allowed the spiritual revival following the ash fall seven decades earlier to slip away from them, like the sliding earth beneath their feet. Measuring days as suns, months by moons, and seasons by snows and grasses, Indians for years to come would reckon events from the time of this unforgettable cataclysm of 1872.

Traumatic as the earthquake was for his people, it was made to order for Skolaskin. It is not too much to say that he rose to prominence on the shaking earth, though untangling the thread of rumor from the fabric of truth as the quake pertained to his rise is no less difficult than ascertaining the cause of his crippling. The facts seem to have been shaken from some informants who, for dramatic effect, telescoped important events of Skolaskin's life around the quake.

Most informants told of the quake in relation to Skolaskin's contest with Suiepkine for the Dreamer leadership. It is difficult to ascertain how long the rivalry between them had been brewing and possibly it did not antedate the quake. After the fact, many informants conveniently related an incident involving the two that they claimed had immediately preceded the quake. According to the published account five years later in a Portland, Oregon, magazine, Skolaskin, on a "black steed," had ridden into the camp of Suiepkine's people in the Kartar valley, where "wild orgies" were in progress. Warning the celebrants of impending disaster because of their wickedness, he supposedly rode off crying, "Warriors beware!"[15] In a less romantic version recorded after the fact by Verne Ray, Skolaskin and four men visited Suiepkine to warn him and his people of a terrible disaster. According to Ray's informants, Skolaskin said: "Warriors, beware, the Manitou is angry with the wickedness of his people. . . . The land is going to shake. Buildings will fall down. People will go out of their heads. You had better tell your people. Warn them as to what is going to happen."[16] The reports of the confrontation with Suiepkine made good fodder to feed frontier newspapers such as the Spokane Falls *Morning Review*, which carried a May 16, 1889, story describing Skolaskin's career and "How He Frightened His People and Became an Absolute Monarch in Washington."

In any case, after the quake, Skolaskin's status was elevated, despite his disability. In an article published over a half-century later, former Colville agent Richard D. Gwydir gave a most colorful account of how the trembling earth elevated the Dreamer-Prophet to a leadership role. As Gwydir recalled it, the Sanpoils approached Skolaskin's lodge at Whitestone hailing him as "Illunigum Skolaskin!" ("Chief Skolaskin!") and offering him horses in homage.[17]

The trauma of the earthquake coincided with increasing governmental threats to the stability of Sanpoil-Nespelem society, demanding leadership that the traditional chiefs, especially those with less charisma and spiritual credentials than Skolaskin, could not supply.[18] By the same token, those threatening his people's freedom could no longer do so without reckoning with him, be they government officials or clergymen seeking to "civilize" them.

11

The Preaching

See that I am crippled and unable to make my livelihood in any other way.

—*Skolaskin to Reverend Urban Grassi, S.J.*

In preaching, Skolaskin reiterated the heavenly credentials that he claimed to have acquired through his illness and subsequent death, ascent to heaven, and return. He buttressed his credentials by reiterating his marvelous recovery and the dreams, revelations, and prophetic powers with which he claimed the deity Quilentsuten had commissioned him to deliver the people from their evil ways. Their sins included drinking, stealing, and committing adultry, and the Prophet believed the deity had shown his displeasure with the people by shaking the earth. Despite the hysteria occasioned by the quake, those who remembered his crippling a decade earlier could not have overlooked the evidence of his twisted limbs that his recovery had not been so complete as he claimed it had been. They must have wondered why he was crippled, if his spiritual experiences had been miraculous. His explanation was that God had cut him up in little pieces, and when he had put him back together, one leg was shorter than the other, but God would straighten out his limbs when he was ready to do so.[1] In their fright the people apparently felt compelled to accept his words at face value. At no time does Skolaskin appear to have encouraged others to emulate his miraculous experiences. To have done so would have been to dilute their impact, possibly weakening his position.

Skolaskin's services were usually held once or twice on Sundays and at other times on other days as well. On entering the meeting place, a crude structure of one storey and a loft, worshippers knelt. Then someone began praying and others joined in. Skolaskin admonished his people to pray when rising in the morning, retiring at night, before eating, and before berry picking and hunting to assure the success of those ventures. It appears that the responsibility for the prayers for the all-important fishing remained with the traditional salmon chiefs, whose leadership in that activity at sites such as those on the lower Sanpoil River was so well established that Skolaskin did not challenge it. On Sundays no one was to work, paint their faces, or even look at their images in the water.[2] All were to be friendly and kind, and they were to shun dancing, unlike the participants in Smohalla's Washat, of which the centerpiece was the dance. Skolaskin's ban on gambling struck at the heart of a practice long engrained in native cultures. Nevertheless, his followers vowed to heed his words, pledging him their allegiance and promising to pray to the God whom he revealed.

There were no curings in Skolaskin's services. In this respect his services were like Smohalla's but unlike those of the Feather Religion and Indian Shakers, who practiced healings. Informants said, however, he did visit homes to minister to the sick, fulfilling a more typical shamanistic role. His puritanical code did not preclude the use of bells but did prohibit instruments and trappings such as candles, drums, and apparently, flags.[3] According to Okanagan informants, at one time he catechized seven young men and seven young women, teaching them Catholic-type prayers and tunes so that they could in turn teach them to others during the daytimes. Each night these disciples carried pitch-pine torches when accompanying Skolaskin to the church, carrying out their tasks with zeal unmatched by devout Catholics counting rosary beads.[4]

Skolaskin's congregation comprised not only Whitestone villagers but also others who traveled there. He is known to have traveled down the Columbia to the more populous lower Sanpoil River to hold services in a men's longhouse.[5] Verne Ray stated that the prayers for help of the kneeling ones closely followed the supplications to the holy sweat lodge, which was a place of both physical and spiritual healing and constituted "the nearest approach to an aboriginal deity."[6] At Skolaskin's services many traditional songs had newly composed lyrics resembling those of love songs, and these also were addressed to the sweat lodge. Protestant ministers, more than their Catholic counterparts, believed songs such as those in Skolaskin's services to be sensual in nature.[7]

Two songs were basic to Skolaskin's worship, one a prayer and the other a funeral song. Services for the dead were very important and were distinguished from regular services because death and the gathering of the faithful in heaven were vital to Skolaskin's religion. The bodies of the dead lay in log houses or in tipis for up to three days, or for shorter periods during warm weather. Services for them were held outside the church building. In contrast, the bodies of Smohalla's Washani worshippers sometimes lay unburied for up to five days, in case they were experiencing a sojourn in heaven and might return to earth. Skolaskin did not advocate a similar experience for his followers.

At a Sanpoil-Nespelem funeral the mourners, in single file, carried the body of the deceased in a blanket held at the corners. The women followed the men, moving in cadence behind their Prophet's handpicked leaders. One of the latter, Tentenamelakin, a member of Skolaskin's own police force, rang a bell and, humming, changed the hymns en route to the graveyard. Dirges for the dead began: "Hisholamaway, Hastsholanawist, Hastsholanawist" ("Heaven is good. We'll all be glad when we die and see our friends in Heaven. And we'll all be glad when we see our Father in Heaven").[8] From those words it may be deduced that Skolaskin's doctrine did not emphasize the mass return to earth of the dead stressed by Smohalla. Instead Skolaskin's foresaw the mass reunion of the faithful in heaven. The adoption of the common graveyard burial seemingly symbolized the collective grouping of the faithful dead as though awaiting resurrection in a common meeting place in heaven. Because Skolaskin was unable to march in processions, he preached his funeral sermons from a horse. His chosen disciples threw dirt into the grave, and mourners shook hands with the dead. Then the men circled one way and the women the other, crossing in front of each other to end the services.[9]

Skolaskin believed that his control over his followers was as important to his ministrations as preaching his creed and the practice of his ceremonials. To keep his people true to the faith, he found it necessary to safeguard and enforce it by gathering about him a corps of policemen such as Tentenamelakin. This was a common practice among Indian leaders. Even their government agents selected policemen to help them control the people. Like Americans of that era, Pacific Northwest Indians also condoned whippings, often by designated whippers, to punish errant individuals. The rods consisted of several sticks tied in a bundle.[10] Because of his debility, Skolaskin relied on others to administer this kind of discipline. Indians were revolted by the white practice of hanging guilty ones. Skolaskin continued the traditional punishments of children for picking berries on Sundays, for contradicting their elders, and for trying to join in the games and other activities of these seniors.[11]

Skolaskin controlled his people by a mixture of the physical and the psychological, of chimera and charisma, of fear and hope. According to informants, among his bizarre and subtle means of control were his threats to turn wavering ones into birds, rocks, and other nonhuman beings. On occasion he summoned to his house those wishing to hear a prophecy only to charge them a dollar for predicting an eclipse, the date of which he had gotten from an almanac as Smohalla had done.[12] Informants related that in later years he also claimed to prophesy an eclipse about which he had learned from soldiers at Fort Spokane, and to have a "magic tube," which was an anise plant into whose hollow steam he had put burned glass. When held to the sun, the plant showed the colors of the rainbow in a kaleidoscopic design that was changed by turning the stem. He told the people that the bright light that they saw through the tube was the "Great Chief Above." He would never let others hold it.[13] He comforted them with the promise of escape with him to heaven from earth, which he said was soon to be destroyed. Indian observer Edward S. Curtis pointed out that the Indians of the Colville Reservation were known to have destroyed their winter supply of dried fish at Skolaskin's command in the belief that the end of the world was at hand.[14] Lest they stray from the faith, he would ride around Whitestone Village on a white horse while someone following called attention to his person by ringing a bell.[15] His high visibility and the sound of the instrument in their ears reminded them of his power and authority which he kept intact by constant reminders of the white encroachers who were coming ever closer to destroy their independence.

The continuing government encroachments only gave more impetus to Skolaskin's preachments and made his people more willing to heed his words. In August, 1872, the then Washington territorial superintendent of Indian affairs (and later Simcoe agent), R. H. Milroy, traveled to meet Skolaskin, but was met instead by a large mounted and armed Indian party that descended on Milroy's camp. When the Indians refused to shake the superintendent's hand, the Colville agent, Simms, grabbed Milroy's clothing before releasing his grasp with a warning "to go easy." Milroy began by using the standard means of intimidating Indians, telling them they were like leaves in the winter against whites who were as numerous as the sands of the shore. He then lectured them on the government's policy in general and its particular proposal to headquarter an agency at the head of the Nespelem River. After those words the Indian party rode away.[16]

On May 11, 1873, a native delegation including Sanpoils warned a thirteen-man party which was under contract to survey the reservation, that, should it disobey their chief's order to leave, many Indians in the area would force them to stop their surveys.[17] The surveys continued, however. Since Skolaskin knew that physical retaliation against government employees would only bring more retaliation, his preaching was nonviolent, with opposition to the American foe limited to complaint rather than combat.

Possibly because he believed that it would not concern them, or possibly wishing to avoid confrontation with them, Agent Simms did not call the Sanpoils to a council held on August 2, 1873, where the tribesmen asked for an extension to the first Colville Reservation to include missions and fisheries on its edge near the Columbia River. Agent Winans had suggested that three tribes who preferred Protestant to Catholic teachers—the Sanpoils, certain Spokanes, and the Methows,—be given a reservation separate from the Colville. Catholic tribes such as the Colvilles proper, the Senijextees, the Kalispels, and the Okanagons would be assigned to the Colville.[18]

It appears that Simms had as many apprehensions about the Sanpoils as they had about him and about other Indian Office personnel. Simms proposed to the commissioner that punishment be meted out to Sanpoil-Nespelem Dreamers. The "speediest and most effectual means of bringing them to terms," he suggested, was "to arrest the ringleaders [who were not over six in number] and send them to some distant reservation, and forbid them to their country." Such a policy, he wrote, "would strike terror among them, as an Indian dreads nothing so much, as to be forced from his home and friends." He explained that the Sanpoil-Nespelems, whom he regarded as one tribe, were

> under the control of their Preachers or Prophets who are called dreamers, and are distinct from the drummers who live lower down on the Columbia. They tell their followers that truth is revealed to them (the prophets) directly from Heaven, and all that is necessary to secure their well being in this world, and happiness in the next is to obey them implicitly, and that they do almost without an exception. A distrust of white men, and a disregard of their teaching and laws, seems to be the foundation of their faith, and no one is permitted to acknowledge any authority eminating [sic] from them. They are having a bad effect upon the surrounding tribes, offering to the turbulent and disorderly a place of refuge and immunity from punishment. . . . The Chief [Quetalikin] is a well meaning man, but has lost his influence, and blindly follows the Prophet [Skolaskin].[19]

Most important evidence of the effectiveness of Skolaskin's preaching and his hold over his people was their continuing obeisance to him, out of a mixture of fear and faith, as he sought to implement a most bizarre plan, in the words of Simms, "to secure their well being in this world, and happiness in the next."

Skolaskin's Ark and Church

Skolaskin proposed to build an ark to save his followers from the world-inundating flood that he predicted was to come. Never again, he proclaimed, would they reach the hereafter by death and funerals. His belief in the second such world cataclysm was not unique with him. The Paiute Ghost Dance prophet Wovoka, for example, described a dream that he had in January, 1889, in which he claimed that God assured him that water and mud would wipe the whites from the face of the earth, which would shake like a dancer's rattle under the influence of smoke, lightning, and thunder to be reborn in a heavenly era.[20] Closer to Skolaskin, the Southern Okanagons, and very possibly his own people, believed that the world would return to a life-ending aquatic void.[21] Skolaskin's creed offered individuals hope for survival, but only for those who would follow him.

Some scholars believe that since the story of the flood was universally handed down among American Indians long before white contact, it was based less on the biblical account than on native tradition. Skolaskin would have had ample opportunity to hear the story from missionaries or other whites who tried to impress natives with biblical stories such as that of the creation or the fall of man. At any rate, natives were familiar with the Bible story, and they adapted the Mount Ararat resting place of Noah's ark to peaks in their various homelands.

Skolaskin's ark-building proposal provided him the dramatic means with which to direct his people at a time when they were willing to accept control because their world was in crisis. Questions arise, nonetheless, about the motives underlying his proposal. Probably Skolaskin believed that a world flood was coming in the same way that he believed miraculous spiritual experiences had brought him to his place in life, but did he propose to launch an ark mainly to launch his own ministry? Or did he honestly seek to save himself and his people from what he believed was a real, not an imaginary, catastrophe? Was his plan a means of salvation or subordination for his people? Only later, when his taciturnity weakened, would he give an inkling of what lay within the recesses of his mind.

One account had it that, although Skolaskin's heavenly mandate was to build an ark, he had his people build a church instead when the deluge failed to materialize.[22] Some informants believed that was why he was forced into a second revelation of a soon-coming deluge.[23] To give the story a stronger Noah-like flavor, some informants went so far as to state that Skolaskin ordered his people to gather aboard the craft a male and a female of each species. In any case, his disciples initiated the project as outlined by their leader. With how much willingness on their part or coercion on his is unclear.

A white settler, for whom one of Skolaskin's wives picked and shucked corn, stated that the Prophet sent the husbands of the more comely wives greater distances to harvest trees to prepare timber for the ark.[24] The tribe had learned how to whipsaw lumber for the project and for Skolaskin's church from observing the Chinese miners digging and sluicing gold along the Columbia. Skolaskin discouraged unions of his women followers with the Chinese, as he had those with white men, but he was not averse to Chinese help in carrying out his projects. The whipsaw, broad axes, and other tools for preparing the lumber were carried on horseback from Walla Walla. He and his people avoided acquiring tools or other goods from the much-nearer Colville Agency because of their wish to have nothing to do with the United States. Money to purchase the supplies came from sales of bunchgrass-fattened horses and cattle, which Skolaskin often requisitioned from his people, as he did other things of value.[25]

The *Walla Walla* (W. T.) *Union* on February 10, 1883, carried an account by Special Indian Inspector Robert S. Gardner that fifty thousand feet of timber to be whipsawed had been set aside for both the church and the ark building. The newspaper reported the dimensions of the proposed ark as 50 or 60 feet by 150 feet, a size roughly one-third the length and two-thirds the width of Noah's craft. Unlike his ship-building predecessor, Skolaskin received no heaven-sent directive concerning the ark's dimensions. One account had it that, after driving horses and cattle to Walla Walla to exchange for nails to build the ark, Skolaskin returned home with word that the Great Spirit, who had changed his mind about the flood, had ordered him to trade some of the logs to the Chinese for gold dust. According to this version, gambling losses had forced Skolaskin to send for a horse to carry him home. Were such the case, he would have found it convenient to blame the Great Spirit for his change of plans.[26]

The church eventually was constructed, unlike the ark, which was never built. One elderly Sanpoil panelist recalled that its one storey and loft, were begun when he was seven or eight years old, which would have been about 1877. The arduous tasks of cutting the logs, having horses haul them in, and whipsawing the lumber prolonged construction of the ark, and each passing day left more of the one-by-six-inch planks rotting in a pile. Skolaskin had talked about floating the craft down the Columbia to the mouth of the Sanpoil to rescue the people there along with those from Whitestone and from other villages where the faithful lived. That day never came, and of course, the funeral dirges continued. Remaining land-bound, the Dreamer's disciples had the face-saving last word after the great Columbia River flood of 1894. More conclusive yet were the waters of Roosevelt Lake behind Grand Coulee Dam, which buried Whitestone Village, the very place where the Prophet had uttered his predictions of a coming flood.[27]

12

The Black-Robe Challenge

> I supposed that they [Presbyterians and Roman
> Catholics] will punish me when I die, but I will
> stand it when it comes.
> —Skolaskin, *Seattle Post-Intelligencer,*
> July 9, 1905.

Skolaskin's opposition to the federal government that was taking
the natives' land was no more intense than his conflicts with those
who threatened their souls or his religion. His most important
Christian rivals were the black-robe missionaries of the Roman
Catholic Church, whose first representatives in the Pacific Northwest interior had been the Reverends François Norbert Blanchet
and Modeste Demers, who visited the Sanpoils and neighboring
peoples at Kettle Falls in November, 1838,[1] the year before the
Prophet's birth. The black robes, in turn, had been as much concerned by the presence between 1838 and 1848 of the Reverends
Elkanah Walker and Cushing Eells and their wives at their Tshimakain Mission below Kettle Falls as they were by the natives' "pagan-
ism." The flight of the protestants from that mission precipitated by
the Whitman massacre in 1847, which resulted in the Cayuse War,
left only Dreamers and other native religious leaders as threats to
the black robes' attempts to spread the Christian faith. The appearance of a Dreamer at Kettle Falls, where the Catholics had a mission station, set them on edge after he proclaimed that he had experienced a six-day "death" in which he claimed to have seen
Christ, his horse, and heaven, which he said abounded with game
and salmon. The black robes breathed easier after this Prophet's ex-
pulsion from the country.[2]

Because large numbers of natives visited Kettle Falls during sal-
mon-fishing seasons, that place was well suited for a mission, from
which black robes ministered more successfully to Salish-speaking
Colvilles, Coeur d'Alenes, Flatheads, Pen d'Oreilles, and Senijextees than they did to the Sanpoil-Nespelems (who also were Salish-
speaking). Before Skolaskin became their leader, however, the Sanpoils appear to have had no visible animosity to the black robes.
Responding to a visit to Kettle Falls of several Sanpoils who were

seeking Catholic prayers for protection from the terrible smallpox epidemic ranging along the Columbia River in 1853, the Reverend Joseph Joset, S.J., came to their lands to vaccinate them against that disease and against the cholera as well. The smallpox is believed to have been carried back to the Sanpoils by a party who returned from a trading trip to Portland in the late 1840's or early 1850's. All of the party succumbed to the disease except for the one who exposed his tribe to it. In an October 18, 1855, letter to the Reverend Peter J. De Smet, S.J., the Reverend Adrian Hoecken, S.J., wrote: "During the late prevalence of the small-pox, there were hardly any deaths from it among the neophytes, as most of them had been previously vaccinated by us, while the Spokans and other unconverted Indians, who said the 'Medicine (vaccine) of the Fathers, was a poison, used only to kill them' were swept away by the hundreds. This contrast, of course, had the effect of increasing the influence of the missionaries."[3]

On another occasion when a Sanpoil delegation came to Kettle Falls seeking religious instruction, Joset sent them home with Christian names, a prayer, and a promise to see them in the spring. With the death that winter of the delegation leader none of them came again seeking instruction from the missionary, although he visited them in June, 1870. From that visit he returned "displeased, though not discouraged, at the coldness of the Simpoilshi."[4]

From a Nespelem village, shortly after the middle of the nineteenth century, the native evangelist Slaybebtkud (also Skubebtkud or Satbabutkin) brought the mass and other Catholic ceremonials westward across the Cascade Mountains to the Salish-speaking natives of the upper Skagit River. Slaybebtkud prophesied that white men would come there bringing evil, and he exhorted the people to lead good lives to avoid succumbing to it. The prophecies of another Upper Skagit, Haheibalth, in the 1860's and 1870's caused great concern among the Catholic fathers, who regarded such ministrations as detrimental to their own. Although the black robes claimed successes in converting natives, especially near their missions, they faced problems on the plateau in gathering and holding the natives within their flocks, especially in isolated places such as the Sanpoil-Nespelem country. As in the interior, black robes west of the Cascade Mountains were fearful lest native religious leaders inject pagan elements into Catholic worship or lead the people away from it altogether.[5]

With the earthquake of 1872 and the emergence of Skolaskin, Sanpoil relations with the black robes, like those with government officials, took a sudden turn for the worse. Opposition to the clerics and to black robe attempts to convert them seemingly rose in direct ratio to the natives' adherence to the Dreamer faith. And they were no more willing to heed the ministrations of Presbyterian ministers after the earthquake, which helped stimulate a Christian revival among the Nez Percé and Spokane Indians. In the summer of 1874 the Presbyterian Reverend H. T. Cowley, with a party out of Spokane Falls, visited Skolaskin's Whitestone Village. The Prophet permitted his visitors to camp overnight, but in the morning told them to move on.[6] Over the years the Spokanes kept a cool religious distance from Skolaskin and his Dreamers. In June, 1880, their chief, Lot, under Presbyterian influence, told Special Indian agent H. Clay Wood of the "annoyance" to which Lot was subjected by the Sanpoil Dreamers and their religious practices.[7]

The Reverend Urban Grassi, S.J., was one black robe whose zeal compelled him to rescue the natives from the "devil-sent" doctrines of Dreamer-Prophets emerging from the quake. Not only did his zeal fit him for the task, but also his mastery of native languages, with which he sought to draw them away from their Dreamer leaders and follow his faith. During the summer of 1873 one of his objectives, as he itinerated northward from the Ahtanum Mission in the Yakima country, was to restore to his faith members of the Wenatchee band of "Sinpesquensis" under the Dreamer-Prophet Patoi. Like other religious leaders, Patoi used the earthquake to try to dislodge his band from the Catholic faith to follow him, and he refused to turn over their names to Grassi. When the priest told him that only those espousing the Catholic "prayer" would go to heaven, Patoi replied that Catholic fathers (possibly because of the isolation of the Wenatchee peoples between the Kettle Falls and Ahtanum missions) had abandoned his people. Moreover, he chided, his people did not need the Catholic prayers, since they led good lives, not only because of his preachings against gambling, stealing, lieing, and drinking but also because they kept Saturday sacred as well as Sunday. Grassi commended Patoi for the virtuousness of his people but remained unconvinced of the efficacy of their prayers.

During Grassi's visit to the Wenatchees a woman suffered a convulsive seizure. Patoi rang a bell to assemble the people and had her carried in to pray over her. Both young and old, Grassi observed, prayed over her as though in a "trance of devotion." Some of them, he recorded, closed their eyes, some looked heavenward, and others put their arms over their breasts while Patoi prayed aloud and led a hymn. After another prayer Patoi began preaching, and his people stood entranced as though hearing from God. The woman's recovery made Grassi's challenge of Patoi all the more difficult. "Black-gown," said the Prophet, "I have two things in my heart, one of which I will tell you now. Four months ago when we felt the earthquake, one night while my people slept I watched and

prayed. During my prayer there appeared to me three persons clad
in white robes. One of them did not speak; the second spoke and
told me many things and among them, that if I prayed well the
third person would protect me." Grassi said that he was that "third
person" who had come to teach the good prayer. This outwardly
pleased Patoi.

When Grassi asked if he might return and establish a mission
among Patoi's people, the Prophet replied that he could, but that
Grassi could spend only the winter with them. Patoi may have felt
secure in making such a stipulation because he was aware of a pattern of itinerancy among Catholic priests. His followers and those
of other Dreamer-Prophets, having not experienced the ecstasies of
"heavenly sojourns" themselves, were more prone than were the
Prophets to accept the warnings of Catholic priests that the tor-
ments of hell awaited the unbaptized. Grassi returned to the Wenatchees as he promised. During his visit five medicine men ministered over the sick and the dying in the aftermath of an epidemic,
preferring their own "medicine" to that of the priest. But Grassi's
persistence and "heavenly patience" enabled him to win over to his
faith members of the tribe, including Patoi himself, who was baptized on April 5, 1874, in his forty-fifth year, three months after the
rite had been administered to six of his children. During the same
year Grassi baptized 186 other Wenatchees, performed 28 marri-
ages, gave Christian burial to 10 adults, and cited the deaths of 39
baptized babies. In an October 4, 1873, letter to his superior, he
told of his two-day sojourn among the tribe to repair a chapel and a
small house that he had built for them about three years previously. More important to him were the spiritual repairs that he administered to keep these tribesmen within the Catholic fold and
away from the flames of hell.[8]

On his northern tour in the late spring and early summer of
1876, Grassi was met by Suiepkine's Southern Okanagon Kartar
band. Of their Dreamer-Prophet chief, he wrote that he was "one of
those to whom the devil appeared four years ago, teaching him
some kind of prayer, he adopted the prayer and made it to be
adopted by his small nation." At about that time his people began
making the sign of the cross and leaving their children unburied
three days after death. Grassi was impressed with their well-
watered, sheltered Kartar valley, where their livestock wintered
well. He was equally impressed with the livestock owners, who
showed "signs of more civilization" than did neighboring tribesmen
because their well-built wooden houses sheltered them on returning from excursions.[9]

Despite the opposition of Suiepkine and his rival, Skolaskin, to
the black robes, they and their priestly antagonists shared a common fear of the growing influence of the government in Indian af-

fairs. The failure of its church-oriented Peace Policy in the 1870's, in which Indian-agency governance was delegated to contesting church bodies, contributed to a growing secularism in government and in American society at large. This threatened Catholics in their efforts to advance a Christian way of life on Indian enclaves. Skolaskin, especially, feared the growing hand of government, for it threatened his own hand in leading the Sanpoil-Nespelem-oriented society. Worse yet for him was an awareness that the government was now in league with his old nemesis, Chief Moses, for whom it had plans on the Colville as alarming to the Dreamer as was the presence of black-robed priests.

A day's journey brought the Reverend Grassi to the Sanpoils, who numbered two hundred souls. Since their chief (Quetalikin?) and their "man of prayer" (Skolaskin) were absent, none of the tribe were cautious about voicing any religious opinions. Grassi described Skolaskin to his superior as this "man of prayer" who "nourished the minds of his tribe with fables," making them prepare an ark to save themselves from a second flood. Wrote Grassi:

> That the devil might have talked to him, there seems no doubt, but also there is no doubt that there is much more of it that he adds himself; He told a White, worthy of faith and who reported it to me: "See that I am crippled and unable to make my livelihood in any other way." He makes himself pay. . . . [by] his dreams with horses, and cattle which he sells and from it he procures an elegant table and fine suits. He refuses to see the Black Robe, and says often to his own: "Do not become annoyed if the Frenchmen and the Americans laugh at us, the day will come when we will laugh at them."[10]

Grassi remained with the Sanpoils no longer than two days, June 22 and 23. During Skolaskin's absence, the Sanpoils felt safe enough visiting the priest's tent. Their headmen assured their guest: "We do not hate you, Black Robe, you want to lead us to God and make us good, our man of prayer wants to lead us to God and make us good, both of you tend to the same goal, and how can we hate you, both of you are equally dear to us." After that diplomatic explanation, Grassi moved hopefully on to Kettle Falls, praying that, like spiritual dominoes, Suiepkine's people, whom he believed the most disposed to Catholic teachings, would fall under the "influence of Grace," to be followed in turn by the Nespelems, who would cause the Sanpoils to "open their eyes to the Truth" and fall under that influence.[11]

In December, 1877, a year and a half later, the persistent Grassi returned to the Sanpoils. He reported that there remained much work to do among them and the Nespelems, especially since the Sanpoils' leader "some years ago. . . . told his people that God ordered him, as Noe of old, to build an ark, because there would be another deluge; those who would follow his prayer, he would receive into the ark and save. In consequence of this order from above he set his young men to sawing lumber during the whole winter. . . . [and] tells his people that he can read, though he never learned how, and that, were the whites to fire at him, they would not hurt him, as God had made him invulnerable." A census prepared by the Reverend Paschal Tosi, S.J., stated that in the year 1877 the Sanpoils were composed entirely of "infidels" and no converts and among the Nespelems there were forty "infidels" and thirty-five converts.[12] En route to the Sanpoils, Grassi fell in with one of their number who was struggling with an overburdened pony. The Sanpoil chided the priest that God, who made innocent babies, would no more cast them off unbaptized at death than would their parents. "What good can Baptism do a person?" he chided, adding that there were "very good people among the unbaptized, and very bad ones among the baptized." In a meeting with the main body of Sanpoils, which began with the customary bell ringing, Skolaskin warned Grassi not to speak – that he had already spoken too much, that the people would reject his prayers, and that he did not blame the priest for adopting the prayer of Jesus Christ, but he had no right to impose it on others. To prove that the Great Spirit protected him as it did the black robes, Skolaskin told his unwelcomed guest that God had made him invulnerable to the bullets that whites might fire at him – a belief long engrained in the thinking of Pacific Northwest prophets, priests, and chiefs. Skolaskin admitted that God had spoken to Jesus Christ, but said that lately God spoke to his chosen ones only through Skolaskin himself. Okanagon informants stated that in one of his nightly dreams Skolaskin was assured that, like Christ, he too had been to purgatory and had returned to teach mankind. During this awkward meeting others, emboldened now by Skolaskin's presence, arose to speak even more vehemently than he did against Grassi, reiterating their belief in the rightness of their native prophets' prayers. Some of them said that baptism was worthless. The meeting ended with the final ringing of a bell and intonations of benedictory "aahs!" After a fruitless two-day sojourn, Grassi left warning the people that by continuing Skolaskin's prayers they would never go to heaven.[13]

In December, 1879, the Reverend Alexander Diomedi, S.J., was on a tour west to the mouth of the Okanogan River from the Saint Francis Regis Mission near Kettle Falls, which he described as "the advanced post for conquering the Sempuelsh (Sanpoil) and Okinagan Indians." East of Whitestone, Diomedi encountered a five-lodge camp of Sanpoils – and trouble. The Sanpoil wife of a storekeeper fumed at him: "Why have you come here among us? To convert us, I suppose! You are always preaching against our dreaming, but your own religion is worse than ours. I know how to read; I have been to Portland, and I know that you priests are thieves! Where do you get your coat, your pants, your clothing?"[14]

Holding his temper, Diomedi replied, "Did you ever know me to ask anything from you? or from any Indian you know? If I go around, it is only for God's sake and to help those who wish to become good and upright; those, however, who prefer to remain pagans and dreamers are never molested by me." These words antagonized the Sanpoil woman to respond so vociferously that her children had to calm her down. At his guide's insistence, Diomedi pushed on. When the subject of Skolaskin came up, he told his guide: "Kolaskin is a poor wretch who has greatly deceived his own people. He is a dreamer who sometimes shuts himself up in his tent and allows no one to see him. Then he comes out and tells his people that he has had a revelation from heaven during his seclusion."

The priest proceeded to tell of Skolaskin's proposed ark, his opposition to Catholics, and the dangers that priests faced by visiting him. A case in point the Reverend James Vanzina, S.J., whom Skolaskin, despite his crippled condition, allegedly had tried to strike with a knife, forcing the cleric to stop preaching, jump to his horse, and ride off. At the suggestion of his guide, Diomedi gave Skolaskin a wide berth and retreated down the Columbia River.[15] The Sanpoils' boast that they had never killed a white man did not convince Diomedi.

In an April 19, 1881, letter to his superior, Joseph Cataldo, S.J., Grassi wrote that about ten years before (actually, earlier) Skolaskin had fallen ill with a nervous, crippling disease. During that time (which would have been about that of the great quake), wrote Grassi, the Dreamer-Prophet claimed to have received visions of paradise and messages that were to be communicated to the people. Skolaskin claimed God had chosen him to make his wishes known to them in order to save them, and that God in anger had commanded him, like a second Noah, to build an ark in which all believers were to be rescued from the deluge. The greater part of the tribe, wrote Grassi, believed Skolaskin, but when no flood came, he had another revelation—that he was first to build a church and then an ark, after which the deluge would come. The poor Sanpoils, wrote Grassi, "swallowed it all [and it] hurts my heart to see the veneration that these poor people have for this imposter." Grassi further recalled that Skolaskin believed he was second only to God and that he invoked Jesus and Mary as intercessors. "The code which he promulgates," wrote Grassi, "is a mixture of things Indian, Protestant and Catholic [and] thus he satisfies the conscience of everybody."

Further on in his letter to his superior, Grassi revealed his attendance "some years ago" at a "prayer" at which Skolaskin and all the other Sanpoils were present. The Prophet had objected to Grassi's preaching. Grassi had continued undaunted, proclaiming the divinity of Jesus Christ and the need for baptism. Skolaskin warned him that he had spoken long enough, especially as Grassi spoke without the Prophet's permission. Skolaskin did not, however, deny the merits of baptism, stating instead that his people were as yet unprepared for the rite. He then summarily dismissed the meeting, and Grassi, believing it prudent to moderate his own zeal in the face of this opposition, had circulated among the lodges warning their occupants that, should they not become Christians, they would never enter heaven.

Grassi narrated how he had pushed on from the Sanpoils to the Nespelems. On learning from them that one of their chiefs had become a fervent believer in Skolaskin's revelations, he moved on to Suiepkine and his Kartar band, who permitted him to spend a fortnight in a house whose owner was away on a hunting trip. Grassi remembered that during his stay he was comforted by seven or eight Catholics of the band, until they informed him they had received ample instruction for the time being—that they had gone to confession and that he should leave, since Suiepkine did not want them to be baptized. When Grassi told this delegation's leader that he would like to hear about Suiepkine's "revelation" and the latter's many journeys to heaven in or outside the body, the leader left, confused. Then, after Grassi had retired for the night, Suiepkine and a dozen or so headmen woke him and asked if Grassi wanted to hear about the visions. When the priest replied affirmatively, the Dreamer said that he actually had seen no one in his visions, but he had heard a man who taught him things which, in turn, he taught to his people. Then, more or less precisely, Suiepkine recounted the stories of the creation, the flood, and Christ. Grassi received Suiepkine's promise to surrender the "dream-up" prayer and accept baptism. But when Grassi expressed the wish that his people follow the Dreamer in the rite, Suiepkine's people responded coldly. The Dreamer also turned colder as the winter of 1881–82 progressed, and by the spring the priest had departed.

Grassi recalled for his superior that, after an absence of three months visiting various Indian tribes, he had returned to Suiepkine and his people and had reiterated his wish to build a chapel. Suiepkine had responded with polite evasiveness, having changed none of his religious beliefs. Grassi then called on Gilkagan, a headman and the only tribal member with carpentry skills, to build the structure. Revealing the democratic spirit that characterized deliberations among Salish speakers, Suiepkine called the headmen together to discuss the project. They responded by expressing fears that, were Grassi to have a chapel, other white men would come to take their lands as they had those of other Indians. Okanagon informants recalled that Suiepkine warned his people not to let the priest perform baptisms, since priests were "only after money." Grassi concluded his narrative by telling how, after spending the winter among the Indians, he returned to the Saint Francis Regis Mission near Kettle Falls, promising to return to these tribesmen as soon as possible.[16]

In 1890, his fifty-ninth year, Grassi died of pneumonia on the Umatilla Reservation, far to the south of his earlier ministrations. An Indian of a band between the Sanpoil and Okanogan rivers had tried to drown him by upsetting the canoe in which they were crossing the Columbia.[17]

Black-robe successes would have to wait the coming of later Catholic priests. One of them, the young Reverend Etienne de Rougé, S.J., could not bring Suiepkine and Skolaskin into his fold, yet he persisted with some success in ministering to their Okanagan and Sanpoil-Nespelem peoples from his Saint Mary's Mission, which he founded at Omak Lake in 1889.[18] In the summer of 1890, the year of Grassi's death, Suiepkine requested that a white man, Francis (Frank) Streamer (described by his biographer Ann Briley as an eccentric pedestrian and self-instructed amenuensis for heavenly powers), write General Howard, warning him of the Okanagan Dreamer's continued defiance in the face of his threatened defeat:

> The priests build Catholic churches on my peoples' land at the Omack, and take all their money for their church, make them neglect their work, to spend days and weeks there, to get them prejudiced against the whites and the George Washington [American] people. The church is a King George [British] church, and the priests make enemies of the Indians. My lands will soon be taken from me and my people, because we mind our own business, and never fight the Soldiers. Tell General Howard that I am no priestman. I am a true Indian, and object to priests stealing lands for churches.[19]

Without mentioning Suiepkine by name, an article in the Portland, Oregon, *Catholic Sentinel* on March 9, 1911, told of the "Liar" and his dreamings and opposition to the Saint Mary's Mission.[20]

It was trouble enough for Skolaskin, as it was for Suiepkine, that he had to face Catholic inroads among his people, but there was always the threat posed by the United States government, which threatened him in a new way. The government was in league with old foes of the Dreamers, the Columbia Sinkiuse chief Moses and his followers, for whom it had plans that alarmed the Prophet as much as the presence of black-robed priests.

13

The Coming of Moses and Joseph

Our boast that a white man's blood has never
been shed by a San Poil is true.
— *Skolaskin to Major R.G. Gwydir.*

When Chief Moses in 1877 asked Skolaskin if he were going to join
Joseph and his Nez Percés in their fight against American forces,
the Sanpoil Dreamer-Prophet replied, "God made the world for us
to live on, not to fight or sell."[1] A headman, named Klikitas (perhaps the Nespelem Quequetas), warned white settlers of the impending trouble as Nez Percé emissaries went among northern interior tribes seeking recruits in their struggle against the American
troops.[2] John C. ("Virginia Bill") Covington returned from Walla
Walla to inform Skolaskin of a hitch in obtaining supplies and
equipment: Walla Walla merchants in that time of panic were forbidden to purchase guns to sell to the Indians. On hearing of the
ban, the Prophet dispatched Sanpoil chief Komotalakia and five
men to Walla Walla to explain their need for powder and shot,
which by now largely had replaced the bows and iron-headed arrows that the tribe had used for hunting. On arriving in Walla
Walla on July 10, Komotalakia assured its nervous citizenry that
the Sanpoils had no intentions of joining the Nez Percés in war.
Said Komotalakia:

> I talk for myself and my people; we came down to tell the white people
> that we have heard of the troubles with Joseph's Nez Percés, and to find
> out how the white people feel toward us. We wish to know whether the
> whites are angry with us on account of what the hostile Indians have
> done? In the last Cayuse war [the Yakima War, 1855–1858?] none of
> our tribe fought the whites; we are now opposed to fighting the whites;
> it makes no difference how many other Indians fight the whites, we will
> never fight them. There are perhaps a hundred of us; we shall follow
> our usual occupations and remain at home in our country. We must
> return home to our people, and we wish the white people not to suspect

our friendship. We do not wish to die fighting, but to die in peace. We don't lie, but speak the truth, and white men on the Columbia river know it. It is now new that our hearts are good to the whites; our hearts have always been so in the past. We have been constant and true to the whites. Long ago our chief set us the example and we have always followed it.[3]

Convinced of their sincerity, the merchants allowed the Sanpoils to purchase their needed supplies.

In August, as the Nez Percés continued their fight, representatives of the Okanagons and the Sanpoils were among the bands that met at Spokane Falls with the federal Indian inspector, Colonel E. C. Watkins, and Colonel Frank Wheaton, who led five hundred troops of General O. O. Howard's command. With such a force confronting them, the Indians were in no position to withhold signatures from an agreement not to enter hostilities.[4] They also agreed to accept the Colville Reservation, provided that a six-mile strip lying immediately east of the Columbia River was included within it, and to go and live on the strip by October 1. They also agreed to live at peace with whites and obey the orders of the Indian Office. According to official reports, Suiepkine was at the council, representing two hundred Dreamers. Two other representatives, named Charley and Snip-kel, signed for the "San Poel and Dreamers."[5]

Most Sanpoils refused to recognize the agreement extending the Colville Reservation, chiding those who would sign such pacts. Fortunately for the Sanpoils, the government failed to incorporate the six-mile strip within the Colville, freeing them from having to move there. Yet, like other Indians, Skolaskin[6] could not understand how the government could so easily make and break agreements.

From the Sanpoils' point of view, the greatest governmental duplicity involved Chief Moses. Because miners had been active on the northern portion of his Moses (Columbia) Reservation, the federal government withdrew it from the public domain without consulting the native inhabitants. Moses and his people were never welcome there, nor did they settle there, although some of them fished for salmon on the Methow River within the reservation during the summer, and Moses collected fees from stockmen for letting them run their cattle on the confine. Since his reservation was to be taken from him because miners and then settlers wanted to have it opened, he knew that the government was duty-bound to move him and his people elsewhere, most likely to the Colville. The government's subsequent action was in part a reward to Moses for his pro-American stance during the turbulent 1870's.[7]

Anticipating a move, Moses, as early as the latter part of 1880, visited the main Sanpoil village near the mouth of the Sanpoil River to inform Skolaskin that he and his people would soon be digging their winter lodges in at Komellakaka on the Columbia right bank, just east of present-day Belvidere, below Grand Coulee Dam. Sanpoil informants stated that, when Moses was given his first reservation, his "brother" had asked Skolaskin about the possibility of bringing his people onto the Colville. Skolaskin had angrily opposed the request. Then the Sanpoil headman Komotalakia had pulled Moses aside saying, "Yes, go there." As a result, Komotalakia fell out with Skolaskin, who berated Moses, saying: "He is just like his people before him. They came to our camps when the men were off on hunts and hanged our people, burned our babies and stole our salmon. They will do us no good."[8] Most likely, Skolaskin was aware of the reservation that Moses had proposed at the Steamboat Council at Priest Rapids. It would have angered him that it encompassed Sanpoil lands, not only on the Columbia right bank, near its confluence with the Spokane River, but also on the Columbia left bank, on the southern plateau, where Sanpoils had hunted and gathered their food for generations.

Ignoring Skolaskin's anger and aware of the strong arm of the government behind him, Moses had his Indians drive their horses and cattle north across the Columbia into the Nespelem River valley and then return to pitch their lodges at Komellakaka. About a mile from there they turned west, selecting a bench about a hundred feet above the river on which to build a longhouse and prepared for winter. During that winter of 1881 and 1882 some of them went to live with Skolaskin, who told them that their evil chief was stealing his lands. Most of Moses' people at Komellakaka, and those who went to nearby Peter Dan Creek and farther west to the Nespelem valley, remained loyal to their chief. All of these places were on Nespelem lands, which were shared by the Sanpoils.[9]

We have a good picture of the reluctant Sanpoils and Nespelems who played hosts to Moses' people during the latter part of 1882 from the pen of the interpreter-guide S. F. Sherwood, who was traveling with Lieutenant William R. Abercrombie to take a census of the Indians. It is possible that in conversing with Sherwood the Indians spoke not only in their native tongues but also in Chinook jargon, which Sherwood observed most of them spoke. As usual the Sanpoils refused to give their numbers. Some of them, reported Sherwood, wore "citizens'" clothing. On his own Sherwood counted 27 Indians at Whitestone, 14 on the Sanpoil River, 15 at its mouth, 17 on the Columbia, and 39 at Nespelem—a total of 112 souls. Although he estimated Sanpoil numbers at 200, other

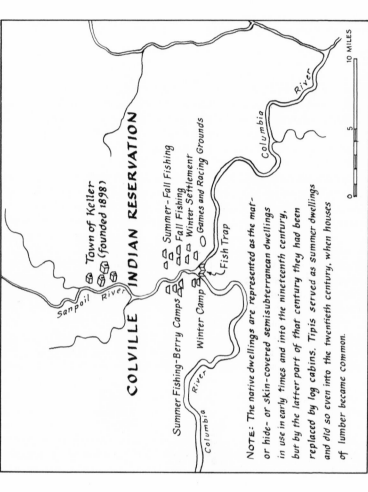

Indian Villages in the Vicinity of the Sanpoil and Nespelem Rivers

estimates ranged as high as 400, including the Nespelems. Inspector Gardner in 1882 reported a wide range of 200 to 400. Although that estimate was nebulous, it was closer than Sherwood's. Census takers such as he had difficulty ascertaining Indian populations because they moved about and refused to tell their numbers.

The Sanpoils, recorded Sherwood, ranged from twelve miles above the mouth of the Spokane River westward down the Columbia to the mouth of the Nespelem. He also reported that they cultivated small patches on about three hundred acres six miles up the Nespelem, as well as at Whitestone and along the Columbia between the Sanpoil and Nespelem rivers. At those places they raised melons, squash, potatoes, corn, oats, and wheat, since these were more easily grown than other crops and more resistant to the climatic rigors of that high country, where summer frosts were common. Unlike Smohalla, Skolaskin did not believe in subsisting solely on the "natural" products of the environment. Sherwood observed that his people also ran many horses and, like other Indians of the region, raised a few cattle. He reported many gamblers and prostitutes among the "saucy and independent" Sanpoils (whom Gardner reported as "doing no good"). Possibly this indicated that Skolaskin was failing to hold them to his moral standards, or perhaps Sherwood overemphasized such practices. At Whitestone, besides observing Skolaskin's log and lumber pile for the proposed ark, Sherwood noted his church, four or five frame houses, a barn, and a stable.[10] Sherwood moved on to visit Suiepkine's Dreamer band, reporting on it as he had on the Sanpoils. He described it as comprising about a hundred Okanagans intermixed with Nespelems. The latter was also drawn to Skolaskin, so that there was a rivalry between the two Dreamers for Nespelem minds and souls. At the time of Sherwood's visit over half of Suiepkine's band was absent from their cultivated sixty acres and eight cabins, visiting in the hills at the head of Omak Lake. One of their number had 120 fenced acres, a fine log house, a barn, and a stable in their Kartar valley home. Like the Sanpoils, Suiepkine's band did not recognize the Colville agent and continued to refuse goods from the government.[11]

Those whom Sherwood visited are best described as isolationists or independents, although they were regarded as renegades by the white community. From the president on down, the American officials who permitted Moses to settle on Nespelem lands revealed an insensitivity to, or lack of understanding of, the natives' territoriality. Agent Simms, for example, believed it proper to settle Moses and his people among the Sanpoils because he erroneously believed that they could more readily affiliate with them than could the other tribes on the Colville Reservation. Simms wanted neither the

Sanpoil-Nespelems nor Moses' people to mix with Catholic Indians, for whose welfare he was most solicitous in his role as Catholic agent under the Peace Policy. Nonetheless, contacts between Catholic and non-Catholic Colville Reservation Indian headmen were inevitable and were often unfriendly.[12] Skolaskin, for example, believed that the reservation was too small for himself and Barnaby, a Catholic chief of the Colvilles proper, some of whom had removed from east of the Columbia River to the reservation. Lieutenant Thomas William Symons of the U.S. Corps of Engineers, who conducted a survey of the Columbia River in 1881, knew more about it than he did about the Indians who lived along it. When asked if there was room enough among the Okanagons, the Sanpoils, and the Nespelems for Moses' band, he replied "most emphatically yes."[13] Obviously, Symons was thinking only in physical and geographical terms.

The federal order to restore a fifteen-mile strip along the northern border of Moses' Columbia Reservation was issued on February 23, 1883. That spring Moses was invited to Washington, D.C., to arrange for his removal to the Colville. Skolaskin was jealous of Moses and angry that no one had invited him to the capital to oppose the move and state his own views on the matter. Aware of his disposition, officials could see no purpose in inviting him, for he would go there, they believed, simply to challenge Moses and cause trouble. Accompanying Moses on his eastern journey in June were the Okanagon chiefs Tonasket and Sarsopkin, both of whom were more amenable to the government than was the Okanagon Dreamer Suiepkine. Resenting any transaction involving his peoples' lands, Skolaskin avoided a council that was held on the Kettle River to discuss the journey to Washington.[14] Far from the U.S. capital, he would perhaps have been unaware initially of the agreements effected there between the Moses delegation and Department of Interior officials. One agreement stipulated that, if Moses and his Indians removed to the Colville and engaged in farming, the government would guarantee them equal rights and protection with all the other Indians of the reservation and assistance in carrying out the terms of the agreement made.

Although American society was entering the industrial age at that time, agriculture was the industry into which Indian Office personnel believed the Indians could best fit. It did not matter that they had no inclination to become farmers. Among various professionals whom the government provided under the agreements were farmers whose difficult task it was to remake Indians into American agrarians. To induce Moses to move to the Colville, the government appeased him with a thousand-dollar anunity. Delays in receiving the money caused him much anxiety, as did the deductions that sutlers at various posts demanded for changing his drafts into cold cash. Certain concessions were also made to Tonasket and Sarsopkin. A year after it was drawn up, the Moses removal agreement was approved by Congress on July 4, 1884. Skolaskin burned with anger that the same Moses, who had fought Americans in his early years, had signed a perfidious contract with those same Americans to invade his lands. Moses' participation in those early wars conjured up in Smohalla's mind stories of his Columbia Sinkiuse predecessors raiding and killing defenseless Sanpoil villagers.

Skolaskin's isolationism was like a two-edged sword. It gave him an edge of independence from the threats of the Indian Office, yet it deprived him of knowledge of the federal government's moves and motives. He thought it better to have contact with the military, who sometimes were called in to reinforce Indian Office decrees, than to have contact with the office that had issued the decrees in the first place. He knew enough English to communicate his concerns to the soldiers.

Accompanied by delegations of his people, Skolaskin began traveling routinely across Johnny George Mountain and the Columbia River to Fort Spokane. That post, established in 1880 as Camp Spokane and renamed a fort on January 12, 1882, overlooked the confluence of the Columbia and Spokane rivers. It served as an information center for Skolaskin not only to learn what the government was planning for Moses and his people but also to find out what else was transpiring in the outside world. He could have learned much at the Colville Agency, but would never go there. On February 9, 1885, he was at Fort Spokane talking with its commandant, Colonel Henry C. Merriam. During his meeting he berated Moses with all the bitterness of Dreamer-Prophets towards hereditary chiefs, stating his opposition to the government's supplying Moses and Tonasket with mills, fearful that such nontraditional things would ensure Moses permanent residency on the Colville.[15] Viewing Skolaskin's jealousy as an Indian Office problem, Merriam wrote the Colville agent, Sidney Waters, at his new Chewelah headquarters, which was south of Fort Colville in the Colville River valley. Merriam suggested that by the spring thaw, or earlier, Waters should meet with the various chiefs. In a March 3, 1885, letter to Indian Commissioner Hiram Price, Waters reported that Skolaskin's Indians said that Moses had twice sold his lands—first, those of his birth and then the Columbia Reservation that the government in Washington, D.C., had given him—and that he would even sell his claim to the Colville if Washington offered him enough money.[16]

Waters followed up Merriam's suggestion by meeting with Skolaskin at Fort Spokane in early April, 1885. He believed that he had arrived none too soon, as Skolaskin, "a fanatic of the worst kind," was trying to arouse the Indians to prevent any building for Moses. "He belongs to a tribe called the Dreamers," wrote Waters, "and has a way of working on the minds of his hearers exciting them to do what if they were let alone they would not attempt."[17] The Prophet found little comfort in confronting Waters, who reaffirmed the government's intention to settle Moses' people on the Colville and to build saw and grist mills and a schoolhouse on the Nespelem River. As if that were not enough bad news for Skolaskin, the agent informed him that the government would also furnish them cattle, wagons, and implements. To quiet the agitated Prophet, Waters sought to intimidate him by accusing him of exerting a bad influence on his people by encouraging them to drink and gamble. Waters also threatened to hold the Prophet in irons at the fort if he did not "behave himself." In his own defense, Skolaskin maintained that, try as he might, he could never stop his people from drinking and gambling as long as Moses encouraged his people in those practices.[18] The Prophet saw better than did his imbibing rival the pernicious effects of liquor, which improvised some of the Moses' people. Moses would later tell an Indian agent that white men made the whiskey, and as long as it was made, people would drink it.[19] As for the gambling charges, Waters must have known that such activities had long been practiced not only by the Sanpoils but by every tribe of his agency.

In late April or early May, 1885, accompanied by several of his people, Skolaskin again met with Waters. This time he apparently was resigned, although nonetheless bitter, that he had not been sent for to accompany Moses' delegation to the national capital. As though trying to save face in a difficult situation, Skolaskin and his delegation told the agent that, had they been called into council at an earlier time to discuss the Moses settlement, they would have acceded to it. When they left the agent, they promised not to obstruct the building of the mills and the schoolhouse. Waters warned the Indian commissioner that they would annoy Moses in any other way they could.[20]

In May, 1885, Joseph and his Nez Percé remnant were sent to the Colville Reservation from their Indian Territory exile. To Skolaskin the arrival of the ninety-two adults, 12 children, and 14 infants added insult to the injury of the coming of Moses, the Nez Percés' benefactor. Military officials at Fort Spokane kept a wary eye on the conflict that appeared to be approaching between the Moses-Joseph people and the native Sanpoils. On May 11, 1886, Colonel J. S. Fletcher, the Fort Spokane commandant, reported that Sanpoils living at Whitestone and on the Sanpoil River had appropriated ten head of cattle from the issue for Joseph's people. Apparently, the man under contract to furnish them the beef had obtained it from "a man named Friedlander," who got it from the reservation "without authority" from those to whom it belonged.[21] In October, Major J. Ford Kent, Fourth Infantry, commanding Fort Spokane, reported Chief Joseph's complaints of "incursions and theft" by Cut-Nose, a Sanpoil Indian, and others.[22] Kent also reported on April 1, 1887, that Skolaskin encouraged his followers to order the Moses Indians off their lands whenever the Moses Indians tried to occupy them.[23]

Indian Inspector Frank C. Armstrong reported that Skolaskin would not permit Joseph to build houses or establish farms and that he blocked the efforts of agency farmers to settle the Nez Percés on the land. Because of Skolaskin's disregard of governmental authority, warned Armstrong, a military force would be required to stop this "smart fellow" who knew he had the best of Joseph and his people. The problem could be solved, the inspector believed, by placing on the spot a military force of sufficient strength to overawe Skolaskin and his people. If they further interfered, Armstrong warned, Skolaskin should be put in the Fort Spokane guardhouse for a month or two to break his influence. Like other officials, especially those who visited the troubled reservation from outside the region, Armstrong recommended that the agency headquarters be moved from Chewelah to the reservation to make the latter easier to govern and control.[24]

The unpleasant and immediate tasks of settling the Nez Percés in the Nespelem valley and trying to placate Skolaskin and his people about their coming fell to Agent Rickard Gwydir, appointed in May, 1887. Before the Nez Percés came, Gwydir had warned Commissioner John D. C. Atkins that the Sanpoils would bitterly oppose their arrival as they had that of Moses' people, and the agent privately believed the government would ignore his warnings.[25] Meanwhile, on the Nez Percé Reservation there were indictments out against Joseph for murder and warrants for his arrest. Among the Christian, "praying" Nez Percés there were those who regarded Joseph's people as troublemakers, and they were happy to see these "long haired ones" settled away from their reservation.

Apprised of the explosive situation on the Colville, Atkins instructed Gwydir to request Colonel Kent to dispatch a troop detail to the Nespelem valley, since Skolaskin had told his people what God would do in the way of punishment should the president give their lands to Joseph's band.[26] Kent detailed two infantry companies and cavalry to assist Gwydir in placing the Nez Percés in the Nespelem valley. The colonel's instructions were to provide every possible protection to Joseph and his band, to warn all others against interfering with them, and should that warning be ignored, "to promptly arrest offenders and send them in irons to Fort Spokane."[27] The troops moved out from the fort under the pretence of practicing maneuvers in order not to arouse Sanpoil suspicions. Meanwhile, Gwydir crossed the Columbia from agency headquarters to a Sanpoil village.

From Gwydir's pen we have a record of a council held on July 21 in a craterlike enclosure which was nearly surrounded by a solid rock wall and lighted by two resinous wood fires, which were attended and kept brightly burning by elderly women. Skolaskin sat on a raised, pelt-covered platform, flanked by his two principal subordinates. In front of them were fifty hand-picked warriors, who were "decked out in all their barbaric bravery, war bonnets, beaded and silk-worked suits of buckskin . . . all the paraphernalia belonging to a well-dressed warrior . . . a formidable looking band of warriors." Their appearance belied the peaceful disposition of their tribe. Skolaskin seated Gwydir and his two companions next to his "latest and favorite squaw." Apparently there was no pipe smoking though that ritual usually initiated such meetings. Skolaskin immediately got down to the business at hand, stating that the land had been Sanpoil-Nespelem territory from the beginning and it would be until the end of time. "When God made dry land," he declaimed, "when there was water, it was our land, and here our forefathers hunted the cougar, bear and deer, ages and ages before the white-face race was known." Alluding to his Prophet predecessors, he continued:

> Our medicine men prophesied to our forefathers of the coming of a new race with white faces like the snow, and warned us never to injure them, but to help them and be their friends. The white man of to-day is the race our medicine men prophesied were to come, and we have lived up to their advice, and have always been friends to the whites, and our boast that a white man's blood has never been shed by a San Poil is true.[28]

Skolaskin asked why the white race should want to take Sanpoil lands and give them to their enemies. He appeared to be alluding to Moses and Joseph, both of whom had warred against the United States. Perhaps with these arch rivals in mind, he emphasized that certain Indians had warred against the president, murdering white settler families, burning their houses and stealing their cattle – and the president, instead of punishing them for their evil deeds, took care of them by placing them on Sanpoil-Nespelem lands where they became "fat, lazy and good-for-nothing." Skolaskin unsuccessfully tried to wring from Gwydir a confession that the president had done wrong. His final words were: "The cougar, the wolf and the bear will fight for their young, and why not the Indian? Does he care less for his offspring than the wild beast does for its young?" Then he sat down, exhausted. His followers approved his words by saying, "Onah, onah sha" ("Yes, we understand").

Masking his anxiety, Gwydir rose like a debater for a rebuttal to explain the traditional U.S. government position that it was foolish to think the Sanpoils or any other people could hold large portions of land without putting them to use for themselves, and for others. "I say to you," he declared, "they [the whites] have come to stay." Trying to get them to join the bandwagon, he told the assemblage that other important chiefs, among the Spokanes and Okanagons, as well as Moses, had received protection and gifts such as mills and schools by taking the president's advice. Emulating the picturesque Indian oratory, Gwydir concluded with the following warning: "As well might a few trees on the mountain try to stop the avalanche as for you to attempt to oppose the will of the Great Father."

With those words Gwydir closed the meeting, and he departed for the Nespelem valley on the following morning, July 22, believing that his words were "not well received."[29] About twenty of Skolaskin's men, joined by several others from Whitestone and other Sanpoil villages, accompanied the agent to the Nespelem, where he was met by about two hundred Sanpoil-Nespelems and the Moses-Joseph people. Threatened by the tense situation, he sent runners to the troops that were now in the area, explaining his predicament and asking them to hurry to his aid. Increasing his anxiety was an ominous report from his interpreters, who were circulating among Indian councils on the evening of July 23, that the Indians were in a nasty mood. The next morning Gwydir postponed the showdown meeting for a few hours, telling Indian envoys that he was not quite ready to parley with them. This was a delaying tactic to give the troops time to move closer to the council site. The Sanpoil impatience at his response moved him to remark later that, had the Sanpoil-Nespelem and Moses-Joseph factions fought to the finish, it "would be like the fight of the Kilkenny cats, nothing left but the head dresses."

Finally, as noontime neared, a nervous Gwydir called the council to order at the government mill on the Nespelem River. From his position in a doorway, he conducted the proceedings through his interpreter. He directed the factions to position themselves so that Joseph and his Nez Percés sat at his right and Moses and his people on his left, and Skolaskin and his followers directly in front of him. His opening statement that Joseph and his people were to be permanently located on the reservation by order of the president evoked an immediate shouting match, with the Moses-Joseph people crying "Origh!" ("Yes!") and Skolaskin's followers exclaiming "Tah!" ("No!"). When quiet was restored, Skolaskin managed to rise to his feet shouting vituperations against the president, whom he called a thief for giving lands to murderers such as Moses and Joseph—an allusion to their previous wars against the United States. Gwydir interrupted this blast against the president by warning that, should Skolaskin persist in maligning the American leader, the agent would stop his talk altogether. Skolaskin then shifted his indictments to Moses, saying little about Joseph. Possibly he hoped to drive a wedge between them.

Moses rose to explain how he had helped his people by taking what the government gave them and how he was cooperating with the United States in return. Then he confessed that at one time he had been as ignorant as a child, not understanding the ways of the "Great Chief" (the president), but now, enlightened like Joseph, he understood, and henceforth he and his people would do as the president wished. He said that he was glad his people were not ruled like the Sanpoils, whose Dreamer chief "could not make a talk without frothing at the mouth like a dog" and, moreover, was not as good as one. His cutting remarks sparked immediate boiling anger among Skolaskin's people, but because of a command from their now-silent leader, they made no move.

Afraid that further talk from Moses would worsen the already tense situation, Gwydir silenced him. Such inflammatory words not only might have led to open conflict but might have turned the agent into "the goat, for the [Interior] department would have one." At the critical moment, a bugle sounded. With traditional cavalry flair, Lieutenant Curtis Bushrod Hoppin rode up with an advance guard, ordering his men to picket their mounts and align themselves in front of the mill. Gwydir believed that the Indians had been unaware of the presence of the troops who had followed a circuitous route to Nespelem. They had crossed the Columbia to the reservation farther downstream on "Wild Goose Bill" Condit's (or Condon's) ferry. Those Indians who could not see what was transpiring, heard, in Gwydir's words, "the military click as breech of the carbine was closed." Gwydir and Hoppin entered the mill. The agent closed the council, believing that the hastily departing Skolaskin had been outgeneraled.[30] On July 25 and 26, accompanied by Hoppin, but without a military escort, Gwydir located Joseph and his band on 160-acre family plots. Thanks to the presence of the troops to reinforce Gwydir's policy of firm diplomacy, a crisis had passed—but for Skolaskin and his Dreamer Sanpoil-Nespelems, only for the time being.[31]

14

A Tale of Two Prisons

> My heart is broken and I want to go home to
> my wife and my three children.
> — *Skolaskin in prison cell to newspaper reporter.*

In a January 25, 1888, letter to Colville Agent Rickard Gwydir, Commissioner of Indian Affairs, John D. C. Atkins, echoing the agent's low-key response to Skolaskin's wrath, asked him to tell the Prophet that he was pleased that evil reports about Skolaskin were groundless. The commissioner also requested Gwydir to encourage Skolaskin to retain his reputation for intelligence and good sense as an example to his people and to assure Skolaskin that his problems could be solved by pursuing the "civilized" life and encouraging his people in achieving that goal.[1] The commissioner was obviously trying to mitigate the ill-feelings of Skolaskin and his people by dealing with them in a positive manner. On November 21, 1887, Gwydir had reported to the commissioner the Sanpoils' negative reaction to rumors of the opening of the Colville Reservation to white settlement. Yet the agent had expressed the opinion that Skolaskin was "too smart" to war against whites, because he had frequently associated with them. The "cheapest way" to change his attitude, reported Gwydir, was to allow Skolaskin to go to Washington, D.C.[2] In an April 14, 1888, letter the agent restated his opinion that officials would be wise to invite Skolaskin there to unruffle his feathers and soothe his hurt pride over the settling of Moses' and Joseph's people on his lands.[3] Like other officials, Gwydir perhaps believed that in the capital Skolaskin would be impressed by the power of the government and the endless westward stream of whites, whose coming it would seem to be as futile to prevent as it would be to stop the Columbia River.[4]

In early March, Gwydir met Skolaskin in council at the agency headquarters, which was now removed from Chewelah to the left bank of the Columbia at the mouth of the Spokane River, across the latter river from Fort Spokane. Skolaskin was outnumbered in council by Moses and other Colville Reservation chiefs who wanted him out of the way; they stated in essence that they would submit to the wishes of the government. Untouched by Moses' repeated confession that his "hands had been dipped in blood; that his arms had been bloody to the elbow, but Washington had made them clean," Skolaskin interrupted the proceedings by talking with Gwydir. After leveling verbal blasts at Moses, he confessed that he and his people were all alone – different from the others, with whom they had nothing in common – that if the others wanted to accept government aid, that was well and good, but he wanted nothing from the government or anyone else. Ironically, by the new year, 1889, according to an Indian inspector, the Sanpoils had "progressed" further than had Joseph's people, who had received rations, clothing, and agricultural implements from the government.[5]

Gwydir suggested in the March, 1888, council that the chiefs establish a court. Even Joseph acceded to the suggestion, but Skolaskin responded with a resounding "No!" He feared that such an institution would replace his own law-and-order system with puppets whose strings the government officials would pull at will. Later in the day Skolaskin told his people that, should the agent put him in jail, he would cause a wind to blow its doors open and destroy the building, and if shipped off by train to confinement, as the other Indian leaders wished him to be, the Almighty would stop the wheels when he, Skolaskin, commanded the cars to stop. Should the agent put him in jail, he would cause a wind to come up and blow its doors open and destroy the building. When agency officials learned of his words, they dispatched their Indian policemen to catch him and let him fulfill his boastings. They were too late. He had crossed the Columbia River to the temporary safety of his homeland.[6]

On October 29, 1889, the commissioner, basing his report on that of the Colville agent, Hal Cole, who had assumed his duties on May 27, catalogued complaints of the chiefs that with his own laws Skolaskin had opposed establishing an agencywide jail and had imposed cruel and oppressive penalties on his people for trivial offenses.[7] In the floodless aftermath after the stockpiling of whipsawed lumber to build the unfinished ark, Skolaskin had found a new power symbol in his jail at Whitestone, the most notorious feature of his penal system. He had forced men and women to dig the hole in the ground that was its main feature. Southern Okanagon informants related how, like an Egyptian taskmaster, he stood over the workers, one of whom, like the biblical Moses, killed one of Skolaskin's overseeing policemen.[8]

The side poles of the windowless jail were planted in the ground and covered with sawn boards to form the stockade. Of the two sections, one atop the other, the upper level was for the punishment of lesser offenses, and the lower for more serious wrongdoers. Inmates underwent no semblance of a hearing or trial and had little more than a starvation diet. Confinement was mainly on Skolaskin's charges. The offenses ranged from those minor in nature to more serious ones such as adultery, philandering, stealing, and intoxication.[9] Skolaskin seems to have had some success in suppressing drinking and gambling among his people, but it was commonly believed that he confined men on the slightest pretext so that he could take their wives and daughters.[10] He had a double standard in sexual matters – one for himeself and one for his people.

Considering the makeshift nature of his jail, it is a small wonder that escapes from it were frequent. Once a woman threw a long pole into it to allow some prisoners to escape. To assure that wrongdoers received the punishment that he believed they deserved, Skolaskin dispatched his policemen to search them out and return them to the crude place of confinement. When a woman ran away from her husband to the Okanogan River country, his policemen returned her, tied her to a pole, and whipped her. Fortunately, she was not confined to the jail.[11] Unable to administer his judicial system by himself, because of his physical condition, the Prophet depended on his assistants, such as Ka-osalikin and Celumkinlalalak.[12] The latter would soon turn against Skolaskin.

According to a July 9, 1905, article in the *Seattle Post Intelligencer*, Skolaskin's undoing began at his jail when a Sanpoil man, failing to obtain a legal divorce from the Indian agent, appealed to Skolaskin, who supposedly advised killing the woman. According to the article, the resulting murder led to the Prophet's own jailing.[13] A more credible explanation, however, centers around events at his little prison after two inmates had escaped and one of them, Sqwielumpquen, returned to his home nearby. The other escapee, Qotalakias, fled southward. Possibly the two had been unable to purchase their release in the customary Indian fashion – with horses. Moses lodged many complaints that Skolaskin arrested Sinkiuse people and made them pay for their release with these animals. When Skolaskin discovered that his prisoners had escaped, he assembled his policemen to run them down. They succeeded in capturing Sqwielumpquen, whom Skolaskin ordered tied and returned to jail.

At that time Sqwielumpqen's cousin Ginnamonteesah, who was Moses' nephew, went with a gun after one of Skolaskin's policemen, the powerful Kannumsahwickssa, who had been the one most responsible for the jailing of the two escapees. In an ensuing altercation, Ginnamonteesah struck Kannumsahwickssa in the

face. The latter struck back with a scythe, barely missing his attacker. Then, on July 14, 1889, Kannumsahwickssa shot Ginnamonteesah dead, hastily buried his body, and returned to Whitestone to report the deed to Skolaskin, who took no action. Two
friends of the deceased exhumed the body and took it to Whitestone for reburial. While they were there, they broke down the jail
door, released prisoner relatives of the victim, and told them of his
fate. With no matches to fire the jail, the rescuers ripped off its
roof, allowing the other prisoners to escape.[14]

After a hearing before government officials, Kannumsahwickssa
was released. The United States commissioner at Spokane Falls refused to issue warrants for his arrest, stating that the case properly
belonged to the Territory of Washington, but the district attorney
said that he wanted nothing to do with this "inconsequential" affair,
since it was a case of one Indian killing another. In what may have
been a different case, Skolaskin was subsequently jailed at Fort
Spokane. He was released on September 4 on the condition that he
arrest and deliver up within four days an Indian who recently had
committed murder at a Colville River mission. After failing to meet
the condition, Skolaskin was rearrested, then released.[15]

Skolaskin's control over his people was the last straw frustrating
government officials in their efforts to "civilize" and assimilate them
with the other peoples on the Colville Reservation. Interior and
War Department authorities agreed that such a dangerous leader
should be banished from the reservation. Unfortunately for the
Prophet, the two departments, although they sometimes worked at
cross-purposes, were in accord about the necessity of his removal,
and initiative for such action came from anti-Skolaskin Indians as
well as the U.S. government. At Lake Chelan, southwest of the Colville Reservation, Moses and Joseph in September, 1889, unburdened to General John Gibbon, the commander of the Department of the Columbia, their complaints about the Prophet, whom
they accused of stealing Indian livestock.[16] On September 29, Gibbon fired off a letter to Agent Cole, suggesting that he see to it that
Skolaskin be sent to "some distant point where he can no longer
exercise his pernicious influence over his followers in interfering
with the designs of the Government."[17]

On October 9, Cole dispatched a letter to General Gibbon at Vancouver Barracks, expressing full agreement that Skolaskin should
be removed and assuring the general that the Interior Department
would concur in the action, which he claimed would have benefitted the Indians had it been taken long before. On October 10,
Cole dispatched to the commissioner correspondence that he had
received from Gibbon and Kent relative to Skolaskin, whom he
described as "a very troublesome and disagreeable Indian" totally

unfit to live among the Indians of the Colville Reservation. He reminded the commissioner that this was his third letter with reference to the murder of an Indian by a Sanpoil. Cole had written the first letter on July 29, just fifteen days after the murder of Ginnamonteesah of Moses' band by Skolaskin's policeman, Kannumsahwickssa. Cole wrote that the murder would not have occurred (to use Gibbon's words) without Skolaskin's "pernicious influence."[18]

In an October 29 letter to the secretary of the interior, Commissioner T. J. Morgan explained Skolaskin's judicial system, including his jail, his court, his police, and the payment of fines in horses, and he reiterated that the American legal system legitimized the federal government's action in sending Skolaskin off to confinement. The justification for doing so, wrote Morgan, came under section 2149 of the *Revised Statutes*, from which reference had been made in the case of *United States* v. *Crook* (5 Dill 465), which held that the commissioner of Indian Affairs, with the approval of the secretary of the interior, could cause to be removed from Indian reservations all persons who were there in violation of the law, or whose presence was deterimental to the peace and welfare of the Indians. The secretary therefore recommended that Skolaskin be imprisoned until he was thoroughly disciplined and had been taught to respect and obey government officials.[19] One would think that he should have been able to cope with the injustice of not having access to fair legal procedures since he had meted out such to his own prisoners.

On October 30, Acting Secretary of the Interior George Chandler wrote the secretary of war enclosing papers from the Indian commissioner, who complained that Skolaskin was "a most dangerous and turbulent element among the Indians" and suggested his banishment under military custody.[20] On November 21 the Prophet was arrested at his place near Snuke'ilt by a lieutenant and fifteen privates of the Second Infantry out of Fort Spokane, who brought with them a mule on which to carry their prisoner back to the fort.[21] On the following day, guarded by a detachment commanded by a captain of the Fourth Infantry, Skolaskin was conducted to Vancouver Barracks. The detachment arrived there on October 24 and turned its prisoner over to the post guard for his journey to incarceration in the military prison on Alcatraz Island in San Francisco Bay.[22]

Skolaskin had prophesied that the late fall chill would turn to cold and deep snow to stop the train carrying him away. It was not severe enough to do so, but the winter, one of the coldest on record, brought much suffering to the Colville Reservation Indians and the loss of many of their livestock. On the day when Skolaskin left for Vancouver, his wife came to the fort complaining to Major

Kent that she and her helpless children were left with no support other than a few supplies and four or five dollars that her husband had left behind. She said that she wanted to visit Skolaskin, but would not consent to absent herself permanently from her people. In a November 23 letter to the adjutant general at Vancouver, Kent suggested that, after Skolaskin's people were settled, to assure his wife and her people of his safety, she and the children should be taken for a time to Fort Spokane and put under the care of one of its Indian scouts, one of whom was Skolaskin's brother-in-law. Kent thought that, in "common justice and for its effect upon the tribe," the government should provide rations to support the "helpless" family.[23]

More than the welfare of Skolaskin's family was at stake in his absence. There was a possibility that his followers, especially those on the periphery of his cult, would lend support either to the tribe's traditional chieftains or to rising, aspiring progressive leaders. It was also possible that both groups of leaders, emulating Skolaskin's arch foe, Moses, would cooperate with government officials and permit their people to adopt white ways. This might seem a better alternative to them than submission to Skolaskin's restrictive code, authoritarian actions, and domineering will.

The commandant of the Alcatraz Island military prison Major W. L. Haskin, First Artillery, in an April 6, 1890, letter to the assistant adjutant general of the Department of California, San Francisco, stated that Skolaskin, then in the fourth month and twentieth day of his confinement, was being held until military officials were assured that he would cause no further trouble. Skolaskin, he wrote, had requested an application to the proper authorities to allow him to return home, claiming that he had been charged because he had made his people work (as the government wished them to do). Haskins stated that Skolaskin objected to the Moses-Joseph card-playing, whiskey-drinking people and that he denied the charges that he had maintained a jail, encouraged the stealing and killing of livestock, and connived at murder. Furthermore, stated Haskin, Skolaskin said that he should be allowed to confront his accusers and be heard in his own defense. Haskin stated that Skolaskin's physical debility and mental makeup precluded his doing physical harm; in short, that any good from detaining him had already been accomplished.[24]

In a May 4 letter to the assistant adjutant general of the Department of Columbia, Major Kent stated that, in following their tradition of choosing hereditary chiefs, the Sanpoils had thrown their support to Celumkinlalalak, under whose rule they had "settled down" and "bettered themselves." His statement possibly indicated that Skolaskin's return home could upset Celumkinlalalak's chieftaincy. In his letter Kent told of an April 22 meeting at Fort Spokane at which that chief had requested aid from the government and had promised to encourage his people to avail themselves of its services and work their farms.[25] This Sanpoil disposition to receive goods and services is interesting since as recently as the first of the previous year (1889) under Skolaskin's influence they had refused such offers. One Indian inspector reported on January 17 of that year that their steady advancement was due not to government aid but to pride in greater accomplishment than that of neighboring tribesmen such as Joseph's Nez Percés, and from fear that if they showed no advancement the government would force them to it.[26]

Kent assured his correspondents that Sanpoil promises of cooperation with government officials had come not from Celumkinlalalak alone but from eight influential and apparently previously covert opponents of Skolaskin. Having held their tongues in the Prophet's presence, they now felt free to reveal their true feelings toward this one whom they now called an evil man. It had been Skolaskin's practice to seek frequently votes of confidence, albeit while pressuring his people. His absence prevented this practice and further stimulated their independence from him. In the emerging anti-Skolaskin faction was Long Bill, who said that their erstwhile leader had probably done enough against the "Washington D.C. Law" to suffer the death penalty. Considering such sentiments, Kent thought it risky to return Skolaskin, not only for the sake of the Sanpoils but also for that of the Moses-Joseph people, who might feel the brunt of his wrath on returning home. Kent wrote: "Skolaskins whole history is a bad one and his influence for bad, has, up to the time of his removal, been very great. He is called the 'dreamer' and pretends to have communication with the Spirit land and has given messages from thence with promised indication of signs, which have been singularly fulfilled; and hence his influence over his Indians and the increase of his following, which was constant. . . ."[27] General Gibbon believed the favorable progress made by the Sanpoils and their opposition to Skolaskin's rule could be upset by his return home. On May 8 he wrote that "it would be the worst possible step" to return the Prophet to the Colville Reservation.[28]

Unaware of the correspondence stretching from the Pacific to the Atlantic coast pertaining to his confinement, Skolaskin was left to ponder and brood about not only his own fate but also that of his flock back home. In conversing with a military convict, Clarence S. Duvall, he claimed that Moses and Joseph had conspired with others to usurp his authority and estrange him from his people, leading them into debauchery, drunkenness, gambling, and general dissoluteness. By contrast, he explained that he had pursued their best interests and welfare by instilling in them the principles of temperance, honesty, industry and frugality. His real crippling, he implied, came from those who had thwarted his efforts by having him unlawfully confined much in the same manner of a bear that the Colville trader, Herman Friedlander, once kept chained at his store.[29]

Skolaskin's lamentations fell on official ears that were, if not deaf to them, hard of hearing, such as those of General Nelson A. Miles, who now commanded the Military Division of the Pacific. In a May 23, 1890, statement forwarded to the adjutant general of the army, Miles admitted that Skolaskin had been treated unjustly, but he suggested that, if his influence was detrimental to the Colville Indians, he should be removed to some other reservation.[30] On July 10, Acting Adjutant General Samuel Breck, in correspondence with the commandant of both the Department of the Columbia and the Division of the Pacific, General Gibbon, explained the Prophet's application to return home. He also explained that it was the view of the major general commanding the army that the prisoner should be treated as kindly as circumstances would permit and the rigors of confinement should be relaxed, but that he should not be returned to the Colville, where he had "created trouble," until such time as its agent and the commandant of the Department of the Columbia believed such a return would not cause a recurrence of the difficulty necessitating his removal.[31]

In accordance with the view of the secretary of war that the rigors of Skolaskin's confinement should be relaxed, General Gibbon reported that, "The good effects of the removal of the Indian 'Skolaskin' from the Colville Reservation are marked, and the commanding officer of Fort Spokane reports that he has heard of no difficulties such as 'Skolaskin' caused, since his arrest." Gibbon added that as "a disquieting element on the reservation his removal was deemed essential to the welfare of the rest of the Indians, and it is recommended that he be not returned to his tribe so long as the present condition of affairs exists." Gibbon also added that there was "no desire, however, to treat him with needless severity," suggesting that he be allowed the freedom of Alcatraz Island and, should he desire it, his wife and children be sent to join him.[32]

Back in his homeland there were those who sympathized with Skolaskin's plight, not so much because his incarceration had interrupted and damaged his position but because of the way the government literally and figuratively had railroaded him out of the country. They reasoned that, if it could treat him in such singular fashion, then why could it not treat others the same way? At a large Indian council at the mouth of the Wenatchee River in the summer of 1890 a large number of chiefs from many tribes of the upper interior aired grievances against the government. One complaint aired in council was that the government officials had "stolen" Skolaskin and imprisoned him without explaining their actions to the Indians. The story resurfaced that during Skolaskin's absence a "squawman" had tried to file on his lands in order to take them from their absent owner. The Indians requested that the peripatetic Francis Streamer, who was in attendance, write to their friend General Howard about their various complaints, telling him to send no more soldiers to their lands and demanding that they be treated fairly in the white courts before being punished or imprisoned.[33]

In 1891, Skolaskin's plight had become known outside of army and Indian Office circles thanks to an April 21, 1891, letter from the Alcatraz chaplain, W. H. Pearson, to Herbert Welsh, the corresponding secretary of the Indian Rights Associaton. Pearson's letter was also forwarded to the Indian commissioner on May 5. Pearson believed that Skolaskin would cause no more trouble if he were returned to his home.[34] It may have been through Pearson that Skolaskin's plight came to the attention of the press and the public, or possibly a newspaper article about his incarceration prompted Pearson to action. At any rate, the public became aware of it when the *San Francisco Chronicle* on April 10, 1891, carried a story under headlines that were obviously calculated to stir sympathy among its readers for the unfortunate Prophet: "Chief Skolaskin/A Lonely Indian Prisoner of Alcatraz/Confined Without Hearing or Trial/His Heart Is Breaking and He Wants to Be With His People." In his story the reporter carried a statement by General Gibbon to another newspaper man on the previous day, in which Gibbon sought to defend the government's position regarding their prisoner: "This man was taken to Alcatraz as a prisoner upon my own request, when I was in command of the Department of the Columbia. He is a ward of the nation and not a citizen of the United States, therefore the military authorities, with the consent of the Department of the Interior, have a perfect right to place him where he can do no harm." Since the government by this time dealt with Indians through executive orders that established, removed, or abolished reservations, instead of effecting treaties with sovereign Indian tribes as it had formerly, government officials regarded them as "wards" whom they could control at will. Gibbon refused the reporter a pass to visit Skolaskin to investigate the case. Then, relenting, he sent an accompanying letter to Major Abram C.

Wildrick, the Alcatraz commandant, who instructed an orderly to allow a reporter an uninterrupted interview with the prisoner. Wrote the reporter:

> Down inside the heavy stone walls in the gloomy corridor of the military jail Skolaskin, the Indian chief, was found sitting on a stone step. All of the native nobility which this specimen of the noble red man may have once possessed has evidently left him, for he is now a very crestfallen and mild-mannered creature. His fellow-prisoners, all soldiers, crowded around Skolaskin when he in broken English unfolded his tale of woe to the reporter [who also had visited him the previous day].

To the reporter Skolaskin unburdened the agony of his imprisoned body and soul:

> My heart is broken and I want to go home to my wife and my three children. I am all alone here and no one to talk to and nobody to keep up my spirits. I am lame and cannot walk much, so that the freedom of the island which is given me does not do me much good. I am nearly always in my cell pining for my liberty. I do not know why they keep me here. I never did any harm. One time somebody killed a cow. It wasn't me that did it, but Chief Joseph, who hates me, wrote a paper to the old soldier chief [General Gibbon] at Vancouver, and the next thing I knew I was brought here.[35]

To another Alcatraz official Skolaskin poured out a similar lament: "Why am I confined here? If a white man steals a cow or pony he is tried and sent to jail one year, two year, three years, why not try an Indian and send him to jail if he has done wrong?"[36] He also claimed harassment by a "large black man" who peered through a hole in his cell. Skolaskin thought this a government stratagem to cause him to give up his preaching and his church.[37]

On May 5, 1891, Secretary Welsh and the Indian Rights Association forwarded to the commissioner a letter from Chaplain Pearson and a newspaper clipping of the reporter's interview with Skolaskin.[38] In a May 21 letter to the secretary of the interior, the commissioner recommended that the matter of Skolaskin's release be laid before the War Department for such action as the commandant of the Division of the Pacific should recommend. On July 7 the secretary of war informed the secretary of the interior that it was suggested that their prisoner not be returned until the North Half of the Colville Reservation was officially opened to settlement and the Sanpoils had accepted the opening.[39] On June 15 the Fort Spokane commandant, Colonel Frederick Mears, suggested that it would be foolish to return Skolaskin, considering the highly agitated state of his followers.[40]

Skolaskin sat out the winter of 1891–1892 in a mental fog as thick as that surrounding his rocky prison. As the crisis over the opening of the North Half was passing, and as he was evincing a passive spirit, Agent Cole in a June 4, 1892, correspondence assured the commissioner that he had no objection to Skolaskin's returning home, provided he agreed to conduct himself among the Indians and agency personnel in a "proper manner." Cole apparently hoped that the long absence from his people had worked a great change in Skolaskin.[41]

After the exchange of correspondence between the war and interior departments it was evident by mid-1892 that Skolaskin would soon be returning home on the condition that he sign a pledge to alter his ways. He would have signed such a statement at Alcatraz, but with no interpreter there to inform him of the specifics of what he was signing, the pledge would have to wait until he reached Vancouver. The authorities, believing that their military interpreter, Arthur Chapman, could adequately explain the document to Skolaskin, had the text sent northward to Vancouver. On June 22, 1892, the Prophet put his X on the following statement:

In case the authorities will permit me to return to my people, I promise to obey the Indian agent; to treat the employees of the Agency well and to make no threats against them; also that I will not make any trouble amongst the Indians nor between them and the white people, nor give any advice or talk to the Indians that will make them discontented or not willing to obey the agent.[42]

After that he was on his way home.

15

The Exile Returns: *The Shearing*

I originated a religion. Conditions changed. I
am the only one left. I want to be a Catholic.
—Skolaskin to the Reverend Celestine Caldi, S.J.

Skolaskin approached his homecoming happy to be free from
prison, but angered at Moses and Joseph, whom he blamed as
much as he did government officials for his incarceration. His own
statements indicate that he did not understand the reasons for it.
The opposition of the two chiefs and the accusations of government officials that he had broken some criminal code did not seem
sufficient causes for confining him so long and so far from home.
Although his imprisonment appears to have been initially for
"troublemaking," it was extended for another reason—namely, to
keep him from hindering the smooth implementation of governmental policies regarding the lands of the Colville Reservation. In
the dark of his Alcatraz prison cell he was also much in the dark
about what the government was up to.

On May 1, 1891, the nineteenth month of his imprisonment, a
council was held in the Nespelem valley at the request of visiting
commissioners who were seeking to negotiate with the Indians the
sale of the 1.5 million-acre North Half of the Colville Reservation
for as many dollars. The commissioners agreed that Indians living
and owning improvements there should be permitted to remain
and that they should receive 80-acre allotments, a schoolhouse,
grist and saw mills, a blacksmith shop, and water and hunting
rights on lands held in common. Their Sanpoil-Nespelem spokesman, Posahli, made long-winded, time-consuming speeches in
council, attempting to block the sale of the North Half. The Sanpoil-Nespelem opposition to it caused Moses to chide them for "acting like a lot of fools." Placing one hand above the other to illustrate
his point, he said, "Don't you know that Washington is right on top
of you, and if they want the land they are going to take [it] whether
you are willing or not!"[1]

The Nespelem valley council wore on for three days. Except for the Sanpoil-Nespelems, the other reservation tribes agreed to cede, provided that the purchase price was paid in five annual installments, that eighty-acre allotments were made to Indians wishing to live on the North Half, and that thousand-dollar annuities were granted the chiefs, plus an additional five hundred dollars per year for Moses, Joseph, and Barnaby. For the Sanpoil-Nespelems this added amount recommended for their arch foe Moses and Joseph capped an ignominious transaction.[2] The editor of the *Wilbur* (Wash.) *Register* noted that dissatisfied Indians of the Colville had sent a remonstrance to President Benjamin Harrison relative to the transaction. He wrote, "It is claimed that a majority of the signatures obtained by the commissioners were thro' threats and misrepresentation."[3]

With Skolaskin confined, the government had indeed chosen an opportune time to secure the North Half. In a July, 1891, letter to the secretary of the interior, his war-department counterpart, L. A. Grant, relayed remarks to the commanding general of the Division of the Pacific that it would be wiser if Skolaskin were not allowed to return home, since in the recent council with the commissioners all the members of the Sanpoil tribe had refused to sign the agreement, and because of the warning of Colonel Mears at Fort Spokane that Skolaskin's untimely return would stir discontent and trouble among the people. The commanding general of the Division of the Pacific further advised that, when the ceded portion of the Colville was opened to settlement and Skolaskin's Indians had "practically accepted the new condition of things," then Skolaskin could be returned home without any concern that he would harm arrangements there.[4] The commanding general also stated that he assumed from the report of the medical officer at Alcatraz that Skolaskin had suffered no physical or mental harm from his confinement. No physical or mental harm? Such would hardly have been the case of the badly crippled Skolaskin, much depressed by his imprisonment.

Although that May, 1891, agreement between the Indians of the Colville and the visiting commissioners was never ratified, an act of July 1, 1892 (27 Stat. 62), at the time of Skolaskin's return, restored the North Half of the reservation to the public domain by presidential proclamation on October 10, 1900. On December 1, 1905, 350 of an estimated 551 adult Indians living on the Colville would sign what was known as the McLaughlin Agreement (for Major James McLaughlin), relinquishing to the United States all Indian rights, title, and interest to lands within the Diminished Colville Reservation, or the South Half, provided that eighty-acre allotments were made to each Indian having tribal rights on the confine. The 1891 agreement had provided that the Indians be paid $1.5 million for the North Half that was restored to the public domain by the July 1, 1892, act. When allotting was completed on the North Half, 660 tribesmen received a total of 51,653 acres, leaving 1,449,268 open to the settlement.[5]

The Fort Spokane commandant reported that no disturbances had occured on the Colville during the absence of Skolaskin, whom he described as a "disquieting element" whose removal he "deemed essential to the welfare of the rest of the Indians."[6] On his return, discovering that drastic changes on the reservation had been effected behind his back, Skolaskin condemned the Indians who had had any part in what he believed to be a perfidious transaction. During that summer of 1892 he was in the Okanogan River country inciting its Indians against it. His crusade there was of little avail, for it was opposed by his latest Catholic nemesis, the Reverend Etienne de Rougé, S.J., who, in a September 16, 1892, letter requested Agent Cole to tell Skolaskin to "mind his own business" and not excite "our" Indians as he had in former years.[7] De Rougé also wished no opposition to his mission from Suiepkine, Moses, or any other chiefs, be they Dreamers or traditionalists.

During Skolaskin's absence his flock received the ministrations of two of his disciple chiefs, Umtosoolow and Charlie Skmoautkin. The latter reportedly prayed three times on Sundays.[8] One informant claimed, however, that Umtosoolow changed his religion during the Prophet's absence.[9] Verne Ray was of the opinion that when Skolaskin returned home he urged his people to disband, confessing his religion to have been false, after which he assumed a traditional shamanistic role.[10] The presence of opponents among his own people, who took advantage of his absence to vent their pent-up feelings against him, may have been one reason he jettisoned his role as Prophet-leader, if indeed he did abandon that role so suddenly.

Just as the earthquake had propelled Skolaskin to prominence, it appears that his leadership was diminished during his imprisonment although he subsequently remained a force in Sanpoil-Nespelem affairs. He continued to be adamant against government officials and refused their offers of aid. His people continued to subsist on traditional foods and produce from their small farm patches, plus goods that they purchased with gold dust received from Chinese miners in exchange for beef from their herds. Disregarding Skolaskin's admonition against theft, some of his people appropriated gold from the "Celestials," perhaps rationalizing their action on the grounds that it had been extracted from their own lands.[11]

Skolaskin's loosened spiritual hold was not the only problem he faced on returning home. The extremely cold winter of 1892–1893, like that of the time of his departure for Alcatraz, left Sanpoil horses easy prey for wolves.[12] As he resumed his practice for accumulating livestock, he would have been among those suffering the effects of the cold weather.[13] To add to his other woes, his wife, in December, 1894, ran off with one whom the editor of the *Wilbur Register* described as "some handsomer, if more humbly titled brave." Skolaskin dared not seek help from the Colville agent, but he told his troubles to Mr. Short, the postmaster in the town of Wilbur on the Big Bend of the Columbia. Short wrote several letters inquiring about the missing spouse.[14]

When what informants called his "last wife," Quinspeetsa, was about to leave him, he pleaded with her: "No, I need your help. I need somebody to get my firewood and cook for me." When she insisted on leaving, he threatened to kill himself. He went a short distance from his house, fired his gun in the air, and lay as though wounded. When she did not come to his aid, he picked himself up and returned to his house to discover that she had taken a blanket roll and ridden off on a horse.[15]

On August 23, 1891, while Skolaskin was at Alcatraz, the editor of the *Wilbur Register* had written: "Across the Columbia on the reservation all is quiet and peaceful except for a lively dispute over the building of a sawmill. The government had decided that nothing would do the Sans Poil tribe half as much good as a sawmill with a white man to run it and teach the savages how to build frame houses instead of tepees of their ancestors. But somehow the San Poils don't see it that way."[16] The Sanpoils did not oppose wooden houses as such, especially in winter, but they did not want the government to build them. Shortly after the turn of the century they began replacing their log houses with ones made of lumber, which they obtained from private mills that were springing up in the area.

Such developments are further proof that Skolaskin and his Sanpoils were never averse to business dealings with nongovernment whites. Where formerly they had purchased goods directly from Walla Walla or indirectly through "Virginia Bill" Covington, they now transacted business with other merchants in the Big Bend. In 1899, for example, they sold salmon from the Sanpoil River to a white man of the area for ten cents apiece.[17] They also worked for white farmers along the Columbia left bank and sold produce to the whites. They also traveled to the Yakima valley to pick hops and buy goods at stores there.[18]

Whereas Sanpoil transactions with whites had been largely on the latter's turf, in the 1890's whites began invading the reservation to conduct their business. When the North Half was to be opened to mineral entry on February 20, 1896, Wilbur merchants and other town leaders promoted the Sanpoil River valley on the South

Half as the best route to the North Half mines. Some Sanpoils cooperated with the gold seekers by building for a fee a wagon road running fifteen miles up the Sanpoil River, and for a time tribal members served as guides and furnished miners with dressed beef. In anticipation of a mining rush three ferryboats began crossing the Columbia to the Sanpoil River in March, 1896, and by April a ferry had been installed to transport miners across the Columbia to Skolaskin's Whitestone Village, from which they took the well-worn Indian trail westward to the Sanpoil River. Shortly thereafter numerous ferryboats crossed the Columbia to reservation points. In defiance to federal law, many of them were run by whites who acted as "dummy" owners using Indians to operate the craft.[19] The problem of the invading miners with their roads and diggings became more acute for the Sanpoils before the July 1,1898, opening of the South Half to mineral entry.[20] The Sanpoils (without waiting for agency police to patrol their lands) took matters into their own hands by pulling up miners' stakes after one of many false rumors of the opening of the South Half to mineral entry; they were "in no good humor" as sooners staked mineral claims to their farms and gardens.[21] After the South Half opening miners brazenly took Sanpoil women and cattle and made agreements with the Indians that they had no intention of keeping. In their haste to extract gold, they dug up Sanpoil burials and blasted out fishing places.

With such encroachments, it was clear that the historic association of Skolaskin's Sanpoils with nongovernment whites had taken an unfortunate turn indeed. The weakening of Skolaskin's hold over the Sanpoil-Nespelems may have spared him involvement in violent reactions to white incursions. The latter caused the editor of the *Wilbur Register* to write an epitaph for the native cultures that were falling before the restless "superiority" of his own race:

As the white man advances, so the red man retreats far into the deep recesses of the forest or the lonely solitude of the mountains. Where once could be seen the teepe [sic] on the banks of the Columbia scattered up the banks of the Sans Poel from its mouth; indian children playing along the edge of the running water; the women drying fish, weaving willows; the sing song chant of the buck as he rides slowly down the mountain trail; now all is silent and the stream and mountainside deserted; naught is seen except an occasional prospector as he appears over the crest of the hill and slowly descends to the landing and hails the ferryman. "They have folded their tents like the Arab and silently stolen away." But on this side of the river the noble white man is making racket enough for a hundred tribes, the measured plash of the water wheel; the labored puff of the engine and the rattle of the rocks as they gaily roll down the length of the sluices; the scream of the steam whistle

as it sounds the hour of work and rest, are music to the ear of the cau-
cassin [sic].[22]

Whites came to the Colville Reservation primarily to advance
themselves and not its original inhabitants. In 1898, J. C. Keller
opened a store in the town bearing his name on the east bank of the
Sanpoil River about six miles from the Columbia confluence. The
following year the immediate area boasted forty cabins under construction as well as a restaurant, two hotels, a feed stable, butcher
and blacksmith shops, and three general stores. The town grew
rapidly after a federal judge ruled that by the act of July 1, 1898,
the South Half ceased to be "Indian country" with regard to the
mineral claims that had caused miners and merchants to establish
themselves there.[23] In 1906 a smelter was built near the town.[24]

Colville Agent John McA. Webster sought to bring his charges into the twentieth century by extending to them the new technology
of the time. He advocated innovations such as transportation facili-
ties so that they could ship produce to the outside world and receive its goods in return. These rail and riverboat transportation
plans never materialized,[25] but that failure did not lessen the implementation of government policy on the Colville. On December 2,
1905, a Sanpoil delegation visited the town of Wilbur to state their
unpreparedness in understanding what the government was planning for the South Half. They wished their headmen to go to Washington, D.C., to learn what was transpiring. They stated that Major
McLaughlin had talked them out of going by warning that nothing
would be promised them in the capital. In a previous council headmen of the Nespelem tribe – which had begun to break their isolation from the government earlier than did the Sanpoils – agreed to
accept eighty-acre allotments to each adult Indian and the division
of proceeds from the sales of surplus lands.[26] On March 22, 1906,
the act was passed authorizing allotments in severalty to Indians of
the Colville and the classification of the lands remaining after allotment. By 1914, 333,275 acres within the South Half had been allot-
ted to 2,505 Indians.[27] On May 3, 1916, the Sanpoils were alarmed
to learn that the surplus lands on the South Half would be sold.

In a January 27, 1906, letter to the commissioner, Agent Webster
included a petition from Sanpoil-Nespelem headmen to let them
carry their grievances to Washington. Webster thought that the
proposed visit there would satisfy "their consuming desires, giving
them a different idea of this great country and its people, and returning them to their reservation with a larger and more correct influence." Among the petitioners was Jim James (Wahkaneetsa), son
of the Nespelem chief, Quela-quela-qua, who assisted Skolaskin in
some of his services.[28] Another petitioner was the persistent Nes-

pelem Charlie Swimptkin, whom Webster described as a "nervous and aggressive Nespilem of correct habits, who aspires to the chieftaincyship, but has a very small following." The third petitioner was Nespelem Frank, who, in Webster's words, was "another strong character." He was amenable to decisions made in Washington, but suffering from lung trouble, he died shortly thereafter.[29] Webster characterized Nespelem Frank's son, Johnny Frank, as a figurehead and a negative character, possibly because, like Charlie Swimptkin, he wanted nothing to do with the government. Skolaskin, whom Webster described as a man "of really strong character and the dominating influence" among the Sanpoils and Nespelems, refused to sign the petition, but seemingly, Webster reported, he had become resigned to the government's actions.[30]

Webster's assessment of Skolaskin's importance among the people did not indicate a corresponding strength in his church, which had suffered from his imprisonment. Even in what would appear to be secular matters, its erstwhile leader must have realized that changing times demanded tribal representatives who could deal with American officials more ably than he. His background had left him ill prepared for that task.

With Nespelem Frank, Nespelem George had helped breach the wall of Nespelem isolation from the government in December, 1897, by agreeing to accept sixty dollars' worth of supplies per month for keeping eleven of the government's oxen. This was perhaps a small concession, but it served to divide Nespelems from Sanpoils in the matter of accepting government money.[31] Webster gave George a paper that, in essence, recognized him as chief, with this added authority, he was to counsel his people to obey the laws, live in the right manner, and prepare for American citizenship. Webster described George as "an intelligent, sensitive and progressive man" who adopted civilized habits (in contrast to Skolaskin whom Webster characterized as "shrewd and tricky").[32] George's new position incurred the enmity of the Sanpoils and some of their Nespelem sympathizers, for they knew it would increase the agency's influence among the Sanpoils, who numbered 189 in 1910, and would hamper continuing opposition to the government. Webster thought that antagonisms against George had prompted whites with grudges against his agency to stir up trouble on the Colville in the national capital.[33] He also maintained that for a long time the Indian Office had terminated the chieftaincy so that the Indians could "acquire the individual habit of thinking and acting for themselves instead of allowing their thoughts and actions to be controlled by a chief. . . ."[34] The agent knew better than did George that, as far as the government was concerned, the chieftaincy was more honorary than powerful. The inability or refusal of native leaders to discern the difference between the honor and the reality served only to further weaken their control.

Despite its titular character, certain Sanpoils still aspired to the chieftaincy. Skolaskin's favorite was the young Jim James, whom Webster characterized as a man of "excellent habits and character." He might have added that he was more cooperative than Skolaskin,[35] although he too refused to sign the McLaughlin Agreement. James would later claim that Skolaskin passed the leadership mantle over to him, but there were those who said that James assumed leadership before Skolaskin was willing to yield it to him.[36] One informant stated that Skolaskin wanted his friend and interpreter, Henry Covington, as chief, but changed his mind on finding that he lacked leadership ability.[37] James attributed his own rise to leadership to his speaking out against agency officials for taking Sanpoil-Nespelem children for schooling without parental knowledge and approval. In 1908, along with other Sanpoil headmen, he complained to officials about the closing of the Fort Spokane boarding school.[38] He perhaps believed it better to send the students the short distance there than to schools at greater distances where they would have suffered more homesickness and even death, or from which they might return home after a long absence to find family members had died in their absence. The eventual establishment of day schools in the Keller and Nespelem districts was more to the liking of progressives such as James.[39]

The allotting system continued to rankle Skolaskin so much that he held meetings to protest it. He succeeded in collecting $450 from his tribespeople to finance a trip to Washington, D.C. He must have known it was futile to try to convince the government to abandon its allotting on the South Half, but he tried to induce it to establish allotments of over eighty acres if it was to allot at all. He also wished to protest federal spending on persons of mixed blood. Like Smohalla, he decried the admixture of Indian and non-Indian blood, and many Indians of the Colville believed that mixed-bloods, both on and off the reservation, were responsible for having it thrown open to settlement.[40]

Did he plan to go to Washington for other reasons? Did he wish to prove to officials, who had denied him an invitation to do so, that he could go there uninvited? Did he wish to see the president, about whom he had heard so much and who had so many servants to do his bidding? Was his proposed journey a concession that his long-standing aloofness from the government was no longer viable with changing times?

In late December, 1910, Skolaskin and Henry Covington rode their mounts to Creston in the Big Bend, from which they traveled to Spokane by rail. They spent a short time there cloistered in a hotel, apparently celebrating the arrival of the new year, 1911, before entraining for the East. In Chicago, Skolaskin changed trains in a wheelchair, probably because the journey had been difficult on his crippled limbs. When he learned of his departure, Webster on December 30 fired off a telegram to the Indian Office requesting that it censure Skolaskin and send him home from his unauthorized journey. On January 10, 1911, Webster received a telegram from the capital stating that Skolaskin had arrived there on Saturday, January 7, and had already left for home "satisfied." Like so many other Indians visiting there, he could not help but be awed by the power of the government shown by the capital's massive buildings, growing bureaucracy, and large numbers of people. His stay was indeed short, but he knew that he had little business to transact and little authority with which to do it. Ironically, this chief who opposed the division of his peoples' lands would receive allotment number S-1478.[41] Like other Indians of the Colville, the Sanpoil-Nespelems would travel to Washington for many years to air grievances. Typical was a Colville delegation in January, 1917, when the Sanpoil Peter Suimtakam complained that the town of Keller was built on lands that he had selected for his allotment.[42]

Shortly after Skolaskin returned home, "Portuguese Joe" Enos died on May 30, 1911, in the Azores, the place of his birth. He had become wealthy ranching in the Big Bend, and Suzanne, his former mate and also Skolaskin's, sought to gain a share of his property, which was appraised at $137,000 at the time of his death. Suzanne argued that the money represented what she and Enos had acquired during their marriage. Witnesses on her behalf maintained that the marriage had been solemnized around 1870 by the Sanpoil headman and preacher Quetalikin. During court proceedings it was alleged that Enos had said he married her because, as a squawman, the Indians would leave him alone in times of trouble with whites and, as a Sanpoil tribal member because of his marriage, he would be allowed to run cattle on the Colville.

The case was tried in a Spokane County, Washington, superior court. Suzanne's marriage to Skolaskin was introduced into the proceedings by the defendants, who sought to portray her marital experiences with him as temporary like her relationships to Enos and other men with whom she lived. To strengthen her claim of marriage to Enos, her attorneys sought to minimize her relations with Skolaskin, claiming that she and other women came to him only to cook and perform other domestic chores. Trying to discredit him further before the law, her attorneys told how he had said that all good people would float to heaven on an ark and how he claimed to be descended from God – statements that Skolaskin then denied, as though trying to blot from his mind this tenet of his former religion. During the Spokane trial two attorneys cloistered him in a hotel to prevent him from testifying against a daughter, Alice, whom he had with Suzanne. Bent from the toils of her sixty-five years, Suzanne received from the jury a verdict that her marriage to Enos was legal, only to have the court on the defendants' motion set aside her favorable verdict. With this reversal she appealed her case to the Washington state supreme court in 1914.

Before the supreme court she claimed three children by Enos, of whom two had died and the whereabouts of the third was unknown. The respondents undertook to show that after the appellant, Suzanne,

> had married some seven or eight different men, Skolaskin, the alleged chief of the Spokane [sic] tribe, the man who was most looked up to and feared, this religious man, who built a church and an ark, picked out appellant as his wife and married her and lived with her. It is impossible to believe that this chief, this religious man, the head of his tribe, would select for his wife a woman, who if respondents' other witnesses are telling the truth, was nothing more or less than a common prostitute.

The court did not believe Suzanne's testimony, and it ruled that she was not the legal wife of Enos and was thus barred from sharing in his estate.[43]

A sordid aspect of the case involved the murder of Sarah "Salley" Nee, a Carlisle Indian School graduate and a cattle entrepreneur in the Sanpoil valley, who had been Skolaskin's interpreter on his return from Alcatraz. She was murdered to prevent her from testifying for the defense. Her killer was said to have received several thousand dollars to prevent her from taking the stand.[44]

The verdict against Suzanne may have allowed the Prophet to breathe more easily, but at the same time he had cause to reflect that officials, such as those at Alcatraz and in the U.S. Army, the Indian Office, and now the white courts, had made obsolete his own system of law and justice, negating any effort on his part to revitalize it. In Whitestone Village his rotting jail symbolized his failure.

Hair and Power: The Shearing

An event at the fishing site near Keller marked Skolaskin's submission to the forces that had eroded his authority and his independent spirit: he permitted Nespelem George to cut his waist-length braids at the shoulders.[45] This grooming was one of the last concessions that traditionalist Indians made to white men. Braids were a sign of their Indianness, and at the time of Skolaskin's shearing most other Sanpoils continued to wear long, braided hair. Cutting

his hair off at the shoulders represented at least a halfway surrender by Skolaskin to the whites. Like that of the biblical Sampson, his shearing symbolized his loss of power. He had already conceded to wearing hand-sewn cloth shirts, but like most elderly Indians, he would not wear white men's shoes, thus avoiding a head-
to-foot surrender. Among the personal possessions that whites had
given him was an old black army belt, which he adorned with blue
and white beads and brass studs to represent flags. Similarly, it was
probably from Fort Spokane soldiers that he had obtained an old
shell-pouch that he attached to the belt. His corn husk bag, however, was made by his former wife, Suzanne. He also had a red
wool saddle blanket, which was decorated with a wild-flower design, and a wooden pipe.

On May 30, 1918, the aged and long-debilitated Skolaskin made
an even greater concession to white culture. Earlier events had led
him to this day when, in 1915, the Reverend Edward Griva, S.J.,
had founded Saint Rose's Mission at Keller. Griva had come there
from Saint Francis Regis Mission near Kettle Falls as early as January, 1902, but he spent several years in Montana before returning
to the falls area in July, 1913. In May, 1916, he was in Keller seeking to finish a mission house in which to celebrate the Feast of Corpus Christi, which always attracted Indians from miles around, especially because it coincided with spring salmon fishing, horse racing, and other gaming. During this period, Griva ministered to the
Nespelems, despite their opposition to his efforts. Three days before the church building at Keller was completed, smallpox broke
out among the local Indians, frightening many of them away, but
undaunted, the Sanpoils received communion from Griva on Sunday, May 28, 1916. The high mass was celebrated in the native tongue. Whites, such as those living across the Columbia in the Big
Bend, often visited the Sanpoil River area to picnic and attend Indian ceremonials, but they were avoiding the services because they
feared contracting the disease. The church building was dedicated
by the Reverend Celestine Caldi, S.J., on October 26, 1916. Griva
did not like its smallness, nor its dampness because of its proximity
to the Sanpoil River. On May 4, 1917, he was again in Keller,
where, with Bob Covington, he worked on a new Saint Rose's
Church, preparing it for a mass held on November 1, 1917. It
would be dedicated on May 3, 1923.[47]

At the feast of Corpus Christi on Thursday, May 30, 1918, Skolaskin, whom Griva called "Mr. Kullaken," permitted himself to be
carried to the rail of Saint Rose's Church to take communion and
the Christian name "Frank."[48] Accounts of his conversion do not reveal the troubling thoughts that led him to this new spiritual experience. Was he motivated by a sense of failure? Or, by guilt for his
sins, not the least of which were the deceit that he confessed and

his use of people as means to an end? Was he seeking to assure himself of a safe hereafter and escape from the punishments of hell? He must have given increasing thought to the afterlife as he neared the end of his life. We find no clue to his terse statement: "I originated a religion. Conditions changed. I am the only one left. I want to be a Catholic."[49] His conversion was a significant step not only for one who had so stubbornly resisted the Roman Catholic Church, but also for that institution itself, which, more successfully than ever, was nearing its goal of achieving religious unity among Indians of the Colville Reservation.

Time continued to ravage and mottle the Prophet's skin. His eyes no longer pierced those of his opponents, nor did his stare hypnotize. In his last years he rode around on an aged gelding or commandeered the nearest horse he could find, as he formerly had other things he wanted. A friend recalled that Skolaskin had made such demands on his followers to test their tolerance of him.[50] He indeed had ridden far from the trail that he once had followed. Besides jettisoning his own preachments for those of his erstwhile Catholic foes, he came to accept the presence of mixed-bloods, and he halfway made peace with Moses' people by marrying into that band, as had other elderly Sanpoils.

Skolaskin spent his last winters at Omak, visiting the daughter, Alice, whom he had by the oft-married Suzanne. He did not live to learn of Suzanne's death, nor that of his son by Ceeapeetsa, William, or "Billy," who froze to death in a jail.[51] The winter of 1922–23 was severe on human beings and beasts, and he never lived to see another snow. He died the evening of March 30, 1922, at home on his allotment near his birthplace, Snuke'ilt, a short distance upriver from Whitestone. Some claimed that he was driven from Whitestone by men with whose wives he had had affairs.[52]

Skolaskin had reached the apex of his career depending on others, but he died alone. He was buried in his own yard, not in the common graveyard that he had once advocated for his dead followers. Having found no rest in life, he found none in death: when the waters of Lake Roosevelt threatened to cover his grave, it was exhumed and his bones were reburied in the Keller cemetery. Henry Covington, his interpreter on his journey to Washington, D.C., commissioned a funeral home in the town of Colville to remove the remains and with others paid $155 for a headstone for the new grave. The funeral services, attended by nearly three hundred people, revealed some Roman Catholic concessions to native traditionalism for this soul recently gathered within the Christian fold, Tohosalks from Whitestone chose ten men to throw dirt on the Prophet's grave as in the old-time burials.[53]

The waters of Lake Roosevelt also forced removal of the

.Prophet's church building, the first such structure on the Colville Reservation, to Nespelem, where it was reassembled. It stands today as a memorial to not only Skolaskin and his followers but all Indian tribespeople of the past. Other landmarks obliterated by Lake Roosevelt were the age-old Whitestone rock and the Hell Gate rapids. In 1925 about five families remained in Whitestone. The last person to leave, in the mid-1930s, was Arcot Francis, who went to live with her son.[54] In 1959, Indians dedicated a monument to Skolaskin near the former Whitestone Village, with the Reverend Caldi in attendance.[55] Following the Pacific Northwest penchant for naming boats for Indians, an operator named his craft *Skolaskin*.

Unlike Smohalla, Skolaskin did not stand by his Dreamer religion to the end. Feeling it slipping beneath his feet, and more concerned with saving his soul than saving his creed, he scrambled aboard another ark, this one not of his own designing – the Roman Catholic ark of salvation. Thus he and his followers submitted to the very things that they had once feared, an alien church and an alien government. By the 1980's only a small core of traditionalists were still clinging to hopes for a revitalization of the kind envisioned by Smohalla and Skolaskin, foreseeing the day when nonbelievers may be snared in a web of civilization-threatening technology. There may yet arise among the descendants of Smohalla and Skolaskin others who emulate the likes of the Tuscarora Wallace (Mad Bear) Anderson, who in the 1950's revitalized the prophecies of the ancient Iroquois Deganawidah by seeking unity of all Indians.

Skolaskin's greatest tragedy was his failure to persuade either Indians or whites of the rightness of his teachings. It was his interior blindness, not his crippling or the blindness of his eyes in old age, that prevented him from seeing that what he considered his best interests were not necessarily those of his followers. In maneuvering people like pieces on a chessboard, he lost the game to the whites, although he could have done more poorly. From the study of his life and of Smohalla's we may learn to be more tolerant of the shortcomings of prophets who express our eternal quest for freedom and our regard for life. In 1937 an anonymous journalist wrote an epitah for Skolaskin's Sanpoils that many whites would have extended to the Dreamer-Prophet himself. He described the tribe as "probably the least colorful, least artistic and least ambitious of any Indian who ever inhabited the Pacific Northwest."[56] It is hoped that the winds of time will blow away chaff sentiments such as this and that Americans will see the good that grew from the seeds the Dreamer-Prophets planted.

Postlude: *Dreamer-Prophets Today*

> Do not become annoyed if the Frenchman and
> the Americans laugh at us, the day will come
> when we will laugh at them.
> — *Skolaskin to his people.*

The Dreamer-Prophet phenomenon, offering hope for Native Americans, may yet continue into the future. Although the infusion of white American Christianity was important during the anguished culture-altering era of the nineteenth century, the resulting syncretism did not destroy all vestiges of the message of Smohalla and Skolaskin. Those seeking to perpetuate the Dreamer religion have apparently become resigned to the predominance of the alien race, and unlike their predecessors, they no longer seek its destruction. Washat dancers gathering at Priest Rapids and other places seem no longer to cling to the belief expounded by Smohalla that the earth will return to its pristine state. They no longer find efficacy in the trance. Yet, despite the predictions in 1964 of Frank So-Happy, a modern Washani practitioner, that within four decades its drums would be silenced just as Skolaskin's bells were hushed, what appears moribund in the Dreamer-Prophet phenomenon may prove to be merely dormant. Perilous times ensure a platform on which charismatic leaders orchestrate their religions. Their liturgies, although strange in the modern world, may yet attract those who search for a more harmonious way of life – and for hope in the future.

The messages of twentieth-century American Indian Prophets and other leaders are quite similar to those of the preceding century. They cling to traditionalist beliefs such as respect for the Earth Mother. They do not, as their predecessors did, believe that the Creator will destroy the whites. Instead they feel that it is incumbent on Indians to educate whites about the inevitable consequences of their ascendance and prominence. Such a message does not constitute a separate religion, but fits within the framework of traditional worship.

199

This posture is revealed in the following interview with Leonard Crow Dog, a Brulé Teton Sioux, who, like the Hunkpapa Sioux Sitting Bull during the Ghost Dance of 1890, has led his and other tribesmen of the North American continent in a contemporary revival of the visions and messages of the Ghost Dancers. At the second battle of Wounded Knee in 1973, Crow Dog's spiritual leadership inspired his fellow Indians to stand up to the whites. One of the victims in the ensuing confrontation, which resulted in death and injury, was Buddy Lamont, whose burial ceremony Crow Dog conducted, laying the body to rest at the common grave site of victims of the 1890 Wounded Knee massacre.

The Indians chose the 1890 Wounded Knee site of the massacre of Ghost Dancers to stage their 1973 confrontation with the U.S. government. As a result some Indians are integrated "into a spiritual and ideological program that is known as the Traditional-Unity movement [which] is political, seeking national and international recognition of tribal sovereignty, as well as religious [sovereignty]."[1] Today rituals from various tribal traditions are combined into the movement that Crow Dog calls the Ghost Dance. This was evident in our October 12, 1986, conversation with him:

Q.: What do you call your religion? We once read that you use the name Ghost Dance.

LCD: The original Lakota (Sioux) people are Ghost Dancers. We call it the Indian Religion to inform White America. In a hereditary way, I am Mr. Crow Dog. I represent eighty-nine tribes as their spiritual leader.

Q.: Yes, you represent the Colville Tribes and you gave the initial peyote ceremony on the Colville Reservation in Ferry County [Wash.] in Skolaskin's territory. This was on October 1, 1977. Are you familiar with revitalization movements?

LCD: Yes.

Q.: Well, how is it that you combine with the Prophet Religion that of the traditionalists, the Yuwipi?

LCD: In Yuwipi worship the sacred pipe comes from the earth; it could not be started from any other way but to come from the earth. Today we call it Keeping the Soul. It is the same as the Ghost Dance and the Sun Dance; it is all one spirit. There are categories that go along with this way of life. So we live according to seasons. God created seasons which never change. Seasons never change. Our traditional ways never change.

Q.: Are you saying that you live according to tradition? Do you have any code as did the prophet, Handsome Lake of the Seneca tribe nearly two hundred years ago?

LCD: We have laws. The greatest law has been given to the red man. Original instructions have never changed. It has never been written down, but it came from dreams and visions.

Q.: Do you use anything equivalent today to Ghost Shirts?

LCD: Yes, we use these symbols to communicate, to relay the spirit of the Ghost. We wear them in ceremony when we offer sacred food or sacred instruments to the Creator.

Q.: Is this symbol a gown, or do you paint on symbols?

LCD: It is a garment that has been handed down through many generations.

Q.: You use drums, of course. Do you use bells in your ceremonies as did Skolaskin?

LCD: No, we use gourds.

Q.: Are you still preaching a revitalization theme or message?

LCD: Yes–we the nation, Lakota people. My grandfather met with Wovoka. Yes, we still talk about this in a ceremonial way. For those that hear the Ghost Dance teachings picturize in their feelings, in their hearts and souls, the message. It has never strayed from what our grandfathers had left; has never changed. But the individual has to hear with his eyes, his mind, his heart.

Q.: The prophet teachings then are to restore for the Indians his Indianness–to be Indians?

LCD: It is in us to want to live that way.

Q.: Is it still a viable part of your religion that the Creator will take the white man from the earth?

LCD: Not in those terms. There is in the today world a soul which is of the white man. According to spiritual understanding, there is a difference in the cells of the red man and the white man. The white man has to come to know, to be taught, to be educated. Somebody has to educate the white man.

Q.: Is your ministry then to educate the white man, or is it basically to serve the Indian?

LCD: We have to educate the white man and we have to educate the Indians. A lot of our people now, today, do not understand. Even the Lakotas, even the Comanches, Kiowas, Ottawas, Chippewas, Cheyennes, Crows, even. They misdreamed the red man's generation [hereditary message]. In today's world, we Indians have to help each other in order to survive.

Q.: With a revival of Indianness, there seems to be a turning of many Indians from Christianity to their traditional religion?

LCD: Christianity is good. if you want to be a good Christian, let's be a good Christian. If we are going to be traditional, let's be a traditional. Let's not misinterpret Crow Dog's words, misinterpret God's teachings–and massacring red man's knowledge and spiritual communications. There is a right and wrong. What is happening to us [Indians] is genocide. The Indian is confused. God Himself is all right, but it is the white man's teaching to the [Indian] nations of God's words which are misconstrued [by whites].

Q.: Since the 1973 crisis at Wounded Knee, when Indian and non-Indian confronted each other in hostility, do you feel there has been any improvement in relations? Is the white man less intent on genocide for the Indian, which, of course, has to be in the forefront of the cultural crisis for the Indian today?

LCD: Yes, that is why you are here. You want to see if we are still surviving here in our land. We survive on this land to preserve our way of life and culture that will never change. When I was a little boy in this valley [along the Little White River (the South Fork) on the Rosebud Reservation] there was only one sweat lodge. Today we have twenty-six sweat lodges. Families have them. They have understanding [through spiritual visions] from their grandmothers and grandfathers, and they talk to the stones. They don't talk like you, but talk to the stones in a spiritual sense of their feelings.

Q.: Smohalla and Wovoka "died" for three days while their spirits went to heaven and returned with a message from God to the people. They went into a trance. Do you do this?

LCD: Our message today come when we speak with our [dead] ancestors, who bring messages from the Creator. I speak with my grandfather. I speak with my [dead] father in a ceremony. I relate to my people the message from the Great Spirit. The white man taught us that if we did not communicate correctly we would go to hell. There is no hell in the red man's dreams and visions. You [the Indian] are part of the land, are part of Mother Earth. So we have a part here in this western hemisphere. There is a place here for the soul. For many years the United States government told us that we were wrong.

Q.: Do you prophesy as did Smohalla and Wovoka?

LCD: Yes, this is "today world." I follow through with what is going to happen in the seasons of our lives. There is a message which comes from tobacco, cedar, with fire, to communicate with our Maker through our loved ones to our people, not only to the Lakota, but to every tribe in the western hemisphere.

Q.: Is there any part of your ceremony which is comparable to confession?

LCD: Yes, yes, we balance our feelings of right and wrong with each point of the Morning Star. We must repent, we must confess our wrongs from rights, take the right and live our life. We cannot confess today and do it [the wrong] again tomorrow.

Q.: The white man can commit a sin, confess, ask forgiveness, and repeat it and repeat it and go through the healing process again.

LCD: That is the difference in the white man's thinking and the red man's thinking.

Q.: What you are saying then is that what is sinful for whites is not the same thing for the Indian?

LCD: My grandfather is the one who killed Spotted Tail. He confessed and he said that from that day on his grandkids will not go through what he went through. It was wrong. It was wrong in our way. It was the right for the [U.S.] government. The world is filthy. The Mother Earth is nice, and the Great Spirit's teaching is nice, but the red man surrendered the "today world."

Q.: Smohalla's message was for the Indians not to surrender the land.

LCD: Our message is to survive in "today world." We must relate the message to our people of what is right and wrong. We have to live the right life.

The Dreamer religion bore more of the whites' stamp than its Prophet would have acknowledged, and sadly, the faiths that Smohalla and Skolaskin fashioned with great promise lay shaken at their deaths. Nevertheless, their teachings had an important place in the history of their race in crisis, forming what Deward E. Walker has described as the essential conceptual and emotional bridges between the aboriginal and Euro-American cultures.[2] Also, in our concern for the effects of their words on native cultures, we should remember that as chieftains the Prophet-leaders definitely influenced American governmental policy. Finally, the most significant aspects of Smohalla and Skolaskin's careers, besides their claims to supernatural experiences and powers, were their unique personalities, which they exploited in blazing a trail of salvation for their troubled peoples. In societies in crisis there is, as the anthropologist Peter Farb pointed out, a proliferation of their kind of message.[3] The world has not seen the last of their kind.

Notes

Chapter 1. Introduction: *The Dreamer-Prophet Milieu*

1. Philleo Nash, "The Place of Religious Revivalism in the Formation of the Intercultural Community on Klamath Reservation," 374; Ralph Linton, "Nativist Movements," 230; David F. Aberle, "The Prophet Dance and Reactions to White Contact," 74–83; Christopher L. Miller, *Prophetic Worlds*, 42ff.

2. Revitalization is discussed in Anthony F. C. Wallace, "Acculturation: Revitalization Movements," 264–81; Ralph Leon Emerson, "A Chronology and Interpretation of Nineteenth Century Plateau History," Master's thesis, University of Washington, 1962; and Weston La Barre, *The Ghost Dance Origins of Religion*, 206ff., 253–76. Linton discusses what he terms *magical nativism* and *rational nativism*. He maintains that the former arises in societies under stress where individuals assume prophet roles and lean heavily on the supernatural, usually adopting apocalyptic millennial concepts. Rational nativism also is associated with frustrating situations, and its practitioners also look forward to happier times, but they use symbolic elements that are psychological rather than magical. See also Linton, "Nativistic Movements," 230–40. In *Studies in Prehistory: Priest Rapids and Wanapum Reservoir Areas, Columbia River, Washington*, 2: 95–103, Robert E. Greengo has applied Wallace's structuring of the revitalization process to Wanapam–Columbia River cultural development. Sociologist Russell Thornton has pointed out that demographic processes produced differential participation in revitalization during both the 1870 and 1890 Ghost Dances ("Demographic Antecedents of a Revitalization Movement: Population Change, Population Size, and the 1890 Ghost Dance," 88–96; and "Demographic Antecedents of Tribal Participation in the 1870 Ghost Dance Movement," 79–80).

3. Delaware and other eastern American tribal prophets are discussed in Anthony F. C. Wallace, "New Religious Beliefs Among the Delaware Indians, 1600–1900," 1–21. Americans have long been fascinated by the literature pertaining to Tecumseh and his brother Tenskwatawa, from the time

of Benjamin Drake's *Life of Tecumseh, and of His Brother, the Prophet*, published in 1841, pp. 107–109, to modern-day publications such as Wayne Moquin and Charles Van Doren, "A System of Religion: Tenkswataya, or the Propeht (Shawnee)," in their *Great Documents in American History*, 34–35. See also Glen Tucker, "Tecumseh."

4. A good account of revitalization in Seneca culture at the hands of Handsome Lake is Anthony F. C. Wallace, *The Death and Rebirth of the Seneca*.

5. W. P. Clark, *The Indian Sign Language*, 301.

6. Interview, Ella McCarty, September 21, 1966; Robert H. Ruby and John A. Brown, *The Spokane Indians: Children of the Sun*, 31–33.

7. Accounts of Shining Shirt are found in Robert Ignatius Burns, S.J., *The Jesuits and the Indian Wars of the Northwest*, 16, and in Harry Holbert Turney-High, "The Flathead Indians of Montana," pp. 41–43.

8. "Vision of Wat-Til-Ki" (July, 1918), MS. 1514, McWhorter Papers.

9. "Tem-Tie-Quin and the Black-Robes," MS. 1527, p. 28, McWhorter Papers.

10. Cora Du Bois, *The Feather Cult of the Middle Columbia*, 8, 9.

11. Ibid., 10. on p. 5ff., Du Bois lists several prophets, some of whom were Smohalla's contemporaries. Among the tribes from which they came were the Palouses, the Skins, the Wallawallas, the Warm Springs, the Wishrams, and the Yakimas.

12. Spier, *Prophet Dance*, 21–22.

13. Margery Ann Beach Sharkey, "Revitalization and Change: A History of the Wanapum Indians, Their Prophet Smohalla, and the Washani Religion," master's thesis, Washington State University, 1984, 26–29.

14. John Fahey, *The Flathead Indians*, 27.

15. Deward E. Walker, Jr. *Conflict and Schism in Nez Percé Acculturation*, 35.

16. The anthropologist David Chance has shown the importance of Hudson's Bay company personnel and policies to Christian-nativist syncretism among the Indians of the Columbia plateau, especially those of the upper reaches ("Influences of the Hudson's Bay Company on the Native Cultures of the Colville District"). Indians held their services at or near Hudson's Bay Company posts such as Vancouver, Walla Walla, Colvile, Hall, Boise, and Nisqually. During the 1830's such services were observed and recorded by whites, including the Americans Nathaniel Wyeth, a trader; John K. Townsend, a scientist; Captain B. L. E. Bonneville, an army officer; Samuel Parker, a clergyman; and William Fraser Tolmie, a British physician-trader.

17. Du Bois in "Feather Cult," 11, cites Spier's contention. The Iroquois who moved to the West are not to be confused with the French-Canadian voyageurs who returned to their eastern homelands after serving fur companies on western waters. Despite the differences in the religious beliefs of the Iroquois who came West and the followers of Handsome Lake, there is the intriguing possibility that the former may have been influenced by the latter's teachings.

18. Miller, *Prophetic Worlds*, 54, and Wayne Suttles, "The Plateau Prophet Dance Among the Coast Salish," 352–96.

19. The numbers of Immigrant Road travelers to the Oregon Country are cited in Robert H. Ruby and John A. Brown, *The Cayuse Indians: Imperial Tribesmen of Old Oregon*, 94n.

20. Robert H. Ruby and John A. Brown, *The Chinook Indians: Traders of the Lower Columbia River*, 33–34. For accounts of diseases ravaging the Pacific Northwest in the late eighteenth and early nineteenth centuries, see S. F. Cook, "The Epidemic of 1830–1833 in California and Oregon," 303–25; Leslie M. Scott, "Indian Diseases as Aids to Pacific Northwest Settlement," 144–61; Herbert C. Taylor, Jr. and Lester L. Hoaglin, Jr., "The 'Intermittent Fever' Epidemic of the 1830's on the Lower Columbia River," 160–78. What one writer has called the Ghost Cult of the lower Columbia River corresponds possibly to death cults among eastern American Indians. It may have been due to onslaughts of later-eighteenth-century diseases. (William Duncan Strong, "The Occurrence and Wider Implications of a 'Ghost Cult' on the Columbia River Suggested by Carvings in Wood, Bone, and Stone").

21. Eli L. Huggins, "Smohalla, the Prophet of Priest Rapids," 214. Huggins's military career is chronicled in Carolyn Thomas Foreman, "General Eli Lundy Huggins," 253–65.

22. In Elliot Coues, ed., *History of the Expedition under the Command of Lewis and Clark*, a "map of Lewis and Clark's track" places the number of Sokulks as high as 3,000. The name Sokulk is unfamiliar to twentieth-century descendants of the Wanapams, however. For Wanapam population figures that are as conveniently well rounded as they are tenuous, see John R. Swanton, *Indian Tribes of Washington, Oregon, and Idaho*. See also Mooney, *Ghost-dance Religion*, 716, and Robert H. Ruby and John A. Brown, *A Guide to the Indian Tribes of the Pacific Northwest*, 261.

23. In Christian chiliasm Christ would return to earth with his saints and the planet would be under divine governance for a thousand years. Smohalla foresaw a permanence in his millenarianism, whereas that in Christian belief precedes the end of Earth's existence.

24. Leslie Spier, *The Prophet Dance of the Northwest and Its Derivatives: The Source of the Ghost Dance*," pp. 1–73. See also Deward E. Walker, Jr., "New Light on the Prophet Dance Controversy." Verne F. Ray points out the difference in the dance content in Smohalla's and Skolaskin's religions in his "The Kolaskin Cult: A Prophet Movement of 1870 in Northeastern Washington," 67 and nn. The Prophetic process is discussed in Thomas W. Overholt, "The Ghost Dance of 1890 and the Nature of the Prophetic Process," 37–64. For a discussion of Native American prophets and their religions, see also James Mooney, *The Ghost-dance Religion and the Sioux Outbreak of 1890, Fourteenth Annual Report of the Bureau of American Ethnology to the Secretary of the Smithsonian Institution, 1892–93*, pt. 2, pp. 641–1110. For a discussion of what Christopher L. Miller calls "prophetic worlds" in the Pacific Northwest, see his *Prophetic Worlds: Indians and Whites on the Columbia Plateau*.

25. Clifford E. Trafzer and Margery Ann Beach Sharkey, "Smohalla, the Washani, and Religion as a Factor in Northwestern Indian History," 234.

26. In his "Acculturation: Revitalization Movements," 272, Wallace explains the limitation of powers of prophets.

Chapter 2: The Yantcha

1. Mooney, "Ghost-dance Religion," 717; Click Relander, *Drummers and Dreamers*, 32.

2. In the Shahaptian dialects, the northeastern *walula* corresponds to the *walawala* of the Columbia River and northwest. Bruce J. Rigsby, "Linguistic Relations in the Southern Plateau," master's thesis, University of Oregon, Eugene, 1965.

3. Andrew D. Pambrun, "Notes from Mss. etc.," MS. 1193, Pambrun Papers. Throughout *A Chronology And Interpretation of Nineteenth-Century Plateau Culture History*, Emerson cites the observations of nineteenth-century white travelers on the Columbia River in the Priest Rapids–Columbia–Snake River area. He also discusses tribal boundaries and the composition of the tribes inhabiting that area.

4. Click Relander, "Puck Hyah Toot and Other Wanapams: Performance of Smowhala's Washat Dance," Click Relander Papers, Yakima Valley Regional Library. Among other sources in which renditions and meanings of Smohalla's name appear are Du Bois, "Feather Cult," 5; Mooney, *Ghost-dance Religion,* 717; and Leta May Smith, *The End of the Trail*, 197.

5. Huggins, "Smohalla, the Prophet of Priest Rapids," 212.

6. Major J. W. MacMurray, U.S.A., "The 'Dreamers' of the Columbia River Valley, in 'Washington Territory'," 246.

7. Coues, *History of the Expedition Under the Command of Lewis and Clark*, 3: 978.

8. As noted, Smohalla's Prophet role differed from that of a shaman. Shamanism is discussed in Willard Z. Park, *Shamanism in Western North America*, 8-10, and in L. V. McWhorter, *Hear Me My Chiefs*, 78.

9. Click Relander, *Drummers and Dreamers*, 64; Relander, "The Wanapums and Priest Rapids," p. 38, Relander Papers, 25-12, Yakima Valley Regional Library.

10. Gabriel Franchère, *Narrative of a Voyage of the Northwest Coast of America in the Years 1811, 1812, 1813, and 1814*, 276-77. See also Alexander Ross, *Adventures of the First Settlers on the Oregon or Columbia River*, 134.

11. Events leading up to the massacre and its aftermath are discussed in Ruby and Brown, *Cayuse Indians*, 84-127ff.

12. In the annals of the American West no group was more colorful than the voyageurs in the employ of the fur companies. Slight of build, yet often carrying loads equaling their own weight, they could be heard singing as they paddled their bateaux down the Columbia River.

13. MacMurray, "'Dreamers' of the Columbia River Valley," 246.

14. For itineraries of priests of Saint Joseph's Mission, as well as information of its establishment and descriptions of mission operations, see in the case file, *Northern Pacific R.R. Co.* vs. *St. Joseph's Roman Catholic Mission, 1895*, MS. 3095, Henry J. Snively Papers.

15. Ibid.

16. Denys Nelson, "Yakima Days," 50.

17. Pambrun's activities are discussed in Ruby and Brown, *Cayuse Indians*, 58ff.

18. MacMurray, "'Dreamers' of the Columbia River Valley," 248; Relander, *Drummers and Dreamers*, 25–29; Relander interview with Puck Hyah Toot, April 11, 1951, pp. 1–2, Relander Papers, 57–25, Yakima Valley Regional Library; Relander, "The Wanapums and Priest Rapids," p. 39, Relander Papers, 25–12, Yakima Valley Regional Library; A. J. Splawn, *Ka-Mi-akin: Last Hero of the Yakimas*, 354.

19. It seems that Smohalla thought these groups had appeared in a chronological sequence. Contrary to MacMurray's view that the Frenchmen were with the Hudson's Bay Company, they may have been French Canadians with the North West Company. The priests possibly were François Norbert Blanchet and Modeste Demers en route down the Columbia in 1838. The "Boston men" of MacMurray's account could have been any American group from the time of Lewis and Clark through that of the missionaries, soldiers, and settlers. The "King George men," rather than being English soldiers, as suggested by MacMurray, may have been personnel of British fur-trading firms; and the "black men," soldiers on the Pacific Northwest frontier. Like York, the black man with Lewis and Clark, they evoked much interest among the region's natives. Finally, the Chinese would have been those digging gold on bars of the Columbia and its tributaries in the 1860's and 1870's. See MacMurray, "'Dreamers' of the Columbia River Valley," 248.

20. Relander, *Drummers and Dreamers*, 64–65.

21. A. G. Tassin, "Lord Jim," 493.

22. For a description and explanation of the habitat of the Wanapams and their subsistence patterns, see Sharkey, "Revitalization and Change," 17–27. For an explanation of Wanapam village sites in precontact days, see Randall F. Schalk et al., "An Archaeological Survey of the Priest Rapids Reservoir: 1981."

23. Coues, *History of the Expedition Under the Command of Lewis and Clark*, 2: 638.

24. Ross, *Adventures of the First Settlers*, 135.

25. Franz Boas, ed., *Folk-Tales of Salishan and Sahaptin Tribes*, 83.

26. Ross, *Adventures of the First Settlers*, 135; Frederick Merk, ed., *Fur Trade and Empire: George Simpson's Journal*, 129, 168.

27. Huggins, "Smohalla, the Prophet of Priest Rapids," 214.

28. This absence of healings in Smohalla's Washani is cited in Du Bois, "Feather Cult," 44. There are numerous references on the Indian Shaker Church and Shakerism. Among them are H. G. Barnett, *Indian Shakers: A Messianic Cult of the Pacific Northwest*; George P. Castile, *The Indians of Puget Sound: The Notebooks of Myron Eells*; Erna Gunther, "The Shaker Religion of the Northwest," in Marian W. Smith, ed., *Indians of the Urban Northwest*; Paul Lenhoff, "Indian Shaker Religion," 283–86; Lee Sackett, "The Siletz Indian Shaker Church"; Robert H. Ruby and John A. Brown, *Myron Eells and the Puget Sound Indians*, 74 and *Indians of the Pacific Northwest: A History*, 264.

29. *Times Mountaineer* (The Dalles, Ore.), July 10, 1886, p. 4.

30. Smohalla's spiritual experiences are narrated in Relander, *Drummers and Dreamers*, 69ff.; the Relander papers in the Yakima Valley Regional Library; Relander interviews with Puck Hyah Toot, March 23, April 7 and

11, May 17 and 23, June 3, 1951, in "The Wanapums and Priest Rapids," 31ff.; Relander Papers, Yakima Valley Regional Library; and Trafzer and Sharkey, "Smohalla, the Washani, and Religion as a Factor in Northwestern Indian History," 310.

31. Emerson presents statements of anthropologists about the identity and location of these Quil-lema, or Kahmiltpah, Indians in *A Chronology and Interpretation of Nineteenth-Century Plateau Culture History*, 56–58, 112. See also Ruby and Brown, *Indians of the Pacific Northwest*, 131ff.

32. Greengo, *Studies in Prehistory*, 2:61. In *A Chronology and Interpretation of Nineteenth-Century Plateau Culture History*, 60ff., Emerson cites several cases where assemblies of warring elements of tribes such as the Palouses, the Yakimas, and the Sinkiuses at Priest Rapids did not indicate participation in the war by the peacefully disposed Wanapams.

33. So-Happy's death is narrated in Relander's record of his interview with George So-Happy on February 14, 1952. ("Indians." MS., Relander Papers, Yakima Indian Nation Cutural Center). An 1847 painting of So-Ha-Pe as an Indian of "Stony [Rock] Island" (on the Columbia River upstream from Priest Rapids), by the famous artist of western American scenes John Mix Stanley, was destroyed in a January 15, 1865, fire that swept the Smithsonian building in Washington, D.C.

34. In his early years Smohalla was said to have fought against British Columbia Indians. Sharkey, "Revitalization and Change," 43.

35. Pambrun discussed the rise and fall of the "confederation" in "Notes from Mss. etc.," p. 6, MS. 1193, Pambrun Papers.

36. For an account of the political situation among Indians at Priest Rapids at this time, see Granville O. Haller, "Diary 1856," August 8 and 16, Granville O. Haller Papers.

37. John D. Nash, "Salmon River Mission of 1855: A Reappraisal," 22–31.

38. Spier, *Prophet Dance*, 40–41.

39. *Weekly Pacific Tribune* (Seattle, W.T.), August 7, 1878, p. 4.

40. Relander, *Drummers and Dreamers*, 180. See also Robert H. Ruby and John A. Brown, *Half-Sun on the Columbia: A Biography of Chief Moses*, 62–63 and n. There was further substantiation that the fight did not occur in an interview with Nettie Showaway, an elderly Indian of the Yakima and Warm Springs reservations, June 25, 1986, and in a June 17, 1986, letter to the authors from Clifford Trafzer, a student of the Shahaptian peoples and the Prophet phenomenon. Like so many other writers in more recent times, La Barre in his *Ghost Dance*, 218, relates the story of the fight by stating that a "shaman," Smohalla, had been making medicine against his great rival Moses, chief of an upriver tribe, and that in a fight provoked by Moses, Smohalla was wounded and left for dead.

41. Interview with Emily Peone, May 1, 1962.

42. Interviews with Billy Curlew, October 8, 1956, and Emily Peone, May 1, 6, 11, 1962.

43. Moses' denunciations of Smohalla are found in the *Morning Oregonian* (Portland), May 25, 1878, and the *Walla Walla Statesman*, (W.T.) July 13, 1878.

Chapter 3. Washani: *The Creed*

1. Hartley Burr Alexander, *The Mythology of All Races* 10: 91.
2. Du Bois, *Feather Cult*, 12.
3. McWhorter evades dating the grafting of the two religions in "The Dreamer Religion of the Yakima Indians," MS. 1519, McWhorter Papers; Spier, *Prophet Dance*, 21. Mourning Dove's statement is found in her *Cogewea: The Half-Blood*, 291.
4. Milroy described the Washani beliefs in correspondence to Price, March 29, 1884, Yakima Indian Agency, Press Copies of Letters Sent to the Commissioner of Indian Affairs, 1877–1921, and in correspondence to the commissioner, August 15, 1884, *Annual Report of the Commissioner of Indian Affairs, 1884*, p. 173. See also Helen H. Schuster, "Yakima Indian Traditionalism."
5. The inception of the Pom Pom religion is discussed in Lucullus Virgil McWhorter's interview with Puck Hyah Toot, April 4, 1951, box 2 of 3, MS. 2511, H. D. Guie Papers: Mad Moon to Mrs. Hedge 6 [no month] Sunday, 1935, MS. 149A, McWhorter Papers; Du Bois, *Feather Cult*, 5ff.; "Vision of Wat-Til-Ki," July, 1918, p. 126, MS. 1514, McWhorter Papers; Sharkey, "Revitalization and Change," p. 2.
6. Du Bois, *Feather Cult*, 9.
7. A. J. Splawn, *Ka-Mi-akin*, 354. In *A Chronology and Interpretation of Nineteenth-Century Plateau Culture History*, 7ff., Emerson traces the close relationship between the Wanapam and Yakima peoples. Mooney states that Kotiakan was the son of Yakima war chief Kamiakin. *Ghost-dance Religion*, 722.
8. The statement about Kotiakan was given by a Yakima Indian, Charlie Selatkrine, and appears in Du Bois, *Feather Cult*, 15. Du Bois renders the spelling of Kotiakan as Kutaiaxen.
9. Mooney, *Ghost-dance Religion*, 721–22, 727.
10. MacMurray, "'Dreamers' of the Columbia River Valley," 248.
11. Indian Inspector E. C. Kemble to commissioner, September 29, 1873, Reports of Inspection of the Field Jurisdiction of the Office of Indian Affairs, 1873–1900, Washington Superintendency, 1873–1880 (no. 1070, roll 56). For an account of the Peace Policy in operation, see Ruby and Brown, *Indians of the Pacific Northwest*, 229–37.
12. Albert Samuel Gatschet, "The Klamath Indians of Southwestern Oregon," xci–xcii.
13. This retort by Smohalla and his other statements to Huggins are found in Huggins, "Smohalla, the Prophet of Priest Rapids," 211–14.
14. McWhorter provides this information from a field trip to Priest Rapids in his record of an interview with Puck Hyah Toot, April 4, 1951, box 2 or 3, MS. 2511, Guie Papers. Sheri Hokanson, librarian in the Yakima Nation Cultural Center in Toppenish, Wash., suggests that *Kinzbick* is phonetically similar to *kuqmiki*, the "season of five moons" that is the "Cold Wind Time." She cites Will E. Everett, M.D., "Division of Time," *Study of Indian Languages* Washington, D.C.: Bureau of Ethnology, September 1, 1883.
15. A. D. Pambrun, who assumed charge of Fort Walla Walla in 1852, claimed to have purchased several head of cattle from the Coeur d'Alene

Mission. "Notes from Mss. etc.," MS. 1193, Pambrun Papers.

16. Case file, *Northern Pacific R.R. Co.* vs. *St. Joseph's Roman Catholic Mission, 1895*, MS. 3095, Snively Papers.

17. MacMurray, "'Dreamers' of the Columbia River Valley," 242, 246.

18. *Walla Walla* (W.T.) *Union*, August 26, 1871, p. 2; *Morning Oregonian* (Portland), June 19, 1879, p. 3.

19. Techniques used by Smohalla in his ministrations are explained in H. D. Guie's account of a field trip to Priest Rapids ("Articles Misc., 7/22/37," MS. 2511, Guie Papers); MacMurray, "'Dreamers' of the Columbia River Valley," 247.

20. Emil T. Voight, report, March 30, 1885, *Annual Report of the Chief of the [U.S. Army] Engineers for 1886*, appendix Q.Q., p. 1954. The actual surveys were conducted under Major W. A. Jones; see pp. 1957-61.

21. *Yakima* (W.T.) *Record*, March 18, 1882, p. 3, and April 8, 1882, p. 3.

22. MacMurray, "Dreamers of the Columbia River Valley," 247-48. In her *Indian Legends of the Pacific Northwest*, 142-43, Ella Clark renders a similar account of these Indian origins.

23. Mooney, *Ghost-dance Religion*, 722. For the legends about the damming of the Columbia River and about the nearby mountains, see Ruby and Brown, *Indians of the Pacific Northwest*, 22.

24. Guie, "Articles Misc., 7/22/37," MS. 2511, Guie Papers.

25. *Pacific Christian Advocate* (Portland, Ore.), May 15, 1873, p. 1.

26. Thomas Kree to Felix Brunot, July 31, 1871, *Annual Report of the Commissioner of Indian Affairs, 1871*, pp. 131-35.

27. "State of Smohalla," *The Northwest* (Saint Paul, Minnesota), 4, no. 7 (July, 1886): 25.

28. "A Visit to the Umatilla," *The Northwest* 11, no. 12 (December, 1893); 6.

29. In her *Feather Cult*, 44-45, Du Bois presents a chart of Smohalla's Washani creed and ceremonies as well as those of the Feather Dance and Indian Shaker religions. The optional use of alcohol among Washani adherents is one of the items on the chart.

30. Charles Reagan Wilson, "Shamans and Charlatans: The Popularization of Native American Religion in Magazines, 1865-1900," 7.

31. Alice Fletcher, "The Indian Messiah," 57-60. James P. Boyd, A.M., took advantage of the growing interest in the Ghost Dance phenomenon to incorporate an account of it within his 1891 publication, *Recent Indian Wars. Under the Lead of Sitting Bull. And Other Chiefs: With a Full Account of the Messiah Craze and Ghost Dances.*

Chapter 4. Washat: *Symbol and Ceremony*

1. Informants tell of the location of other flags at various points surrounding Smohalla's longhouse. Sharkey, *Revitalization And Change*, 71.

2. MacMurray, "'Dreamers' of the Columbia River Valley," 245.

3. The fur man Alexander Ross described such flags among natives on the middle and upper Columbia River in his *Adventures of the First Settlers*, 201.

4. Longhouses were common among Pacific Northwest natives not only in the coastal areas but also in the interior. Perhaps the first white person to

observe them on the middle Columbia was the Nor'Wester David Thompson, who in 1811 visited one below Rock Island, Wash. He recorded its dimensions as 30 by 240 feet. *David Thompson's Narrative, 1784–1812*, ed. Richard Glover, p. 345.

5. Quoted in Du Bois, *Feather Cult*, 13. The remarks of Luls, whose ceremonials, especially in the trappings attending them, were quite similar to those of Smohalla, reveal how dependent the Washani worshippers were on the bounties of nature and how it was incumbent on them to match that dependency with a meticulously proper and responsive worship. According to the anthropologist Theodore Stern, Luls's relationship with the Creator began after he killed a shaman whom he suspected of having caused the death of a beloved daughter. She appeared in a vision to reproach him for his action, which would have denied him entrance into heaven. The Creator benevolently remitted Luls's sins on the condition that he preach to his tribesmen for a decade. During that time he received songs and a vision of heaven, and under his heavenly mandate he established a church. On Sunday and at funeral services he detailed his visions to his adherents and prophesied events, although he placed little emphasis on the messianic in his ministrations. Stern contrasts Luls's worship with the traditional power quest "A Umatilla Prophet Cult: An Episode in Culture Change," 346–50.

6. Relander, *Drummers and Dreamers*, 84.

7. The dance paraphernalia, including the sacred bird, are discussed in Du Bois, *Feather Cult*, 17; Relander, *Drummers and Dreamers*, 73–74; and Spier, *Prophet Dance*, 8.

8. For an account of differences between the Washani and the Feather Dance religion, see Du Bois, *Feather Cult*, 44–45.

9. Ibid.

10. Relander, *Drummers and Dreamers*, 84; Relander interview Puck Hyah Toot, April 11, 1951, p. 2; and "The Wanapums and Priest Rapids," 38, Relander Papers, Yakima Valley Regional Library.

11. Alexander Ross, *Fur Hunters of the Far West*, 203–205.

12. Wanapam numerical symbolism is discussed in Relander, *Drummers and Dreamers*, 84. In some Columbia plateau religions, songs and ritual acts such as dancing were performed in groups of the magic number seven, accompanied by seven drums. Today some groups are associated with the "Seven Drum Religion," of which the songs are in seven segments. In protohistoric times the Nez Percé sacred number was five, and after adopting the Ghost Dance in the 1870's, the Klamaths also used the number five. Smohalla's belief in the trinity of the sun, moon, and stars, was explained by L. V. McWhorter, who interviewed Puck Hyah Toot on field trips to Priest Rapids (McWhorter Papers, interviews with Puck Hyah Toot, July 22, 1937, and April 7, 1951).

13. In his *Ghost-dance Religion*, 725–27, Mooney cites a MacMurray manuscript describing the major's visit with Smohalla.

14. Based on observations by an army officer, the journalist Eugene Smalley tells of the trance experience in his "From Puget Sound to the Upper Columbia," 841–42.

15. E. D. Bannister, report, March 30, 1886, Reports of Inspection . . . of the Office of Indian Affairs, 1873–1900, Yakima Indian Agency, January

19, 1881–January 12, 1885 (no. 1070, roll 59). Kotiakan's ceremonials are also described in Mooney, *Ghost-dance Religion*, 729–31.

16. E. D. Bannister, report, March 30, 1886, Reports of Inspection . . . of the Office of Indian Affairs, 1873–1900.

17. Mad Moon to Mrs. Hedge, [n.d.] 6, Sunday, 1935, pp. 1–5. MS. 149A, McWhorter Papers.

18. Ibid. Among similar ceremonials are those described in Edward S. Curtis, *The North American Indian*, 8, appendix, p. 175; and in Leslie Spier and Edward Sapir, "Wishram Ethnography: Linguistic Relationship and Territory," 252–53, 271.

19. Sharkey, "Revitalization and Change," 80.

Chapter 5. Rendezvous for Renegades

1. Cain's proposals appear in *Annual Report of the Secretary of War, 1877* (45th Cong., 2nd sess., H. Doc. 1, [pt. 2], 1: 639–41.

2. G. H. Abbott to Supt. Edward R. Geary, January 5 and February 6, 1861, Oregon Superintendency of Indian Affairs, 1848–1872. Letters Received, January 3–December 27, 1861, vol. 2 (roll 19).

3. William Vance Rinehart, "Oregon Cavalry (1874–1881)," 9–10, MS. P-A 62, Bancroft Library.

4. Abbott to Geary, February 11, 1861, Oregon Superintendency of Indian Affairs, 1848–1872, Letters Received, January 3–December 27, 1861, vol. 2 (roll 19); Pambrun, "Reminiscences," typescript of MS. 1193, Pambrun Papers.

5. *Annual Report of the Commissioner of Indian Affairs, 1860*, p. 208; Abbott to Geary, February [n.d.], 1861, Oregon Superintendency of Indian Affairs, 1848–1872, Letters Received January 3–December 27, 1861, no. 2 (roll 19); Pambrun, "Family Papers," MS. 1193, Pambrun Papers.

6. William C. McKay to Commissioner E. P. Smith, August 10, 1875, William C. McKay Papers; T. W. Davenport, Umatilla agent, to J. W. Perit Huntington, Oregon Supt. of Indian Affairs, April 28, 1863, Oregon Superintendency of Indian Affairs, 1848–1872, Letters Received, January 7, 1862–June 28, 1863, vol. 2 (roll 20); T. W. Davenport, "Recollections of an Indian Agent," 20.

7. Ritchie and Howe to Geary, March 6, 1861, Oregon Superintendency of Indian Affairs, 1848–1872, Letters Received, January 3–December 27, 1861, vol. 2 (roll 19); interview with Cull White, March 10, 1957. The Wanapams also ferried men and their vehicles across the Columbia on pairs of canoes, catamaran fashion.

8. *Walla Walla Union*, April 29, 1934.

9. *Walla Walla* (W.T.) *Statesman*, August 9, 23, 1862; *Weekly Oregonian* (Portland), August 30, 1862, p. 1; Brig. General Benjamin Alvord to Umatilla agent, W. H. Rector, August 28, 1862, Oregon Superintendency of Indian Affairs, 1848–1872, Letters Received, January 7, 1862–June 28, 1863, vol. 2 (roll 20).

10. Wesley Gosnell, Simcoe agent, to Geary, April 9, 1860, Washington Superintendency of Indian Affairs, 1853–1880, Letters from Employees Assigned to the Columbia River, or Southern District and the Yakima Agency, May 1, 1854–July 20, 1861 (roll 17).

11. A. Brancroft, Yakima agent, to Supt. C. Hale, March 20, 1863, Washington Superintendency of Indian Affairs, 1853–1880, Letters from Employees Assigned to the Yakima Agency, August 16, 1861–December 3, 1868 (roll 18).

12. Huntington to McKay, November 20, 1865, Oregon Superintendency of Indian Affairs, 1848–1872, Letterbook H:10 (roll 8); J. W. Perit Huntington to D. N. Cooley, commissioner of Indian affairs, October 15, 1866, *Annual Report of the Commissioner of Indian Affairs, 1866*, p. 76.

13. *Weekly Mountaineer*, March 2, 1866, p. 1.

14. In 1884, in the aftermath of the Bannock-Paiute war of 1878, several Paiutes formerly incarcerated at the Simcoe Agency were removed to the Warm Springs Agency. No serious troubles occurred there between them and other tribesmen of that reservation. Meacham explained Smohalla's Nevada connections in correspondence with Washington Superintendent of Indian Affairs Samuel Ross, March 22, 1870, Oregon Superintendency of Indian Affairs, 1848–1872, Letterbook I:10 (roll 10).

15. Pambrun narrated the visit to Smohalla in "The Story of his Life as he Tells it," 180–81, copy of MS., Hargreaves Library, Eastern Washington State University. Meacham's correspondence pertaining to Smohalla and other Dreamers is found in his letters to Col. Samuel Ross, Washington Supt. of Indian Affairs, March 22, 1870; to General George Crook, April 26 and May 1, 1870; to Commissioner E. S. Parker, March 22, April 10, and April 25, 1870, and June 23, 1871; to Lieut. W. H. Boyle, May 1, 1870; all in Oregon Superintendency of Indian Affairs, 1848–1872, Register of Letters Sent April, 1866–December, 1872, vol. I:10 (roll 9); and in Boyle to Meacham, May 1, 1870, Oregon Superintendency of Indian Affairs, 1848–1872, Letters Received, March 31–December 1, 1870, vol. 2 (roll 26).

16. Thomas Donaldson, *Idaho of Yesterday*, 340–41; *Walla Walla Union*, June 1, 1872, p. 3.

17. Meacham's description of conditions on the Warm Springs, including that of its Dreamers, is found in correspondence to Commissioner Parker, April 19, 1870, Oregon Superintendency of Indian Affairs, 1848–1872, Register of Letters Sent April, 1866–December, 1871, vol. I:10 (roll 9). In 1875, Meacham was of the opinion that, had Indians of the Warm Springs been permitted to select the more fertile nearby Tygh valley for their homeland, they might have become more "civilized" under the watchful eye of their agents and might have avoided Smohalla's teachings. A. B. Meacham, *Wigwam and War-Path: or the Royal Chief in Chains*, 154–55.

18. Correspondence pertaining to Smohalla and other Dreamers is found in letters from A. B. Meacham to Col. Samuel Ross, Washington Superintendent of Indian Affairs, March 22, 1870; to General George Crook, April 26 and May 1, 1870; to Commissioner E. S. Parker, April 19 and 25, 1870; and to Maj. W. Boyle, May 1, 1870. Oregon Superintendency of Indian Affairs, 1848–1872, Register of Letters Sent April, 1866–December, 1872, vol. I:10 (roll 9); Boyle to Meacham, April 22, May 5, 1870, Oregon Superintendency of Indian Affairs, 1848–1872, Letters Received, March 31–December 1, 1870, vol. 2 (roll 26).

19. Statement of the Indian George Paul, in Thomas Kree, Commission

Secretary, to Commissioner Brunot, July 31, 1871, *Annual Report of the Commissioner of Indian Affairs, 1871*, p. 132.

20. Ibid.

21. *Walla Walla Union*, March 19, 1871, p. 3.

22. E. D. Bannister, report, March 30, 1886, Reports of Inspection . . . of the Office of Indian Affairs, 1873-1900, Yakima Indian Agency, January 19, 1881-January 12, 1885, (no. 1070, roll 59).

23. Meacham, *Wigwam and War-Path*, 181; Stern, "Umatilla Prophet Cult," 346.

24. *Washington Standard* (Olympia, W.T.), March 25, 1871, p. 3.

25. For an account of the confrontation between the commission and the Modocs in which Meacham was wounded and his fellow commissioners, the Reverend Eleasar Thomas and General E. R. S. Canby, were killed, see Ruby and Brown, *Indians of the Pacific Northwest*, 211ff.

26. T. M. Ramsdell, "Indians of Oregon," 28-32, in "Retrospective Reminiscences," MS. 852, Oregon Historical Society; Fairchild to Commissioner E. P. Smith, January 4, 1875, Siletz Indian Agency, Press Copies of Letters Sent to the Commissioner of Indian Affairs by the Siletz Agents, 1873-1914. The *Corvallis Gazette*, January 4, 1873, reported that several months previously a prophet (unnamed) had come among the Indians of the Siletz stating that, were the Indians to dance long and strong, the dead Indians of many previous years would return to, life, after which there would be a successful war against the whites and then a repossession of the Indians' old homes and hunting grounds. The *Gazette* article stated further that the prophecy caused Indians of the Siletz and the Alsea to dance in a "fanatical" fashion for several days and nights.

27. William Bagley to General O. O. Howard, November 20, 1877, Records of the United States Army Continental Commands, 1821-1920, Department of the Columbia, Letters Received from Indian Agents, Entry F. 20, RG 393.

28. A good summation of the Ghost Dance and other religious movements among the Indians at this time is found in Stephen Dow Beckham, Kathryn Anne Toepel, and Rick Minor, *Native American Religious Practices and Uses in Western Oregon*.

29. There has been confusion among scholars such as Mooney (*Ghost-dance Religion*) and Paul Bailey (*Wovoka: The Indian Messiah*) about which prophets were responsible for the first (1870) and second (1889-1890) Ghost Dances. The confusion centered around the identities of four prophets: Wodziwob, Tavibo, Wovoka, and Weneyuga. Wodziwob is credited with initiating the earlier dances. After experiencing trances, he advanced moralistic teachings, as well as the concept of eternal life, in a nativist setting, while stressing the coming extinction of the whites. One of his followers was Tavibo, who was present during the 1870 Ghost Dance and was the father of Wovoka (Jack Wilson), leader of the 1889-90 Ghost Dance. Weneyuga (Frank Spencer) is thought to have been the same person as Wodziwob, perhaps because both preached the doctrine of the return of the dead. Weneyuga's teachings, however, had little effect among his people, the Paviotso and Washo bands of Northern Paiutes. See Inter-Tribal Council of Nevada, *Life Stories of Our Native People: Shoshone, Paiute,*

Washo, 45-46. Spier points out that the 1870 Dance had its inception in Wovoka's family ("The Ghost Dance of 1870 Among the Klamath of Oregon," 43).

30. Wodziwob's preachments spread west to the Klamaths by way of Northern Paiutes on the Klamath Reservation in southern Oregon. The dance was transformed among the Pit River Indians of northern California in the Earthlodge cult, which stressed the end of the world. It also spread to the Shastas, who were mainly in northern California, where it was transformed into the Warmhouse Dance. From the Shastas it spread to the Siletz Reservation, and from there to the Tolowas of northern California. In that state it spread westward among the Patwins, the Pomos, the Wintuns, bringing further distortions to the original dance and encouraging among these peoples the belief in an imminent world catastrophe. Yet another transformation occurred among the Patwins and the Wintuns in the Bolo-Maru cult, which abandoned the concept of world catastrophe for emphasis on the afterlife and a supreme being. Among the several accounts of the Ghost Dances and their ramifications are Cora Du Bois, "The 1870 Ghost Dance;" Frank D. McCann, Jr., "The Ghost Dance, Last Hope of Western Tribes, Unleashed the Final Tragedy"; Mooney, *Ghost-dance Religion*; Omer C. Stewart, "The Ghost Dance," 179. See also Stephen Dow Beckham, Kathryn Ann Toepel, and Rick Minor, *Native American Religious Practices and Uses in Western Oregon*.

31. *Walla Walla Union*, March 25, 1871, p. 2.

32. Ross, *Fur Hunters of the Far West*, 24; W. D. Lyman, *History of the Yakima Valley, Washington, Comprising Yakima, Kittitas, and Benton Counties*, 1: 269-70; Splawn, *Ka-Mi-akin*, 157-58.

33. *Walla Walla Union*, May 17, 1873, p. 3.

34. Ibid., May 24, 1873, p. 3; Frances Fuller Victor, "The Oregon Indians," *Overland Monthly*, 349.

35. G. W. Kennedy, *The Pioneer Campfire . . . Anecdotes, Adventures and Reminiscences*, 198-201. See also *Pacific Christian Advocate*, May 15, 1873, p. 153.

36. *Walla Walla Union*, August 24, 1872, p. 2, and April 5, 1872, p. 3.

37. Ibid., December 27, 1872, p. 3.

38. The rumored story appeared in the *Walla Walla Union*, December 27, 1872. For references to the quake, see n. 14, Chap. 10, below.

39. *Walla Walla Union*, August 24, 1872, p. 2.

40. Odeneal to Commissioner F. H. Walker, August 22, 1872, Oregon Superintendency of Indian Affairs, 1848-1872, Register of Letters Sent, April, 1866-December, 1872, vol. I:10 (roll 9).

41. *Idaho Statesman* (Boise, I.T.), June 30, 1877.

42. Activities of Hackney, or Hehaney, are discussed in correspondence by the Warm Springs agent, Capt. John Smith, to Meacham, August 18, 1871; to Commissioner E. A. Hayt, November 27, December 2, and December 4, 1878, and April 6 and May 1, 1879; and to General Howard, May 2, 1879, Warm Springs Agency, Press Copies of Letters Sent to the Commissioner of Indian Affairs, vol. 1, 1869-74, and vol. 2, 1878-79.

43. Interview with Nettie Showaway, May 30, 1978; E. C. Kemble, report, December 2, 1873, Reports of Inspection . . . of the Office of Indian

Affairs, 1873–1900, Oregon Superintendency, 1873–1877 (no. 1070, roll 33).

44. *Walla Walla Union,* August 16, 1873, p. 2.

45. Kemble to Commissioner E. P. Smith, October 3, 1873, Secretary of the interior, Indian Division, Letters Received, 1873, RG 48, box 82. In a letter to Smith, Kemble furnished the statistics concerning Dreamers shown in table 1.

Kemble's comments on the council preliminaries are in a letter to Smith, September 10, 1873, Reports of Inspection . . . of the Office of Indian Affairs, 1873–1900, Washington Superintendency, 1873–1880 (no. 1070, roll 56). Comments on the council are found in Kemble's "Notes of Council held with Dreamer Indians, at Wallula, Washington Territory Sept 22 [1873]," Secretary of the Interior, Indian Division, Letters Received, 1873.

46. Kemble to Smith, October 3, 1873, ibid.

47. Kemble's "Notes of Council held with Dreamer Indians, at Wallula, Washington Territory Sept. 22 [1873]," Secretary of the Interior, Indian Division, Letters Received, 1873.

48. Smith, report, September 1, 1873, *Annual Report of the Secretary of the Interior, 1873* (43d Cong., 1st sess., H. Doc. no. 1, pt. 5), 4:687.

49. Kemble's visit to the Warm Springs Reservation is also narrated in "White unto Harvest," *Spirit of Missions,* p. 94.

50. William Vandiver, report, November 20, 1874, Reports of Inspection . . . of the Office of Indian Affairs, 1873–1900, Washington Superintendency, 1873–1880, no. 1070 (roll 56).

51. *Annual Report of the Commissioner of Indian Affairs, 1875,* pp. 85–86.

Chapter 6. The Dreamer and the General

1. Odeneal to Commissioner E. S. Parker, August 22, 1872, Oregon Superintendency of Indian Affairs, 1848–1872, Register of Letters Sent, April, 1866–December, 1872, vol. I:10 (roll 9).

2. Wilbur to Milroy, August 26, 1873, *Annual Report of the Commissioner of Indian Affairs, 1873,* p. 313.

3. R. H. Milroy, Simcoe agent, to Commissioner Hiram Price, December 26, 1882, Yakima Indian Agency, Press Copies of Letters Sent to the Commissioner of Indian Affairs, 1877–1921; Henry Ward, report, January 23, 1884, Reports of Inspection . . . of the Office of Indian Affairs, 1873–1900, Yakima Indian Agency, January 19, 1881–January 12, 1885 (no. 1070, roll 58).

4. Such a petition was that cited in John B. Monteith, Nez Percé agent, to John A. Simms, Colville agent, August 13, 1872, MS. 3B, John A. Simms Papers.

5. Relander, *Drummers and Dreamers,* 95–96.

6. *Annual Report of the Secretary of the Interior, 1870* (41st Cong. 3d sess., H. Doc. 1, pt. 4), 486.

7. Curtis, *The North American Indian,* 8:16, 75–76.

8. Herbert Joseph Spinden, "The Nez Percé Indians," 260.

9. For informants' accounts of the prophetess, see Walker, *Conflict and Schism in Nez Perce Acculturation,* 49–51.

10. Joseph's responses are found in the Shanks Commission report, *Annual Report of the Commissioner of Indian Affairs, 1873*, pp. 158–59.

11. The actions of Chief Joseph and other developments in Nez Percé history are also well told in Alvin Josephy, *The Nez Perce Indians and the Opening of the Northwest*, and in Clifford Trafzer and Richard Scheuerman, "Renegade Tribe: The Palouse Indians and the Invasion of the Pacific Northwest."

12. *Annual Report of the Secretary of War, 1877*, pp. 115–16.

13. Howard to Asst. Adjt. General, May 22, 1877, ibid., 590.

14. C. E. S. Wood, "Private Journal, 1879," 167.

15. Howard to Asst. Adjt. General, May 22, 1877, *Annual Report of the Secretary of War, 1877*, p. 590.

16. Ibid., 591; Oliver Otis Howard, *Famous Indian Chiefs I Have Known*, 326, 336. On p. 332 of the latter publication, Howard states that it was on the day after Smohalla's request to him to come for a visit that the Prophet crossed the Columbia River to meet him, hence on April 25.

17. Howard's meeting with Smohalla is recorded in *Annual Report of the Secretary of War, 1877*, 591. The general's meeting with the Prophet and his assessment of him are to be found in his *Famous Indian Chiefs I Have Known*, 333–34, and his *Nez Perce Joseph*, 40–47.

18. Howard to Asst. Adjt. General, Military Division of the Pacific, San Francisco, Calif., May 22, 1877, *Annual Report of the Secretary of War, 1877*, p. 593; O. O. Howard, "The True Story of the Wallowa Campaign," 61. Toohoolsote was among the many Indians who met Spokane Garry on the latter's return from the mission school on the Red River of the North, and Toohoolsote carried back to his Nez Percé people the message of the whites' God. Clifford M. Drury, *Chief Lawyer of the Nez Perce Indians, 1796–1876*, p. 30.

19. Howard, "The True Story of the Wallowa Campaign," 58.

20. Oliver Otis Howard, *My Life and Experiences Among Our Hostile Indians*, 253–55.

21. Young Joseph, "An Indian's Views of Indian Affairs," 421.

22. Ibid., 421.

23. Ibid., 422.

24. Ibid., 422.

25. Oliver Otis Howard, *Nez Perce Joseph*, 54, 64.

26. Young Joseph, "An Indian's Views of Indian Affairs," 412–43; Howard, "The True Story of the Wallowa Campaign," 57.

27. Howard, "True Story of the Wallowa Campaign," 57.

28. Howard to Asst. Adjt. General, May 22, 1877, *Annual Report of the Secretary of War, 1877*, p. 597.

29. The Simcoe Agency headquarters was on the site of the restored Fort Simcoe, about thirty miles southwest of Yakima, Wash. The Klickitat tribe, closely associated with the Yakimas, was brought onto the Yakima Reservation, where the agents found Klickitat chiefs such as Joe Stwyre more amenable than those of the Yakimas in the implementation of government policies. A description of Colwash by a white man of that period appears in Ann Briley's *Lonely Pedestrian: Francis Marion Streamer*, 36.

30. Howard, *Nez Perce Joseph*, 82.

31. The events of the Simcoe council are narrated in Howard, *Nez Perce Joseph*, 78-84. See also Ruby and Brown, *Half-Sun on the Columbia*, 66-68.

32. Wilbur expressed the peaceful disposition of the Indians in letters to Howard on June 21 and 30, and July 3, 1877, Records of the United States Army Continental Commands, 1821-1920, entry F 20, RG 393.

33. Pambrun, "The Story of his Life as he Tells it," 181, 188-190, Hargreaves Library; Pambrun, "Reminiscences," typescript of MS. 1193, Pambrun Papers, Oregon Historical Society. See also Andrew Dominique Pambrun, *Sixty Years on the Frontier in the Pacific Northwest*, 126ff.

34. Young Joseph, "An Indian's Views of Indian Affairs," 423-24.

35. J. Stanley Clark, "The Nez Percés in Exile," 216.

36. "Captain [John W.] Cullen," p. 58, MS. 213A, McWhorter Papers.

37. Drury, *Chief Lawyer of the Nez Perce Indians, 1796-1876*, p. 240.

38. Young Joseph, "An Indian's Views of Indian Affairs," 425.

39. Howard, *Famous Indian Chiefs I Have Known*, 265-66. For an account of further activities of Oytes, see Ruby and Brown, *Indians of the Pacific Northwest*, 249-51, 254-55.

40. W. H. Gray, *The Moral and Religious Aspect of the Indian Question: A Letter Addressed to General John Eaton, Department of the Interior, Bureau of Education, Washington, D.C.*, 3-4.

41. Moses' denouncements of Smohalla are found in the *Morning Oregonian*, May 25, 1878, and in the *Walla Walla Statesman*, July 13, 1878.

42. The Perkins murders, the ensuing hysteria in the white community, and the consequent involvement of Moses in the aftermath of the tragedy are narrated in Ruby and Brown, *Half-Sun on the Columbia*, 86-140.

43. *An Illustrated History of Klickitat, Yakima, and Kittitas Counties*, 164. The activities of Colwash appear in Ruby and Brown, *Indians of the Pacific Northwest*, 228, 235.

44. *Morning Oregonian*, August 8, 1878, p. 3; December 31, 1878, p. 2.

45. *Washington Standard*, March 4, 1879, p. 4; *Weekly Pacific Tribune*, (Seattle, W.T.), August 21, 1878, p. 4; Capt. J. L. Conrad, Comdg. Fort Colville, reported conflict in the spring of 1879 between Umatilla "gambling renegades" and settlers, not far from the mouth of the Okanogan River (Conrad to Adjt. General, Dept. of the Columbia, April 3, 1879, Umatilla Indian Agency, Letters Sent to the Commissioner of Indian Affairs and Other Parties, 1871-1908). Among sources revealing the scenario developed by the white community for coping with the feared Indian attacks are William McKay to Thomas H. Anderson [n.d.], MS. 495F5, Thomas H. Anderson Papers; *An Illustrated History of Klickitat, Yakima and Kittitas Counties*, 164; and *Morning Oregonian*, June 14, August 5, 1878, February 27, 1879.

46. Parnell to Lieut. W. R. Abercrombie, 2d U.S. Inf. Post [Camp Coeur d'Alene] Adjutant, March 12, 1879, "Correspondence relating to the arrest of Chief Moses and the attempts to relocate his band of Indians on the Yakima Reservation, 1878-79," Records of the War Department of the Adjutant General, 1780's-1917, (roll 427), file 6310, AGO 1878, RG 94.

47. S. F. Sherwood to General Nelson A. Miles, May 7, 1878, Washington Superintendency of Indian Affairs, 1853-1880, Letters Received by the Office of Indian Affairs, 1824-1881 (no. 234, roll 918).

48. "The Indians of Simcoe," *San Francisco Chronicle*, July 22, 1878, p. 23.

49. Proceedings of the council are found in Ruby and Brown, *Half-Sun on the Columbia*, 89–97.

50. Ibid., 98ff.

51. Cain to Howard, December 24, 1878, "Correspondence relating to the arrest of Chief Moses . . . ," Records of the War Department of the Adjutant General, 1780's–1917 (roll 427), file 6310, AGO 1878.

52. Rheem to Howard, December 24, 1878, ibid.

53. *Washington* (D.C.) *Post*, April 12, 1879, p. 1.

54. Howard to Ferry, August 8, 1879. "E. P. Ferry State Documents 1876–1880," Elisha P. Ferry Papers.

55. Green to Asst. Adjt. General, Dept. of the Columbia, September 21, 1879, Records of the United States Army Continental Commands, 1821–1920, entry 862, pt. 1, p. 34.

56. Cornoyer to Commissioner, August 10, 1880, *Annual Report of the Commissioner of Indian Affairs, 1880*, pp. 144–47.

Chapter 7. The Demise of Smohalla

1. Miles to Adjt. General Hqrs, Division of the Pacific, July 30, 1883, "Papers relating to reports from white men to dispossess nonreservation Indians settled along the Columbia River and other places within the Military District of the Columbia and to an Interior Department order, May 31, 1884, to U.S. land offices, instructing land agents to refuse to file all entries by whites for lands then settled by Indians, April 1884–March 1885," Records of the War Department of the Adjutant General 1780's–1917, file 1759, AGO 1884, RG 94 (roll 271).

2. Milroy to Grover, April 13, 1883, ibid. There had already been considerable correspondence from Milroy to Commissioner Price regarding the problem of the Dreamer-Renegades on December 26, 1882, and March 17, 27, 28, April 4, 13, 1883. See Yakima Indian Agency, Press Copies of Letters Sent to the Commissioner of Indian Affairs, 1877–1921.

3. McGregor to Post Adjt. (Fort Walla Walla, W.T.), March 29, 1883, Records of the War Department, Office of the Adjutant General, 1780's–1917, file 1468, AGO 1883 (roll 271).

4. McGregory to Post Adjt. (Fort Walla Walla, W.T.), April 15, 1883, Records of the War Department, Office of the Adjutant General, 1780's–1917, file 1759, AGO 1884 (roll 271).

5. Gardner, report, November 27, 1882, Reports of Inspection . . . of the Office of Indian Affairs, 1873–1900, Warm Springs Indian Agency, November 27, 1882–August 31, 1899 (no. 1070, roll 55).

6. Upham to Post (Walla Walla) Adjt., March 18, 1884, Records of the War Department, Office of the Adjutant General, 1780's–1917 file 1759, AGO 1884 (roll 271).

7. Ibid.

8. MacMurray to Asst. Adjt. General, Dept. of the Columbia, August 18, 1884, ibid.

9. Milroy to Price, April 18, 1883, Yakima Indian Agency, Press Copies of Letters Sent to the Commissioner of Indian Affairs, 1877–1921; *Annual Report of the Commissioner of Indian Affairs, 1884*, pp. 172–73.

10. Milroy to Price, July 2, 1884, Yakima Indian Agency, Press Copies of Letters Sent to the Commissioner of Indian Affairs, 1877–1921.

11. *Annual Report of the Commissioner of Indian Affairs, 1884*, p. 172.

12. Milroy to Dear Boys, April 27 and May 4, 1884, MS. 2520, Robert Huston Milroy Papers.

13. Beede to Price, August 28, 1884, Records of the War Department, Office of the Adjutant General, 1780's–1917, file 1759, AGO 1884 (roll 271).

14. Miles to Adjt., Division Hqrs., March 25, 1884, ibid.

15. Statement of Thomas Simpson, Capt. Agency police, and Dave Watlamit, 1st Sgt., September 20, 1884, ibid.

16. Ibid.

17. Milroy to Miles, September 24, 1884, ibid.

18. Ibid.

19. Interview with Hazel Umtuch, March 18, 1983.

20. Milroy to Price, July 28 and October 1, 1884, Yakima Indian Agency, Press Copies of Letters Sent to the Commissioner of Indian Affairs, 1877–1921.

21. *Annual Report of the Commissioner of Indian Affairs, 1884*, p. 173.

22. MacMurray to Asst. Adjt. General, Dept. of the Columbia, September 19, 1884, Records of the War Department, Office of the Adjutant General, 1780's–1917, photocopy of letter in Yakima Indian National Cultural Center Library, Toppenish, Wash.

23. Ibid.; MacMurray to Assst. Adjt. General, Dept. of the Columbia, February 28, 1885, Records of the War Department, Office of the Adjutant General, 1780's–1917, file 1795, AGO 1884 (roll 271).

24. Ibid.

25. Ibid.

26. MacMurray to Asst. Adjt. General, Dept. of the Columbia, March 4, 1885, Records of the War Department, Office of the Adjutant General, 1780's–1917, file 1759, AGO 1884 (roll 271).

27. Pope to Adjt. General, March 26, 1885, ibid.

28. Milroy to Dear Boys, March 20 and 22, 1885, MS. 2520, Milroy Papers.

29. Ibid.; Mooney *Ghost-dance Religion*, 727; *Wash. Standard*, Jan. 10, 1890.

30. Mooney, *Ghost-dance Religion*, 727.

31. Ibid. An account of the visit of Agent Lynch with Tianani is found in *An Illustrated History of Klickitat, Yakima and Kittitas Counties*, 361–62. According to this source, the meeting occurred in 1893, although Mooney stated that Tianani had died in October, 1892 (Mooney, *Ghost-dance Religion*, 727). The "Blower" group is discussed in Mooney, *Ghost-dance Religion*, 760–61.

32. Bernice E. Newell, "A Glimpse into the Yakima Reservation," 12–13.

33. Mooney, *Ghost-dance Religion*, 727.

34. Lynch to Commissioner, June [n.d.], 1893, Yakima Indian Agency, Press Copies of Letters Sent to the Commissioner of Indian Affairs, 1877–1921.

35. Agent L. T. Erwin to Commissioner D. M. Browning, August 28, 1894, ibid.

36. Crawford to Commissioner, December 16, 1891, Umatilla Indian Agency, Letters Sent to the Commissioner of Indian Affairs and Other Parties, 1871–1908.

37. Newell, "A Glimpse into the Yakima Reservation," 12.

38. Stewart Culin, "A Summer Trip Among the Western Indians," 157.

39. Crawford to Commissioner, June 22 and September 28, 1892, Umatilla Indian Agency, Letters Sent to the Commissioner of Indian Affairs and Other Parties, 1879–1908.

40. Milroy to Price, March 29, 1884, Yakima Indian Agency, Press Copies of Letters Sent to the Commissioner of Indian Affairs, 1877–1921.

41. Sharkey, *Revitalization and Change*, 96 and nn.

42. Smohalla's widow died in a Tacoma hospital in January, 1940. *Yakima* (Wash.) *Republic*, January 18, 1940. The newspaper headlined the story, "Prophet's Widow Called by Death."

43. Relander interview with George So-Happy, February 14, 1952, MS. in folder, "Indians" Relander Papers.

44. "Death of Yo-Yonen, Chief of the Wana Pums," p. 1., MS. 1524, McWhorter Papers.

45. "Paiute Vision of the First Wolf People," p. 71, MS. 1514, McWhorter Papers.

46. Guie, "Articles Misc. 7/22/37," MS. 2511, Guie Papers.

47. C. R. Whitlock, Yakima superintendent, to Dean Guie, September 21, 1933, box 1 of 3, MS. 2511, Guie Papers.

48. Robert H. Ruby, who witnessed the ceremonial, gives a detailed account of it in "Ancient First Roots Ceremony of the Dreamers," *Northwest Legacy: The Magazine of Local History*, 1, no. 3 (March 1976): 201–26.

49. The only "treaty" that the Wanapams ever signed was an agreement of January 15, 1957, which men of the four remaining families at Priest Rapids made with the Grant County, Wash., Public Utility District. The Federal Power Commission required the pact to protect the utility from future claims on the project site of Priest Rapids Dam. By the terms of the agreement, the utility agreed to pay the tribal remnant a $20,000 cash settlement to be divided among the survivors, $1,300 of which was to be retained by the utility to finance feasts and religious ceremonies for the survivors and their guests at the damsite. The Wanapams were also assured the right to fish and hunt on the waters and lands of the project, life-long housing in individual homes provided with electricity and water, a longhouse, and employment on the dam. The utility also agreed to remove the ancient pictographs from nearby Whale Island in the Columbia River to new burial grounds and to provide a recreational area as well as employment in coming years for families remaining at Priest Rapids. Sharkey gives a good account of the Wanapam's latter days in her *Revitalization And Change*, 95–113.

Chapter 8. Skolaskin's Sanpoil Heritage

1. Elliott Coues, ed., *New Light on the Early History of the Greater Northwest: The Manuscript Journals of Alexander Henry, Fur Trader of the Northwest Company, and of David Thompson . . . 1799–1814*, 2:711. In *The North American Indian*, 7:64, Curtis renders the name Sīnpoélihuh.

2. Curtis, *The North American Indian*, 7:64. See also Verne F. Ray, *The Sanpoil and Nespelem: Salishan Peoples of Northeastern Washington*, 5; 21–24, for tribal numbers.

3. For accounts on these various attacks, see Ray, *Sanpoil and Nespelem*, 115; James A. Teit, "The Salishan Tribes of the Western Plateaus," 258–59.

4. Verne F. Ray, *Cultural Relations in the Plateau of Northwestern America*, Publications of the Frederick Webb Hodge Anniversary Publication Fund, 3:37.

5. Trading patterns of the Sanpoils and their Salishan neighbors are discussed in James H. Teit, "The Middle Columbia Salish," 121. Whites were intrigued by Kettle Falls and by the natives' methods of catching salmon there. One of several accounts of fishing there is found in the *Walla Walla Union*, August 3, 1872, p. 2. In his *Coast Salish Essays*, 282–86, Wayne Suttles reconciles the opposing views of Verne Ray, who stressed the Sanpoil's peaceful disposition, and those who cite their warring tendencies. There appears to be no evidence that they were involved in early conflicts on the high plains during the horse buffalo-hunting era, but they did not acquire horses until late in the period.

6. Ray gives the location of Sanpoil villages in his *Sanpoil and Nespelem*, 16–21. He gives the name *npui•ʔux* to the village near the mouth of the Sanpoil River to which the Sanpoil historian Clara Moore applied the name Enparaililk in an interview, July 1, 1961. See Ruby and Brown, *A Guide to the Indian Tribes of the Pacific Northwest*, 183.

7. For an account of the Sanpoil acquisition of horses, see Ray, *Sanpoil and Nespelem*, 117.

8. P. J. De Smet, S.J., *Oregon Missions and Travels over the Rocky Mountains. In 1845–46. By Father P. J. De Smet of the Society of Jesus. XIX*, 380–81.

9. Thomas W. Symons, "Reports of an Examination of the Upper Columbia River and the Territory in Its Vicinity in September and October, 1881, to Determine Its Navigability and Adaptability to Steamboat Transportation" (47th Cong., 1st sess., S. Docs. 186 and 188), 30–31; *Wilbur* (Wash.) *Register*, October 18, 1895, p. 4. See also Boas, *Folk-tales of Salishan and Sahaptin Tribes*, 101–02.

10. One of the many legends pertaining to Hell Gate appears in the *Wilbur Register*, August 23, 1895, p. 8.

11. Curtis, *The North American Indian*, 7:77.

12. Ibid.; Spier, *Prophet Dance*, 55–57.

13. Ray, *Sanpoil and Nespelem*, 21–22.

14. The eruption of Mt. Saint Helens and its ash fallout are described in Ruby and Brown, *Indians of the Pacific Northwest*, 22, 62, 67, 74, and 96.

15. Spier, *Prophet Dance*, p. 7.

16. The Dream Dance is discussed in Walter Cline et al., "The Sinkaietk or Southern Okanagon of Washington," 172–76.

17. The confession dance, which was also incorporated in the Smohallan rites of the Tenino Indians, is discussed in Spier, *Prophet Dance*, p. 8 and n., where the bird in Okanagon worship is discussed as well. See also Cline et al., *Sinkaietk or Southern Okanagon*, 175–76. Okanagon cosmological beliefs are discussed in Ross, *Adventures of the First Settlers on the Oregon or Columbia River*, 287–88.

18. Spier, *Prophet Dance*, p. 9.

19. Thompson's visit and his observations are recorded in *David Thompson's Narrative, 1784–1812,* ed. Richard Glover, 339–46.

20. Henry stated that in the summer of 1810 his North West Company had built a post on the Sanpoil River where Nor'Westers met Indians from the south and west who came there to trade the pelts of beaver, bear, otter, and other valuable animals, as well as horses, "on which they appeared to set no value." It seems that Henry was in error about the location of the post, however. He was referring to Spokane House, which was built that summer in the Spokane country east of the Sanpoils. It would have been out of character for the Sanpoils to permit a post in their country. Henry's Nor'Wester contemporary David Thompson, who visited them in the summer of 1811, made no mention of such a post. Neither did other early fur men in the area, such as Alexader Ross. See Coues, *New Light on the Early History...,* 2:711, for Alexander Henry's observations of the Sanpoils.

21. Ross Cox, *Adventures on the Columbia River,* 2: 125–26, 145–46.

22. Lewis, William S. "Information Concerning the Establishment of Fort Colvile," 107.

Chapter 9. The Crippling

1. Inteview with Alice Cleveland, July 22, 1961; Ray, "Kolaskin Cult," 67.

2. There are numerous versions of the story of Skolaskin's crippling, all of them after-the-fact accounts such as that given by a group of elderly Sanpoils on October 27, 1960, at Nespelem, Wash. (a typescript of their "Statement of Sanpoil Panelists," is in the possession of the authors). The panelists revealed Skolaskin's dependence on horses for getting around. He favored those tamed by white men, who he said broke them to ride more skillfully than did his own people. The Sanpoils were less skilled horsemen than were other tribes such as the Columbia Sinkiuses, whose skill was unmatched among the peoples of the region including the Nez Percés and the Cayuses. Interviews with Bill Thornburg, November 21, 1959, and Henry Covington, July 1, 1960.

3. Ray, "Kolaskin Cult," 68.

4. R. D. Gwydir, "A Record of the San Poil Indians," 244. Other accounts of Skolaskin's crippling were given in interviews with Bill Thornburg, November 21, 1959; Luther Jones, October 4, 1960; and Herman Friedlander, May 4, 1964.

5. Ray, "Kolaskin Cult," 67–69. Fred Runnels (or Reynolds), a son of Tenas George Runnels (who was a brother-in-law of Skolaskin) and a grandson of the headman, Quequetas, was told by Skolaskin that his debility dated from a horse accident in his sixteenth year in Walla Walla, W.T. (interview with George Nanampkin, May 14, 1964). Other, nonaccidental causes of Skolaskin's condition are possible: a herb with teratogenic properties taken by his pregnant mother; congenital joint dislocation during birth; joint disease resulting from syphilis, tuberculosis, or bacterial or rheumatoid arthritis; aseptic necrosis of lower-extremity bones, resulting in muscle atrophy and contracture; lack of bone development, or hypoplasia; osteomylitis; and Legg Perthes, an osteochondritis of the capitular epiphysis of the femur.

6. Cline et al., *Sinkaietk or Southern Okanagon*, 173; Ray, "Kolaskin Cult," 67–69.

7. Ray, "Kolaskin Cult," 68–69.

8. Another sister married a Wenatchee.

9. For an account of activities of these missionaries, see Ruby and Brown, *The Spokane Indians*, 59–82.

10. Quilentsuten was the Sanpoil term for the Christian God, although for Skolaskin it meant the god of the natives. Ray, "Kolaskin Cult," 68 and n.

11. "Statement of Sanpoil Panelists," pp. 3, 4. See Spier, *Prophet Dance*, 9. The evening on which Skolaskin was said to have "died," his people reportedly covered his head with towels. Then one morning, after they had dressed him in funeral clothes, he began tugging at them. Shortly he awoke and almost immediately began addressing those present; interview with Henry Covington, [n.d.] 1958.

12. Spier, *Prophet Dance*, 9.

13. "Statement of Sanpoil Panelists," pp. 2–3. See also Spier, *Prophet Dance*, 9.

14. Interview with Herman Friedlander, May 4, 1964.

15. Interviews with Isabel Arcasa, July 15, 1961; and Madeline Covington, July 14, 1961.

16. The Southern Okanagon Dreamer-Prophet Suiepkine was said to have seduced maidens (Cline et al., *Sinkaietk or Southern Okanagon*, 174). The descriptions of Skolaskin's experiences with women are from interviews with George Nanampkin, May 14, 1964, and Madeline Covington, July 14, 1961.

17. Ray, "Kolaskin Cult," 70.

18. In the file on Skolaskin in the Colville Indian Agency records at Nespelem, Wash., is a list of his several wives. Information about his wives is from interviews with Clara Moore, November 22, 1959, March 4, 1961, and July 14, 1961; Henry Covington, July 1, 1960; Harry Nanampkin and Cull White, March 4, 1961; Alice Cleveland, July 9 and July 22, 1961; Madeline Covington, July 14, 1961; Isabel Arcasa, July 15, 1961; Herman Friedlander, May 4, 1964; George Nanampkin, May 14, 1964; Mary Ellen Runnels Wickersham, June 21, 1964. Information about Skolaskin's wives is also found in *In the Supreme Court of the State of Washington In the Matter of the Estate of John Enos, Deceased. Susan Enos, Appellant,* Vs. *Lawrence R. Hamblen, Executor of the Last Will and Testament of John Enos Deceased. Mary Enos, Catholic Church of Santo Antao Topo, San Jorge, Azores Islands, Each of Asylums for the Homeless at Villa das Villa, San Jorge, Azores Islands, and the Young Men's Christian Association of Spokane Washington Respondents. Washington Reports vol. 79. Cases Determined in the SUPREME COURT of Washington March 27, 1914–June 1, 1914 #11738. Dept. Two, May 12, 1914.* See also Ray, "Kolaskin Cult," 70.

Chapter 10. The Encroaching Whites and the Shaking Earth

1. Yantis to Superintendent of Indian Affairs, July 20, 1857, Washington Superintendency of Indian Affairs, 1853–1880, Letters from Employees Assigned to the Columbia River, or Southern, District and the Yakima Agency, May 1, 1854–July 20, 1861 (roll 17).

2. Burns, *The Jesuits and the Indian Wars of the Northwest*, 138; Ray, "Cultural Relations in the Plateau of Northwestern America," 31.

3. *Annual Report of the Secretary of the Interior, 1859* (36th Cong., 1st sess., S. Doc. 2), 1:759.

4. Winans to Samuel Ross, Washington Superintendent of Indian Affairs, June 30, 1870. MS. W-34, 147/4, W. P. Winans Papers, interviews with Clara Moore, February 5, 1958, March 4, May 27, June 30, July 1, and July 8, 1961. Wilson Creek extends south from below the Columbia River into east-central Washington.

5. Winans to Ross, August 1, 1870, MS. W-34, 147/4, Winans Papers.

6. Harvey's activities are narrated in Ruby and Brown, *Half-Sun on the Columbia*, 51–53.

7. Winans to T. J. McKenny, Washington Superintendent of Indian Affairs, June 30, 1872, MS. W-34, 147/4, Winans Papers.

8. Ibid.

9. S. F. Sherwood, interpreter-guide, to Winans, June 30, 1872, Winans Papers.

10. Simms to R. H. Milroy, Washington Superintendent of Indian Affairs, November 20, 1872, MS 3B, Simms Papers.

11. Sherwood to Winans, November 6, 1871, MS. W-38, 147/5, Winans Papers.

12. *In the Supreme Court of the State of Washington In the Matter of the Estate of John Enos . . . .*

13. Winans, "Journal" (Summer, 1870), MS. W-34, 147/4, Winans Papers. Okanagon informants called Suiepkine the "last chief" of the Kartar band. Although not prophesying the coming of white men, since they had already come in his time, he warned his people of the dangers of their coming. Cline et al., *Sinkaietk or Southern Okanagon*, 174.

14. Cline et al., *Sinkaietk or Southern Okanagon*, 173. There is ample evidence that the quake occurred the night of December 14, 1872. See Bechtel Inc., *Investigation of the December 14, 1872, Earthquake in the Pacific Northwest*; Edward S. Holden, *A Catalogue of Earthquakes on the Pacific Coast, 1769–1897*, Smithsonian Miscellaneous Collections, no. 1078 (1898). Among other sources detailing the quake are Ruby and Brown, *Indians of the Pacific Northwest*, 227, and Ray, "Kolaskin Cult," 72 and n. Ray, however, places the major quake on November 22, 1873, nearly a year later. Aftershocks from the major quake of December 14, 1872, did continue into 1873.

15. W. S. Nelson, "The Dreamers," 226.

16. Ray, "Kolaskin Cult," 72. Among the several informants claiming that Skolaskin predicted the quake were the elderly Sanpoil panelists ("Statement of Sanpoil Panelists," p. 4) and Henry Covington, in his interviews on [n.d.] 1958, and July 1, 1960, and Herman Friedlander, in his interview of May 4, 1964.

17. Gwydir, "A Record of the San Poil Indians," 244.

18. An account of how not only heredity but also leadership qualities and physical abilities enabled one to ascend to the chieftaincy may be found in Henry Ruby, "Changes in Ascendency of Lower Plateau Indian Chiefs," MS. in possession of authors.

Chapter 11. The Preaching

1. Gwydir, "A Record of the San Poil Indians," 244.

2. Ray, "Kolaskin Cult," 68–69.

3. Interviews with William Friedlander, April 26, 1964; Herman Friedlander, May 4, 1964, and George Nanampkin, May 14, 1964; letter from Herman Friedlander to authors, May 9, 1964.

4. Cline et al., *Sinkaietk or Southern Okanagon*, 173.

5. Interview with Clara Moore, June 30, 1961.

6. Ray, "Kolaskin Cult," 70 and n.

7. Ibid. L. V. McWhorter described the sweathouse among Yakima Indians as "the center about which circulated a legion of spiritual regulative rulings of hoary antiquity" ("The Dreamer Religion of the Yakima Indians," p. 3, MS. 1519, no. 1, McWhorter Papers). The rationale for the sweathouse and its various implications are explained in Cline et al., *Sinkaietk or Southern Okanagon*, 167.

8. Interviews with Clara Moore, Harry Nanampkin, and Cull White, March 4, 1961, and Clara Moore, May 27, June 30, and July 16, 1961.

9. Interviews with Bill Thornburg, November 21, 1959, Henry Covington, July 1, 1960, and Clara Moore, March 4, 1961.

10. Interview with Clara Moore, July 7, 1961.

11. Interview with Clara Moore, July 16, 1961.

12. Interview with Bill Thornburg, November 21, 1959, and July 2, 1960. Okanagon informants told of Skolaskin's supposed ability to transform people (Cline et al., *Sinkaietk or Southern Okanagon*, 173).

13. Interview with Bill Thornburg, November 21, 1959, and July 2, 1960.

14. Curtis, *The North American Indian*, 7:78.

15. Interview with Cull White, June 12, 1960.

16. An account of Milroy's journey to the new or second Colville Reservation was given by his son, R. B. Milroy. It is included in box 2 of 3, MS. 2511, Guie Papers.

17. Milroy to Simms, May 23, 1873, MS. 5, Simms Papers.

18. Winans to Reverend Linsley [A. L. Lindsley?], December 20, 1875, MS. W-67, 147/9, Winans Papers.

19. Simms to E. P. Smith, Commissioner of Indian Affairs, September 1, 1875, MS. 12A, Simms Papers.

20. David Humphreys Miller, *Ghost Dance*, 27.

21. Ross, *Adventures of the First Settlers on the Oregon or Columbia River*, 286–88.

22. Grassi to Reverend Father Superior, Joseph Cataldo, S.J., April 19, 1881, Grassi Papers.

23. Ray, "Kolaskin Cult," 71.

24. Interview with Bill Thornburg, July 2, 1960.

25. The *Walla Walla Union*, March 22, 1873, p. 3, told of Covington's trading in Walla Walla: "Sunday last a large mule pack train with goods, partly for Mr. Covington's trading post and partly for some Chinese miners started for White Stone on the Columbia River. Accompanied by a pack train of about 30 Chinamen. Both trains heavily loaded."

26. *Spokane Falls Review*, May 16, 1889, p. 6. Inspector Gardner's report of the projected ark is found in the *Walla Walla Union*, February 10, 1883.

27. "Statement of Sanpoil Panelists," p. 7; interviews with Henry Covington, July 1, 1960, Clara Moore, June 30, 1961, and George Nanampkin, May 14, 1964; *Spokane Falls Review*, May 16, 1889, p. 6; *Morning Review* (Spokane Falls, W.T.), May 12, 1889, p. 6.

Chapter 12. The Black-Robe Challenge

1. The Roman Catholic clerics who followed Blanchet and the Demers to the Pacific Northwest made attempts to bring word of the whites' god to the Sanpoils, not bearing out Ray's contention that "the Catholic missionaries do not seem to have opposed Kolaskin" ("Kolaskin Cult," 72n). The Reverend Peter J. De Smet, S.J., who laid the foundations for missions among the upper-interior Salishan peoples, was very solicitous about rescuing them not only from perdition but also from Protestants. In his *Oregon Missions and Travels over the Rocky Mountains*, vol. 29:29, 108, 110–11, 170, and 220, De Smet wrote of the Sanpoils, whom he included within the scope of his missionary endeavors. In *The Jesuits and the Indian Wars of the Northwest*, Burns has many citations of Jesuit missionary work among the Sanpoils.

2. "Colville Missions by J [oset]," MS. folder, Reverend Joseph Joset, S.J., Papers.

3. The account of the exposure of the Sanpoils to the smallpox is found in Ray, *Sanpoil and Nespelem*, 21–22. Hoecken's letter is cited in Sister Maria Ilma Raufer, O.P., *Black Robes and Indians on the Last Frontier*, 73–74.

4. Grassi to Cataldo, April 19, 1881, Grassi Papers; Raufer, *Black Robes and Indians*, 92 and n.

5. Religious personages and their beliefs moved from region to region along the trade routes, and that apparently was how those from east of the Cascade Mountains moved west to areas such as the upper Skagit River. A surveyor in the employ of the Northern Pacific Railroad Company stated in 1870 that, before trading posts were established on Puget Sound, the Indians of the Skagit traded their furs east of the Cascade Mountains at Fort Okanogan (notes by D. C. Linsley on his "Special Examination Cascade Mountains in 1870 – May and June," pp. 25, 96, Chief Engineer Old Vault Files, no. 156, Minnesota Historical Society). The Skagit River tribes traveled, for example, over the Cascade and Ross passes and eastward up the Cascade and Suiattle rivers. Not the least important reason why Indians east of the Cascade Mountains avoided the westward passages was the fear of contracting diseases from the Puget Sound tribes, who had begun trading at Puget Sound posts such as Fort Nisqually, which had been established on southern Puget Sound in 1833. Northern Puget Sound natives had access even early to Fort Langley, established in 1827 on the lower Fraser River in Canada. For accounts of these Skagit peoples, see June McCormick Collins, "A Study of Religious Change Among the Skagit Indians of Washington," in David Agee Horr, ed., *Coast Salish and Western Washington Indians IV*, pp. 682–89, and *Valley of the Spirits: The Upper Skagit Indians of Western Washington*, 32–34. See also Martin J. Sampson,

Indians of Skagit County, 59–60. The Prophet Dance and its relation to the religions of Puget Sound Indians is discussed in Wayne Suttles, "Post-Contact Culture Change Among the Lummi Indians," 48–51. The most complete account of the Prophet phenomenon among Coastal Salish peoples is found in Suttles's *Coast Salish Essays,* 152–98.

6. J. Orin Oliphant, *The Early History of Spokane, Washington, Told by Contemporaries,* 44–45.

7. *Northwest Tribune* (Spokane Falls, W.T.), July 7, 1880, p. 4.

8. Grassi to Rev. and Dearest Father, October 4, 1873, in Grassi, "Indian Missions," *Woodstock Letters,* 3, no. 1 (1874); 68–73. See also Raufer, *Black Robes and Indians,* 155. Grassi's work among the Wenatchee Indians is described in Richard D. Scheuerman, ed., *The Wenatchi Indians: Guardians of the Valley,* 63ff.

9. Grassi to Reverend Father, June 29, 1876, Grassi Papers.

10. Ibid.

11. Ibid.

12. Grassi to Reverend Father, April 23, 1878, in Grassi, "Indian Missions," 174–78. Tosi's enumeration of the Indians is in Raufer, *Black Robes and Indians,* 102–03.

13. Grassi to Reverend Father, April 23, 1878, in Grassi, "Indian Missions." The Okanagon informants' claim that Skolaskin made a journey to Purgatory is found in Cline et al., *Sinkaietk or Southern Okanagon,* 173.

14. Reverend Alexander Diomedi, S.J., "Tour of a Missionary," in Diomedi, *Sketches of Modern Indian Life,* 32. At least two white storekeepers in the Sanpoil country were married to Indian women: "Virginia Bill" Covington, married to the Sanpoil Smillkeen, and Herman Friedlander, married to the Entiat Elizabeth.

15. Diomedi, "Tour of a Missionary," in his *Sketches of Modern Indian Life,* 32.

16. The Okanagons' claim that Skolaskin was mercenary in religious matters is found in Cline et al., *Sinkaietk or Southern Okanagon,* 174, and Grassi to Cataldo, April 19, 1881, Grassi Papers.

17. *Catholic Sentinel* (Portland, Ore.), April 17, 1890, p. 8, and May 1, 1890, p. 5, carried short biographies of Grassi. See also Raufer, *Black Robes and Indians on the Last Frontier,* 171ff.

18. There are numerous references to De Rougé in Raufer, *Black Robes and Indians.*

19. Francis Streamer, "Elsis" notebook, p. 38, Francis Streamer Papers. See also Briley, *Lonely Pedestrian.*

20. *Catholic Sentinel,* March 9, 1911, p. 7.

Chapter 13. The Coming of Moses and Joseph

1. Interview with Clara Moore, February 5, 1958.

2. *Spokesman-Review* (Spokane, Wash.), August 21, 1899, p. 8.

3. *Walla Walla Statesman,* July 14, 1877, p. 3.

4. The Spokane Falls council is reported in *Annual Report of the Secretary of War, 1877,* 1:641ff.

5. Ibid., 646–47.

6. S. F. Sherwood discusses the composition of the mixed bands of In-

dians living in the Columbia, Colville, and Kettle river valleys who were slated for removal to the Colville Reservation. Sherwood, statement, November 6, 1882, Reports of Inspection . . . of the Office of Indian Affairs, 1873–1900, Colville Indian Agency, November 18, 1882–August 27, 1900 (no. 1070, roll 70). The six-mile strip agreement is discussed in John A. Simms to Inspector Robert Gardner, November 9, 1882, ibid.

7. The Moses, or Columbia, reservation is discussed in Ruby and Brown, *Half-Sun on the Columbia*, 156ff.

8. Interview with Clara Moore, March 4, 1961.

9. The events surrounding the removal of Moses and his people and their settlement on the Colville Reservation are discussed in Ruby and Brown, *Half-Sun on the Columbia*, 156ff.

10. Sherwood, statement, November 6, 1882, Reports of Inspection . . . of the Office of Indian Affairs, 1873–1900, Colville Indian Agency, November 18, 1882–August 27, 1900 (no. 1070, roll 70).

11. Ibid.

12. Simms, report, November 10, 1882, ibid.

13. Symons, report, November 14, 1882, ibid.

14. The Kettle River council and Moses' journey to Washington, D.C., are discussed in Ruby and Brown, *Half-Sun on the Columbia*, 203ff.

15. Merriam to Waters, Febraury 9, 1885, Colville Indian Agency Records, Letters Received, 1880–1894, letterbox 19.

16. Waters to Price, March 3, 1885, Colville Indian Agency Records, Letters Sent June 26, 1884–February 10, 1886, letterbox 3.

17. Waters to John D. C. Atkins, Commissioner, April 16, 1885, ibid.

18. Gwydir, report, August 31, 1888, *Annual Report of the Secretary of the Interior, 1888* (50th Cong., 2d sess., H. Doc. no. 1, pt. 5), 2:222.

19. Moses' statement about white men making whiskey is found in Rickard Gwydir, Colville agent, to Commissioner John D. C. Atkins, August 1, 1887, Colville Indian Agency Records, Letters Sent, January 24, 1885–July 19, 1897, letterbook 7. In July 1861 [n.d.] Major Pinkney Lugenbeel, special Indian agent and commandant of Fort Colville, wrote the Spokane County (W.T.) commissioners to complain of the ease with which Indians under his charge could obtain liquor. MS. W-38A, 147/5, Winans Papers.

20. Waters to Atkins, May 4, 1885, Colville Indian Agency Records, Letters Sent, June 26, 1884–February 10, 1886, letterbook 3.

21. Fletcher to Asst. Adjt. General, May 11, 1886, Correspondence and reports relating to the condition of the Chief Moses and Joseph Indians in the Department of the Columbia, including a request that the Department of the Interior supply agricultural implements to them, May 1886–May 1887, Records of the War Department, Office of the Adjutant General, 1780's–1917, file 2458, AGO 1886, RG 94 (roll 452).

22. Kent to Asst. Adjt. General, October 21, 1886, ibid.

23. Kent to Asst. Adjt. General, April 1, 1887, ibid.

24. Frank C. Armstrong, report, June 11, 1887, Reports of Inspection . . . of the Office of Indian Affairs, 1873–1900, Colville Indian Agency, November 18, 1882–August 2, 1900 (no. 1070, roll 70).

25. Gwydir, "A Record of the San Poil Indians," 243.

26. Ibid.

27. General John Gibbon, report, August 31, 1887, in Washington Na-

tional Guard, *The Official History of the Washington National Guard*, 4: 289.2.

28. Gwydir, "A Record of the San Poil Indians," 246.

29. For a description of the San Poil council, see ibid., 246-48.

30. For a description of the Nespelem council, see ibid., 249-50.

31. Gwydir to Atkins, August 1, 1887, Colville Indian Agency Records, Letters Sent, January 24, 1884-July 10, 1897, letterbook 7.

Chapter 14. A Tale of Two Prisons

1. Atkins to Gwydir, January 25, 1888, Selected Documents from Among the Records of the Bureau of Indian Affairs Relating to Skolaskin, chief of the San Puell Indians, Letters Received, 1885-1892, RG 75.

2. Gwydir to Atkins, November 21, 1887, ibid.

3. Gwydir to Atkins, April 14, 1888, ibid.

4. It had long been government policy to invite the Indians to the national capital to impress them with the power of the United States. Pacific Northwest officials had suggested that the region's Indian chiefs make the journey as early as the 1850's.

5. James C. Sanders, report, January 17, 1889, Reports of Inspection . . . of the Office of Indian Affairs, 1873-1900, Colville Indian Agency, November 18, 1882-August 2, 1900 (no. 1070, roll 70).

6. *Morning Review*, March 12, 1889.

7. Commissioner to Secretary of the Interior, October 29, 1889, Bureau of Indian Affairs, "Selected Documents . . . Relating to Skolaskin."

8. Cline et al., *Sinkaietk or Southern Okanagon*, 173-74.

9. Ray, "Kolaskin Cult," 73; interviews with Henry Covington, November 11, 1960, and Emily Peone, November 1, 1983. Skolaskin's granddaughter stated that the jail was rock-walled (interview with Alice Cleveland, July 9, 1961).

10. Interviews with Bill Thornburg, November 21, 1959, and July 2, 1960.

11. Interview with Clara Moore, July 16, 1961.

12. Interview with Jim James, July 28, 1960.

13. *Seattle Post Intelligencer*, July 9, 1905, p. 12.

14. In his "Kolaskin Cult," 74, Verne Ray states that Ginnamonteesah killed a cousin of Kunnumsahwickssa. Other sources state that Kunnumsahwickssa shot Ginnamonteesah, e.g., *Annual Report of the Secretary of the Interior, 1889* (51st Cong., 1st sess., H. Doc. no. 1, p. 5), 2: 284. Clara Moore, a historian of her Sanpoil people, confirmed the account of the shooting appearing in the *Annual Report of the Secretary of the Interior, 1889* (interview, November 22, 1959).

15. A. J. Chapman, military inspector-interpreter, to General John Gibbon, Comdg. Dept. of the Columbia, October 5, 1889, Records of the United States Army Continental Commands, 1821-1920, 2543 DC 1889.

16. Gibbon to Cole, September 29, 1889, ibid., 5/3025 DC 1889; Thomas T. Minor to Cole, September 29, 1889, ibid., 4/3025 DC 1889; Cole to Commissioner, October 10, 1889, ibid., 2/3025 DC 1889. Minor drowned three months later on a hunting trip in Puget Sound, along with the son of the Col. Granville O. Haller who fought in the Yakima War and a brother-in-law of the younger Haller. Hubert Howe Bancroft, *History of*

Washington, Idaho, and Montana, 1854–1889, vol. 31 of *The Works of Hubert Howe Bancroft* (1890). See also James R. Warren, "Famous Young Seattle Pioneers," *Northwest Magazine* in *Seattle Post Intelligencer*, May 11, 1980, p. 12.

17. Gibbon to Cole, September 29, 1889, Records of the United States Army Continental Commands, 1821–1920, 5/3025 DC 1889.

18. Cole to Gibbons, October 9, 1889, ibid., 2616 DC 1889; Cole to Commissioner, October 10, 1889, ibid, 2/3025 DC 1889.

19. Morgan to Secretary of the Interior, October 29, 1889, ibid., 1/3025 DC 1889.

20. Chandler to Secretary of War, October 30, 1889, ibid., 3025 DC 1889.

21. Interview with Clara Moore, November 22, 1959; Henry Covington, July 1, 1960.

22. Gerhard Luke Luhn, Capt. 4th Infantry, to Asst. Adjt. General, Dept. of the Columbia, December 3, 1889, Records of the United States Army Continental Commands, 1821–1920, 3151 DC 1889. It was reported that an Indian named Skolaskin had escaped from Fort Huachuca in Arizona earlier in 1889. Erwin N. Thompson, in his *Golden Gate, The Rock: A History of Alcatraz Island, 1847–1972*, p. 297, states that Skolaskin had arrived at Fort Huachuca earlier that year and was not released until July, 1892. Writes Thompson: "It is not known why Skolaskin had been imprisoned at Fort Huachuca; he was a Sanpoil Indian from the Pacific Northwest." Since the prisoner named Skolaskin was reported to have been in the Arizona prison earlier in 1889, while the Sanpoil Skolaskin was not taken from his homeland until late November of that year on his journey to Alcatraz, it is unlikely that the latter was the one confined for a time in Arizona. Some sources erroneously state that Skolaskin was incarcerated in the federal penitentiary on McNeil Island, Washington. See Raufer, *Black Robes and Indians*, 234, and Ray, "Kolaskin Cult," 74.

23. Kent to Asst. Adjt. General Dept. of the Columbia, November 23, 1889, Records of the United States Army Continental Commands, 1821–1920, 3068 DC 1889.

24. Haskin to Asst. Adjt. General, Dept. of the Columbia, April 16, 1890. Bureau of Indian Affairs, "Selected Documents . . . Relating to Skolaskin."

25. Kent to Asst. Adjt. General, Dept. of the Columbia, May 4, 1890, Records of the United States Army Continental Commands, 1821–1902, 1136 DC 1890.

26. Synopsis of James C. Sander's report, January 17, 1889, Reports of Inspection . . . of the Office of Indian Affairs, 1873–1900. Colville Indian Agency, 1882–1900 (no. 1070, roll 70).

27. Kent to Asst. Adjt. General, Dept. of the Columbia, May 4, 1890, Records of the United States Army Continental Commands, 1821–1920, 1136 DC 1890.

28. General Gibbons, endorsement, May 8, 1890, "Selected Documents . . . Relating to Skolaskin."

29. Duvall to Asst. Adjt. General, Dept. of California, May 15, 1890, ibid.

30. Miles to Adjt. General of the Army, May 23, 1890, ibid.

31. Breck to Comdg. General, Division of the Pacific, July 10, 1890, Records of the United States Army Continental Commands, 1821-1920, 2009 DC 1890.

32. General Gibbon, report, August 19, 1890, Washington National Guard, *The Official History of the Washington National Guard*, 4: 289.2.

33. Accounts of the council and Indian complaints voiced there are found in the "Miscellaneous Notebook" of Francis Streamer, the Indian advocate in attendance, folders 2-4, Streamer Papers.

34. Pearson to Welsh, April 21, 1891, "Selected Documents . . . Relating to Skolaskin."

35. *San Francisco Chronicle*, April 10, 1891.

36. "Skolaskin Memorandum," n.d., "Selected Documents . . . Relating to Skolaskin."

37. Interview with Henry Covington, July 1, 1960.

38. Welsh to Corresponding Secretary Indian Rights Assn., May 5, 1891, "Selected Documents . . . Relating to Skolaskin."

39. Commissioner to Secretary of the Interior, May 21, 1891, ibid.

40. Mears to Asst. Adjt. General, Hqrs. Division of the Pacific, June 15, 1891, "Selected Documents . . . Relating to Skolaskin."

41. Cole to Commissioner, June 4, 1892, ibid.

42. Skolaskin's promise, with his signature, is found among correspondence to Comdg. General, Dept. of the Columbia, July 22, 1892, Records of the War Department, Office of the Adjutant General, 1780's-1917 (roll 271).

Chapter 15. The Exile Returns: *The Shearing*

1. *Wilbur Register*, January 15, 1892, p. 1; *Spokesman-Review*, March 26, 1899, p. 6.

2. *Wilbur Register*, January 15,1892, p. 1.

3. Ibid., June 19, 1891, p. 2.

4. L. H. Grant, Acting Secretary of War, to the Secretary of the Interior, July 7, 1891, "Selected Documents . . . Relating to Skolaskin."

5. Jessie A. Bloodworth, *Human Resourses Survey of the Colville Confederated Tribes . . . Bureau of Indian Affairs*, 44-48.

6. General Gibbon, report, August 19, 1890, Washington National Guard, *The Official History of the Washington National Guard*, 4: 289.2.

7. De Rougé to Cole, September 16, 1892, Crosby Library, Gonzaga University, Spokane.

8. Interviews with Henry Covington, July 1, 1960, and Clara Moore, Harry Nanampkin, and Cull White, March 4, 1961.

9. Interview with Henry Covington, July 1, 1960.

10. Ray, "Kolaskin Cult," 75.

11. Interview with Bill Thornburg, July 2, 1960.

12. *Wilbur Register*, March 3 and June 2, 1893, p. 1.

13. Interview with Guy Dungan, March 3, 1964.

14. *Wilbur Register*, December 14, 1894, p. 5; *Lincoln County Times* (Davenport, Wash.), December 21, 1894, p. 3.

15. Interview with George Nanampkin, May 14, 1964.

16. *Wilbur Register*, August 23, 1895, p. 1.

17. Ibid., October 3, 1890, p. 3; November 29, 1895, p. 1; November 3, 1899, p. 1.

18. In the 1890's the Sanpoil Henry Covington contracted through a railway company to take his Sanpoils aboard boxcars from Ellensburg in the Kittitas valley across the Cascade Mountains to the Puget Sound country to pick hops. Interview with Cull White, July 8, 1960.

19. Robert H. Ruby and John A. Brown, *Ferryboats on the Columbia River*, 132ff.

20. Before the opening of the South Half to mineral entry, Colville Agency police had been called in to remove intruding miners. *Wilbur Register*, May 1, 1896, p. 1.

21. Ibid., March 19, 1897, pp. 1 and 8.

22. Ibid., August 13, 1897, p. 1.

23. Ibid., November 4, 1898, p. 1; *An Illustrated History of Stevens, Ferry, Okanogan, and Chelan Counties, State of Washington*, 423–25; interview with Henry Covington, June 2, 1957.

24. *Wilbur Register*, September 28, 1906, p. 2.

25. Robert H. Ruby and John A. Brown, "Early Twentieth Century Blueprint for Transportation and Electrical Utilities on and near the Spokane Indian Reservation," 32–33; Ruby and Brown, *Spokane Indians*, 223–41; interview with Bill Thornburg, July 2, 1960.

26. *Wilbur Register*, December 8, 1905, p. 2.

27. Bloodworth, *Human Resources Survey of the Colville Confederated Tribes . . . Bureau of Indian Affairs*, 47.

28. Webster to Commissioner, January 27, 1906, Colville Indian Agency Records, Letters Sent to the Commissioner of Indian Affairs, October 5, 1905–July 24, 1906, letterbook 25; interviews with Jim James, July 28, 1960, and Clara Moore, June 30, 1961.

29. Webster to Commissioner, January 27, 1906, Colville Indian Agency Records, Letters Sent to the Commissioner of Indian Affairs, October 5, 1905–July 24, 1906, letterbook 25. Respiratory diseases were common among Indians and the smallpox again struck the Sanpoil-Nespelems and other reservation Indians at about this time. Among the survivors were those who avoided sweat bathing.

30. Ibid.

31. Henry M. Steele, agency farmer, to Albert M. Anderson, agent, December 10, 1897, Colville Indian Agency Records, Letters Received, 1898, letterbox 24.

32. Webster to Commissioner, April 22, 1909, Colville Indian Agency Records, Letters Sent to the Commissioner of Indian Affairs, Janaury 28, 1909–May 12, 1909, letterbook 30.

33. Ibid.

34. Ibid.

35. Webster to Commissioner, January 27, 1906, Colville Indian Agency Records, Letters Sent to the Commissioner of Indian Affairs, Letters Sent October 5, 1905–July 24, 1906, letterbook 25.

36. Interviews with Jim James, July 28 and 31, 1960, and Alex Covington, July 27, 1960.

37. Interview with Alice Cleveland, July 9, 1961.

38. Webster to Commissioner, August 24, 1908, Colville Indian Agency

Records, Letters Sent to the Commissioner of Indian Affairs, July 15, 1908–January 26, 1909, letterbook 29.

39. Frank F. Avery, Day School Inspector, to Webster, November 6, 1908, ibid.

40. Interview with Joe Monoghan, July 29, 1961.

41. Interviews with Henry Covington, January 18, 1958, Bill Thornburg, November 21, 1959, and Alice Cleveland, June 30, 1961.

42. *Spokesman-Review*, January 16, 1917, p. 6.

43. *In The Supreme Court of the State of Washington In the Matter of the Estate of John Enos; Spokesman-Review*, May 13, 1914.

44. Interview with Clara Moore, May 27, 1961.

45. Interviews with Clara Moore, July 14, 1961, and Alice Cleveland, July 22, 1961.

46. Interviews with Bill Thornburg, July 2, 1960, Clara Moore, July 14, 1961, and Alice Cleveland, July 22, 1961.

47. Reverend Edward M. Griva, S.J., "A Brief Account of the Mission of the Sacred Heart of Nespelem," 210–15.

48. Reverend Edward M. Griva, S.J., "History of the 50 Years of My Missionary Life Among Indians and Whites from July 1894 Until the End of September 1944," p. 153, in Memorandum 3, August 1, 1913 to April 30, 1922, Edward M. Griva, S.J., Papers. See also Raufer, *Black Robes and Indians*, 234n.

49. Interview with Alex Covington, July 27, 1960. Skolaskin reportedly told the Runnels, a Sanpoil family, that he had lived a deceitful life. Interview with George Nanampkin, May 14, 1964.

50. Interview with Cull White, January 21, 1958, March 4, 1961.

51. Interviews with Alice Cleveland, July 9, 1961, and Bill Thornburg, July 2, 1960.

52. Skolaskin's death and burial were described in interviews with Henry Covington, February 5, 1958, William Compton Brown, June 12, 1960, Luther Jones, October 4, 1960, and Clara Moore, Harry Nanampkin, and Cull White, March 4, 1961.

53. Whitestone's fate was described in interviews with Bill Thornburg, July 2, 1960, and Henry Covington, November 19, 1960.

54. Interview with John Mires, November 19, 1960.

55. Interview with Cull White, November 22, 1959.

56. "Sanpoils Monopolized the 'Leasts': This Tribe of Indians, of Whom There are But Few Remaining, Has Been Called The 'Digger Indian,'" *Oregonian*, May 9, 1937.

Chapter 16. Postlude: *Dreamer-Prophets Today*

1. Joseph G. Jorgensen, "Ghost Dance, Bear Dance, and Sun Dance," in Warren L. D'Azevedo, ed., *Great Basin*, vol. 11 of *Handbook of North American Indians*, ed. William C. Sturtevent (Washington, D.C., 1986), p. 669.

2. Walker, *Conflict and Schism in Nez Perce Acculturation*, 31–44.

3. Peter Farb, "Ghost Dance and Cargo Cult," 58. Farb briefly discusses Smohalla, the Dreamers, and their role in revitalization in his *Man's Rise to Civilization*, 332–33.

Bibliography

Unpublished Manuscripts Other than Government Documents and Including Theses and Dissertations

Anderson, Thomas H. Papers. Oregon Historical Society, Portland.
De Rougé, Etienne, S.J. Letter to Hal Cole, September 16, 1892. Crosby Library, Gonzaga University, Spokane.
Emerson, Ralph Leon. "A Chronology and Interpretation of Nineteenth Century Plateau Culture History." Master's thesis, University of Washington, Seattle, 1962.
Ferry, Elisha P. Papers. "State Documents 1876–1880." Washington State Archives, Olympia.
Friedlander, Herman. Letter to authors, May 9, 1964.
Grassi, Reverend Urban, S.J. Papers. Crosby Library, Gonzaga University, Spokane, Wash.
Griva, Edward M., S.J. Papers. Crosby Library, Gonzaga University, Spokane.
Guie, H. Dean. Papers. Oregon Historical Society, Portland.
Haller, Granville O. Papers. Suzzallo Library, University of Washington, Seattle.
Joset, Reverend Joseph, S.J. Papers. Crosby Library, Gonzaga University, Spokane.
Linsley, D. C. "Special Examination of Cascade Mountains of 1870–May and June." Chief Engineer Old Vault Files, no. 156. Minnesota Historical Society, Saint Paul.
McKay, William C. Papers. University of Oregon Library, Eugene.
McWhorter, Lucullus Virgil. Papers. Holland Library, Washington State University, Pullman.
Milroy, Robert Huston. Papers. Oregon Historical Society, Portland.
Pambrun, Andrew D. Papers. Oregon Historical Society, Portland.
———— "The Story of his Life as he Tells it." Copy of MS. Hargreaves Library, Eastern Washington State University, Cheney.

Ramsdell, T. M. "Indians of Oregon." In "Retrospective Reminiscences," MS. 852. Oregon Historical Society, Portland.
Relander, Click. Papers. Yakima Valley Regional Library, Yakima, Wash. Yakima Indian Nation Cultural Center, Toppenish, Wash.
Rigsby, Bruce J. "Linguistic Relations in the Southern Plateau." Master's thesis, University of Oregon, Eugene, 1965.
Rinehart, William Vance. "Oregon Cavalry (1874–1881)." MS. P-A62, Bancroft Library, University of California, Berkeley.
Ruby, Henry. "Changes in Ascendancy of Lower Plateau Indian Chiefs." MS. in possession of authors.
Sanpoil panelists. "Statement of Sanpoil Panelists." October 27, 1960, Colville Agency, Nespelem, Wash. Photocopy of typescript in authors' possession.
Schuster, Helen H. "Yakima Indian Traditionalism: A Study in Continuity and Change." Ph.D. diss., University of Washington, 1975.
Sharkey, Margery Ann Beach. "Revitalization and Change: A History of the Wanapum Indians, Their Prophet Smowhala, and the Washani Religion." Master's thesis, Washington State University, 1984.
Simms, John A. Papers. Holland Library, Washington State University, Pullman.
Snively, Henry J. Papers. Suzzallo Library, University of Washington, Seattle.
Streamer, Francis. Papers. Washington State Historical Society, Tacoma.
Trafzer, Clifford. Letter to authors, June 17, 1986.
Winans, W. P. Papers. Holland Library, Washington State University, Pullman.

Government Documents and Publications

Annual Report of the Chief of the [U.S. Army] Engineers For 1886. Washington, D.C., 1886.
Annual Report of the Commissioner of Indian Affairs. 1860, 1866, 1871, 1873, 1875, 1880, 1884. Washington, D.C.
Annual Report of the Secretary of the Interior. 1859, 1870, 1873, 1888, 1889. Washington, D.C.
Annual Report of the Secretary of War. 1877. Washington, D.C.
Bloodworth, Jessie A. *Human Resources Survey of the Colville Confederated Tribes: A Field Report of the Bureau of Indian Affairs, Portland Area Office.* Portland, Ore., 1959.
Colville Indian Agency Records. Letterbooks 3, 7, 25, 29, 30; Letterboxes 19, 24. Federal Archives and Records Center, Seattle.
D'Azevedo, Warren L., ed. *Great Basin.* Vol. 11, *Handbook of North American Indians,* ed. William C. Sturtevant. Washington, D.C.: Smithsonian Institution Press, 1986.
Everett, Will E., M.D. "Division of Time." In "Study of Indian Languages," ed. Will E. Everett. Washington, D.C.: Bureau of Ethnology, Smithsonian Institution, September 1, 1883.
Gatschet, Albert Samuel. "The Klamath Indians of Southwestern Oregon."

U.S. Department of the Interior, U.S. Geographical and Geological Survey of the Rocky Mountain Region, J. W. Powell in Charge. Washington, D.C., 1890.

Holden, Edward S. a *Catalogue of Earthquakes on the Pacific, 1769–1897.* Smithsonian Miscellaneous Collections, 37, no. 5. Washington, D.C., 1898.

In the Supreme Court of the State of Washington in the Matter of the Estate of John Enos, Deceased. Susan Enos, Appellant, Vs. *Lawrence R. Hamblen, Executor of the Last Will and Testament of John Enos Deceased. Mary Enos, Catholic Church of Santo Antao Topo, San Jorge, Azores Islands, Each of Asylums for the Homeless at Villa das Villa, San Jorge Azores Islands, and the Young Men's Christian Association of Spokane Washington Respondents. Washington Reports.* Vol. 79, *Cases Determined in the SUPREME COURT of Washington March 27, 1914–June 1, 1914,* #11783, Dept. Two, May 12, 1914.

Mooney, James. *The Ghost-dance Religion and the Sioux Outbreak of 1890. Fourteenth Annual Report of the Bureau of American Ethnology to the Secretary of the Smithsonian Institution, 1892–93,* pt. 2, pp. 641–1110. Washington, D.C., 1896.

Oregon Superintendency of Indian Affairs, 1848–1872. Letters Received, January 3–December 27, 1861, vol. 2 (roll 19); Letters Received January 7, 1862–June 28, 1863, vol. 2 (roll 20); Letters Received March 31–December 1, 1870, vol. 2 (roll 26); Letterbooks, vol. H:10 (roll 8), vol. I:10 (roll 10); Register of Letters Sent April, 1866–December, 1872, vol. I:10 (roll 9). Microcopy of Records in the National Archives, Washington, D.C.

Records of the United States Army Continental Commands, 1821–1920. Department of the Columbia, Letters Received from Indian Agents, Record Group 393. National Archives, Washington, D.C.

Records of the War Department, Office of the Adjutant General, 1780's–1917, Record Group 94. National Archives, Washington, D.C.

Regulations of the Indian Department. Washington, D.C., 1884.

Reports of Inspection of the Field Jurisdiction of the Office of Indian Affairs, 1873–1900, no. 1070, rolls 33, 55, 56, 58, 59, 70. National Archives, Washington, D.C.

Secretary of the Interior, Indian Division, Letters Received, 1873. Record Group 48. National Archives, Washington, D.C.

"Selected Documents from Among the Records of the Bureau of Indian Affairs Relating to Skolaskin, Chief of the San Puell Indians." Letters Received, 1885–1892. Record Group 75. National Archives, Washington, D.C.

Siletz Indian Agency. Press Copies of Letters Sent to the Commissioner of Indian Affairs by the Siletz Agents, 1873–1914. Federal Archives and Record Center, Seattle.

Symons, Thomas W. "Report of an Examination of the Upper Columbia River and the Territory in Its Vicinity in September and October, 1881, to Determine Its Navigability and Adaptability to Steamboat Transportation." 47th Cong., 1st sess., 1882, Sen. Exec. Docs. 186 and 188.

Teit, James A. "The Salishan Tribes of the Western Plateaus." *Forty-Fifth An-*

nual Report of the Bureau of American Ethnology to the Secretary of the Smithsonian Institution, 1927–28. Washington, D.C., 1930.

Umatilla Indian Agency. Letters Sent to the Commissioner of Indian Affairs and Other Parties, 1871–1908. Federal Archives and Record Center, Seattle.

Warm Springs Agency. Press Copies of Letters Sent to the Commissioner of Indian Affairs. Book 1, 1869–74; Book 2, 1878–79. Federal Archives and Record Center, Seattle.

Washington National Guard. The Official History of the Washington National Guard. Vol. 4 of 7 vols. Tacoma, n.d.

Washington Superintendency of Indian Affairs, 1853–1880. Letters Received by the Office of Indian Affairs, 1824–1881, no. 234 (roll 918); Letters from Employees Assigned to the Columbia River, or Southern, District and the Yakima Agency, May 1, 1854–July 20, 1861 (roll 17); Letters from Employees Assigned to the Yakima Agency, August 16, 1861–December 3, 1868 (roll 18). Microcopy of Records in the National Archives.

Yakima Indian Agency. Press Copies of Letters Sent to the Commissioner of Indian Affairs, 1877–1921. Record Group 75. Federal Archives and Record Center, Seattle.

Books Other than Government Publications

Aiken, George L. The Antelope Boy; or, Smoholler, the Medicine Man. New York, 1873.

Alexander, Hartley Burr. The Mythology of All Races. Edited by John A. MacCulloch. 13 vols. 1916–32. Reprint, vol. 10, New York, 1964.

Bailey, Paul. Wovoka: The Indian Messiah. Los Angeles, 1957.

Bancroft, Hubert Howe. The Works of Hubert Howe Bancroft. 39 vols. Vol. 31, History of Washington, Idaho and Montana 1845–1889. San Francisco, 1890.

Barnett, H. B. Indian Shakers: A Messianic Cult of the Pacific Northwest. Binghamton, N.Y., 1957.

Bechtel Inc. Investigation of the December 14, 1872, Earthquake in the Pacific Northwest. San Francisco, 1976.

Beckham, Stephen Dow; Kathryn Anne Toepel; and Rick Minor. Native American Religious Practices and Uses in Western Oregon. University of Oregon Anthropological Papers, no. 31. 1984.

Boas, Franz, ed. Folk-tales of Salishan and Sahaptin Tribes. Lancaster, Pa.: 1917.

Boyd, James P. Recent Indian Wars. Under the Lead of Sitting Bull. And Other Chiefs: With a Full Account of the Messiah Craze and Ghost Dances. Philadelphia, 1891.

Briley, Ann. Lonely Pedestrian: Francis Marion Streamer. Fairfield, Wash., 1986.

Burns, Robert Ignatius, S.J. The Jesuits and the Indian Wars of the Northwest. New Haven, 1966.

Castile, George P. The Indians of Puget Sound: The Notebooks of Myron Eells. Seattle, 1985.

Chance, David H. Influences of the Hudson's Bay Company on the Native Cul-

tures of the Colville District. Northwest Anthropological Research Notes, Memoir no. 2. Moscow, Idaho, 1973.

Clark, Ella E. *Indian Legends of the Pacific Northwest.* Norman, 1966.

Clark, W. P. *The Indian Sign Language.* Philadelphia, 1885.

Cline, Walter, et al. "The Sinkaietk or Southern Okanagon of Washington." *Contributions from the Laboratory of Anthropology.* General Series in Anthropology, no. 6. In Leslie Spier, ed., Menasha, Wisc., 1938.

Collins, June McCormick. *Valley of the Spirits: The Upper Skagit Indians of Western Washington.* Seattle, 1974.

Coues, Elliott, ed. *History of the Expedition Under the Command of Lewis and Clark.* Vol 2 of 3 vols. Magnolia, Mass., 1965.

———— *New Light on the Early History of the Greater Northwest: The Manuscript Journals of Alexander Henry, Fur Trader of the Northwest Company, and of David Thompson . . . 1799–1814.* Vol 2 of 3 vols. New York, 1897.

Cox, Ross. *Adventures on the Columbia River.* 2 vols. London, 1831.

Curtis, Edward S. *The North American Indian, Being a Series of Volumes Picturing and Describing the Indians of the United States and Alaska.* Vols. 7 and 8. Norwood, Mass., 1907–30.

De Smet, Peter, S.J. *Oregon Missions and Travels over the Rocky Mountains. In 1845–46. By Father P. J. De Smet of the Society of Jesus.* XIX. Vol. 29 in Reuben Gold Thwaites, ed., *Early Western Travels, 1748–1846.* New York, 1907.

Diomedi, Reverend Alexander, S.J. *Sketches of Modern Indian Life.* Woodstock, Md., 1884.

Donaldson, Thomas, *Idaho of Yesterday.* Caldwell, Idaho, 1941.

Drake, Benjamin. *Life of Tecumseh, and of His Brother, the Prophet.* Cincinnati, 1841.

Drury, Clifford M. *Chief Lawyer of the Nez Perce Indians, 1796–1876.* Glendale, 1979.

Du Bois, Cora. *The Feather Cult of the Middle Columbia.* General Series in Anthropology, no. 7. Menasha, Wisc., 1938.

Fahey, John. *The Flathead Indians.* Norman, 1974.

Farb, Peter. *Man's Rise to Civilization.* New York, 1968.

Franchère, Gabriel. *Narrative of a Voyage to the Northwest Coast of America in the Years 1811, 1812, 1813, and 1814.* Edited by J. V. Huntington, New York, 1854.

Gray, W. H. *The Moral and Religious Aspect of the Indian Question: A Letter Addressed to General John Eaton, Department of the Interior, Bureau of Education. Washington, D.C.* Astoria, Ore., 1879.

Greengo, Robert E. *Studies in Prehistory: Priest Rapids and Wanapum Reservoir Areas, Columbia River, Washington.* 2 vols. Seattle, 1982.

Howard, Oliver Otis. *Famous Indian Chiefs I Have Known.* New York, 1908.

———— *My Life and Experiences Among Our Hostile Indians.* Hartford, 1907.

———— *Nez Perce Joseph: An Account of His Ancestors, His Lands, His Confederates, His Murders, His War, His Pursuit and Capture.* Boston, 1881.

An Illustrated History of Klickitat, Yakima, and Kittitas Counties. Chicago, 1904.

An Illustrated History of Stevens, Ferry, Okanogan, and Chelan Counties, State of Washington. Spokane, 1904.

The Inter-Tribal Council of Nevada. *Life Stories of Our Native People: Sho-shone, Paiute, Washo.* Salt Lake City, 1974.

Josephy, Alvin. *The Nez Perce Indians and the Opening of the Northwest.* New Haven, 1965.

Kennedy, G. W. *The Pioneer Campfire . . . Anecdotes, Adventures and Reminiscences.* Portland, Ore., 1914.

La Barre, Weston. *The Ghost Dance Origins of Religion.* New York, 1970.

Lyman, W. D. *History of the Yakima Valley, Washington, Comprising Yakima, Kittitas and Benton Counties.* 2 vols. N.p., 1919.

McWhorter, Lucullus Virgil. *Hear Me My Chiefs.* Caldwell, Idaho, 1952.

Meacham, Alfred B. *Wigwam and War-Path; or the Royal Chief in Chains.* Boston, 1875.

Merk, Frederick, ed. *Fur Trade and Empire: George Simpson's Journal.* Cambridge, Mass., 1931.

Miller, Christopher L. *Prophetic Worlds: Indians and Whites on the Columbia Plateau.* New Brunswick, N.J., 1985.

Miller, David Humphreys. *Ghost Dance.* New York, 1959.

Moquin, Wayne, and Charles Van Doren, eds. *Great Documents in American Indian History.* New York, 1973.

Mourning Dove. *Cogewea: The Half-Blood.* Boston, 1927.

Nash, Philleo. "The Place of Religious Revivalism in the Formation of the Intercultural Community on Klamath Reservation." *Social Antropology of North American Tribes.* Chicago, 1937.

Oliphant, J. Orin. *The Early History of Spokane, Washington, Told by Contemporaries.* Cheney, Wash., 1927.

Pambrun, Andrew Dominique. *Sixty Years on the Frontier in the Pacific Northwest,* Fairfield, Wash., 1978.

Park, Willard Z. *Shamanism in Western North America: A Study in Cultural Relationships.* Evanston, 1938.

Raufer, Sister Maria Ilma, O.P. *Black Robes and Indians on the Last Frontier.* Milwaukee, 1966.

Ray, Verne F. *Cultural Relations in the Plateau of Northwestern America.* Publications of the Frederick Webb Hodge Anniversary Fund. 3. Los Angeles, 1939.

————. *The Sanpoil and Nespelem: Salishan Peoples of Northeastern Washington.* University of Washington Publications in Anthropology, no. 5. Seattle, 1933.

Relander, Click. *Drummers and Dreamers.* Caldwell, Idaho, 1956.

Ross, Alexander. *Adventures of the First Settlers on the Oregon or Columbia River.* London, 1849.

————. *Fur Hunters of the Far West.* Norman, 1956.

Ruby, Robert H., and John A. Brown. *The Cayuse Indians: Imperial Tribesmen of Old Oregon.* Norman, 1972.

————. *The Chinook Indians: Traders of the Lower Columbia River.* Norman, 1976.

————. *Ferryboats on the Columbia River.* Seattle, 1974.

————. *A Guide to the Indian Tribes of the Pacific Northwest.* Norman, 1986.

————. *Half-Sun on the Columbia: A Biography of Chief Moses.* Norman, 1965.

———. *Indians of the Pacific Northwest: A History.* Norman, 1981.
———. *Myron Eells and the Puget Sound Indians.* Seattle, 1976.
———. *The Spokane Indians: Children of the Sun.* Norman, 1970.
Sampson, Martin J. *Indians of Skagit County.* Mount Vernon, Wash., 1972.
Schalk, Randall F., et al. *An Archaeological Survey of the Priest Rapids Reservoir: 1981.* Laboratory of Archaeology and History Series. Washington State University. Pullman, Wash., 1982.
Scheuerman, Richard D., ed. *The Wenatchi Indians: Guardians of the Valley.* Fairfield, Wash., 1982.
Smith, Leta May. *The End of the Trail.* Hicksville, 1976.
Smith, Marian W. *Indians of the Urban Northwest.* New York, 1949.
Spier, Leslie. *The Prophet Dance of the Northwest and Its Derivatives: The Source of the Ghost Dance.* General Series in Anthropology, no. 1. Menasha, Wisc., 1935.
Splawn, Andrew J. *Ka-Mi-akin: Last Hero of the Yakimas.* Portland, Ore., 1917.
Suttles, Wayne. *Coast Salish Essay.* Seattle, 1987.
Swanton, John R. *Indian Tribes of Washington, Oregon, and Idaho.* Fairfield, Wash., 1968.
Thompson, Erwin N. *Golden Gate, The Rock: A History of Alcatraz Island, 1847–1972.* Denver: National Park Service, U.S. Department of the Interior, 1979.
Trafzer, Clifford, and Richard D. Scheuerman, *Renegade Tribe: The Palouse Indians and the Invasion of the Inland Pacific Northwest.* Pullman, Wash., 1986.
Walker, Deward E. *Conflict and Schism in Nez Perce Acculturation.* Pullman, Wash., 1968.
Wallace, Anthony F. C. *The Death and Rebirth of the Seneca.* New York, 1970.

Articles

Aberle, David F. "The Prophet Dance and Reactions to White Contact," *Southwestern Journal of Anthropology* 15 (1959).
Clark, J. Stanley. "The Nez Percés in Exile," *Pacific Northwest Quarterly* 36, no. 3 (July, 1945).
Crowder, Stella I. "The Dreamers," *Overland Monthly* 5 (December, 1913).
Collins, June McCormick. "A Study of Religious Change Among the Skagit Indians of Washington." In *Coast Salish and Western Washington IV,* ed. David Agee Horr. New York, 1974.
Cook, S. F. "The Epidemic of 1830–1833 in California and Oregon." *University of California Publications in American Archaeology and Ethnology* 43 (1955), no. 3.
Culin, Stewart. "A Summer Trip Among the Western Indians." *Free Museum of Science and Art* (Department of Archaeology, University of Pennsylvania) *Bulletin* 3, no. 3 (May, 1901).
Davenport, T. W. "Recollections of an Indian Agent," *Oregon Historical Quarterly* 8, no. 1 (March, 1907).
Du Bois, Cora. "The 1870 Ghost Dance." *Anthropological Records* 3, no. 1 (1939).

Farb, Peter. "Ghost Dance and Cargo Cult." *Horizon* 11, no. 2 (Spring, 1969).

Fletcher, Alice. "The Indian Messiah." *Journal of American Folk-Lore* 4 (1891).

Foreman, Carolyn Thomas. "General Eli Lundy Huggins." *Chronicles of Oklahoma* 13 (September, 1935).

Grassi, Reverend Urban, S.J. "Indian Missions." *Woodstock Letters* 3, no. 1 (1874); 7, no. 2 (1878).

Griva, Reverend Edward M., S.J. "A Brief Account of the Mission of the Sacred Heart at Nespelem." *Woodstock Letters* 48, no. 2 (June, 1918).

Gwydir, Rickard D. "A Record of the San Poil Indians." *Washington Historical Quarterly* 8, no. 4 (October, 1917).

Howard, Oliver Otis. "The True Story of the Wallowa Campaign." *North American Review*, July, 1879.

Huggins, Eli L. "Smohalla, the Prophet of Priest Rapids." *Overland Monthly* 5 (February, 1891).

Lenhoff, Paul. "Indian Shaker Religion." *American Indian Quarterly* 6, nos. 3 and 4 (Fall and Winter, 1982).

Lewis, William S. "Information Concerning the Establishment of Fort Colville." *Washington Historical Quarterly* 16, no. 2 (April, 1925).

Linton, Ralph. "Nativistic Movements." *American Anthropologist* 45 (1943).

McCann, Frank D., Jr. "The Ghost Dance, Last Hope of Western Tribes, Unleashed the Final Tragedy." *Montana the Magazine of Western History* 16, no. 1 (January, 1966).

MacMurray, Major Junius Wilson, U.S.A. "The 'Dreamers' of the Columbia River Valley, in 'Washington Territory.'" *Transactions of the Albany (N.Y.) Institute* 11 (1887).

Nash, John D. "Salmon River Mission of 1855: A Reappraisal." *Idaho Yesterdays* 2, no. 1 (Spring, 1967).

Nash, Philleo. "The Place of Religious Revivalism in the Formation of the Intercultural Community of Klamath Reservation." In *Social Anthropology of North American Tribes* (1937).

Nelson, Denys. "Yakima Days." *Washington Historical Quarterly* 19, no. 1 (January, 1928).

Nelson, W. S. "The Dreamers." *West Shore* 2, no. 12 (August, 1877).

Newell, Bernice E. "A Glimpse into the Yakima Reservation." *Northwest* 12, no. 12 (December, 1894).

Overholt, Thomas W. "The Ghost Dance of 1890 and the Nature of the Prophet Process." *Ethnohistory* 21, no. 1 (Winter, 1974).

Ray, Verne F. "The Kolaskin Cult: A Prophet Movement of 1870 in Northeastern Washington." *American Anthropologist, n.s.*, 38 (1936).

Ruby, Robert H. "Ancient First Roots Ceremony of the Dreamers." *Northwest Legacy: The Magazine of Local History* 1, no. 3 (March, 1976).

_____ and John A. Brown. "Early Twentieth Century Blueprint for Transportation and Electrical Utilities on and near the Spokane Indian Reservation." *Idaho Yesterdays*, no. 1 (Spring, 1976).

Sackett, Lee. "The Siletz Indian Shaker Church." *Pacific Northwest Quarterly* 64, no. 3 (July, 1973).

Schalk, Randall F., et al. "An Archaeological Survey of the Priest Rapids Reservoir: 1981." In *Laboratory of Archaeology and History.* Washington State University, Pullman, 1982.

Scott, Leslie M. "Indian Diseases as Aids to Pacific Northwest Settlement." *Oregon Historical Quarterly* 29 (1928).

Smalley, Eugene. "From Puget Sound to the Upper Columbia." *Century Magazine* 7 (November, 1884–April, 1885).

Spier, Leslie. "The Ghost Dance of 1870 Among the Klamath of Oregon." *University of Washington Publication in Anthropology* 2, no. 2 (November, 1927).

_____ and Edward Sapir. "Wishram Ethnography: Linguistic Relationship and Territory." *University of Washington Publications in Anthropology* 3 (1930), no. 3.

Spinden, Herbert Joseph. "The Nez Perce Indians." *Memoirs of the American Anthropological Association* 2, pt. 3 (November, 1908)

"State of Smohalla." *Northwest* 4, no. 7 (July, 1886).

Stern, Theodore. "A Umatilla Prophet Cult: An Episode in Culture Change." In *Selected Papers of the Fifth International Congress of Anthropological and Ethnological Sciences.* Philadelphia, 1956.

Stewart, Omer C. "The Ghost Dance." In *Anthropology on the Great Plains.* Lincoln, Nebr., 1980.

Strong, William Duncan. "The Occurrence and Wider Implications of a 'Ghost Cult' on the Columbia River Suggested by Carvings in Wood, Bone, and Stone." *American Anthropologist,* n.s., 47, no. 2 (April–June, 1945).

Suttles, Wayne. "The Plateau Dance Among the Coast Salish." *Southwestern Journal of Anthropology* 13 (1957).

_____ "Post-Contact Culture Change Among the Lummi Indians." *British Columbia Historical Quarterly* 18, nos. 1 and 2 (January–April, 1954).

Tassin, A. G. "Lord Jim." *Overland Monthly* 2nd series, 13, no. 77 (May, 1889).

Taylor, Herbert C., Jr., and Lester L. Hoaglin, Jr. "The 'Intermittent Fever' Epidemic of the 1830's on the Lower Columbia River." *Ethnohistory* 9, no. 2 (Spring, 1962).

Teit, James H. "The Middle Columbia Salish." *University of Washington Publications in Anthropology* 2, no. 4 (1928).

Thompson, David. *David Thompson's Narrative, 1784–1812.* Edited by Richard Glover. Publications of the Champlain Society. Toronto, 1962.

Thornton, Russell. "Demographic Antecedents of a Revitalization Movement: Population Change, Population Size, and the 1890 Ghost Dance." *American Sociological Review* 46 (1981).

_____ . "Demographic Antecedents of Tribal Participation in the 1870 Ghost Dance Movement." *American Indian Culture and Research Journal* 6, no. 4 (1983).

Trafzer, Clifford E., and Margery Ann Beach Sharkey. "Smohalla, the Washani, and Religion as a Factor in Northwestern Indian History." *American Indian Quarterly* 9, no. 3 (Summer, 1985).

Tucker, Glenn. "Tecumseh." *American History Illustrated* 6, no. 10 (February, 1972).

Turney-High, Harry Holbert. "The Flathead Indians of Montana." Memoirs of the American Anthropological Association, no. 48. In *Contri-*

butions *from Montana State University,* a supplement to *American Anthropologist* 39 (1937), no. 4, pt. 2.

Victor, Frances Fuller. "The Oregon Indians." *Overland Monthly* 7, no. 4, pt. 1 (October, 1871).

"A Visit to the Umatilla." *Northwest* 11, no. 12 (December, 1893).

Walker, Deward E., Jr. "New Light on the Prophet Dance Controversy." *Ethnohistory* (Summer, 1969).

Wallace, Anthony F. C. "Acculturation: Revitalization Movements." *American Anthropologist* 58, no. 2 (1956).

_____. "New Religious Beliefs Among the Delaware Indians, 1600–1900." *Southwestern Journal of Anthropology* 12 (Spring, 1956).

"White unto Harvest." *Spirit of Missions* 39 (February, 1874).

Wilson, Charles Reagan. "Shamans and Charlatans: The Popularization of Native American Religion in Magazines, 1865–*1900." American Indian Historian* 12, no. 3 (Fall, 1979).

Wood, C. E. S. "Private Journal, 1879." *Oregon Historical Quarterly* 70, no. 2 (June, 1969).

Young, Joseph. "An Indian's Views of Indian Affairs." *North American Review,* April, 1879.

Newspapers

Catholic Sentinel (Portland, Ore.), 1890, 1911.

Idaho Statesman (Boise, Idaho Terr.), 1877.

Lincoln County Times (Davenport, Wash.), 1894.

Morning (Portland) *Oregonian,* 1878, 1879.

Morning Review (Spokane Falls, Wash. Terr.), 1889.

Northwest Tribune (Spokane Falls, Wash. Terr.), 1880.

Oregonian (Portland, Ore.), 1883, 1937.

Pacific Christian Advocate (Portland, Ore.), 1873, 1874.

San Francisco Chronicle, 1878, 1891.

Seattle Post Intelligencer, 1905, 1980.

Spokane Falls (Wash. Terr.) *Review,* 1889.

Spokesman-Review (Spokane, Wash.), 1899, 1914, 1917.

Tacoma (Wash. Terr.) *Herald,* 1878.

Times-Mountaineer (The Dalles, Ore.), 1886.

Walla Walla (Wash. Terr.) *Statesman,* 1862, 1878.

Walla Walla (Wash. Terr.) *Union,* 1871–73, 1883, 1934.

Washington (D.C.) *Post,* 1879.

Washington Standard (Olympia, Wash. Terr.), 1871, 1879, 1890.

Weekly Mountaineer (The Dalles, Ore.), 1886.

Weekly (Portland) *Oregonian,* 1858, 1862.

Weekly Pacific Tribune (Seattle, W.T.), 1878.

Wilbur (Wash.) *Register,* 1890–99, 1905, 1906.

Yakima Record (Yakima City, Wash. Terr.), 1882.

Yakima (Wash.) *Republic,* 1940.

Interviews

Arcasa, Isabel, Coulee Dam, Wash., July 15, 1961.

Brown, William Compton, Okanogan, Wash., June 6, 12, 1960.

Cleveland, Alice, Monse, Wash., June 30, July 9, 22, 1961.

Covington, Alex, Soap Lake, Wash., July 27, 1960.

Covington, Henry, Ephrata, Wash., June 2, 1957; Keller, Wash., n.d., and January 18, 1958; February 5, July 1, November 11, 1960.

Covington, Madeline, Nespelem, Wash., July 14, 1961.

Curlew, Billy, Ephrata, Wash., October 8, 1956.

Dungan, Guy, Ephrata, Wash., March 3, 1964.

Friedlander, William, Elmer City, Wash., April 26, 1964.

Friedlander, Herman, Coulee Dam, Wash., May 4, 1964.

James, Jim, Soap Lake, Wash., July 28, 31, 1960.

Jones, Luther, Wilbur, Wash., October 4, 1960.

McCarty, Ella, Spokane, Wash., September 21, 1966.

Mires, John, Wilbur, Wash., November 19, 1960.

Monoghan, Joe, Soap Lake, Wash., July 29, 1961.

Moore, Clara, Belvidere, Wash., February 5, 1958, November 22, 1959; March 4, May 27, June 30, July 1, 7, 8, 14, 16, 1961.

Nanampkin, George, Nespelem, Wash., May 14, 1964.

Nanampkin, Harry, Belvidere, Wash., March 4, 1961.

Peone, Emily, Auburn, Wash., May 1, 6, 11, 1962; Cashmere, Wash., November 1, 1983.

Showaway, Nettie, Warm Springs Reservation, Oregon, May 30, 1978, June 25, 1986.

Thornburg, Bill, Lincoln, Wash., November 21, 1959; July 2, 1960.

Umtuch, Hazel, Toppenish, Wash., March 18, 1983.

Wickersham, Mary Ellen Runnels, Tonasket, Wash., June 21, 1964.

White, Cull, Moses Lake, Wash., March 10, 1957; Elmer City, Wash., January 21, 1958; Nespelem, Wash., November 22, 1959; Okanogan, Wash., June 12, 1960; Moses Lake, Wash., July 8, 1960; Coulee Dam, Wash., March 4, 1961.

Index